HUMAN RIGHTS IN AMERICAN AND RUSSIAN POLITICAL THOUGHT

Arpad Kadarkay

UNIVERSITY
PRESS OF
AMERICA

To Leszek Kolakowski

iii

The extent of (Russian) Dominion requires
an Absolute Power to be vested in that
Person who rules over it . . . Every other
Form of Government whatsoever would not
only have been prejudicial to Russia, but
would even have proved its entire Ruin.

>   - Catherine the Great, Nakaz

Human rights invented America.

>   - President Carter, Farewell Address

What god was it then set them together in
bitter collision?

>   - Homer, The Iliad.

CONTENTS

TABLES

Preface

The political conscience and morality bite deep in the American experience. Founded by religious dissenters, America had entered the family of nations convinced of divine protection and mission. Like Socrates, America has a stronger sense of mission than policy. The Socratic gospel, exhorting others to lead an examined life, has an unbreakable grip on the American political mind.

Socratic America, on self-display through profligate, prodigous self-examination and pressing on with the quest of what America is and stands for, has met its match in Soviet Russia. This study is premised on the conviction that nations resonate to the vibrations that flow through and over them as the stream of thought.

One of the tasks of political theory is to understand the relation of political life to thought. Hence this book's primary aim is to investigate the formative ideas that shaped and continue to shape American and Russian political thought. When a scholar looks at his work, it is sometimes a swan that has hatched out a duck; sometimes vice versa. It sensitizes me to define, modestly, this study as an essay in comparative political thought.

As an essay, the book makes no claim to a comprehensive, systematic study of the American and Russian political thought. Only those aspects of political thought are discussed which, in my view, explicate the recurrent American-Russian conflict over human rights.

The U.S.-Soviet rivalry is unbearably sad, if not tragic, because though times and leaders change, they change nothing. The superpower adversary relations is a tragic world, but it is a world without guilt for its tragic flaw is not a flaw in the American or Russian human nature, still less a flaw in individual leaders, but a flaw in the antimonial nature of American and Russian political thought.

Though America and Russia recognize and ritualize their responsibility for peace, they continue to hurl challenges at each other like spear-shaking Homeric heroes who dared the most awful deeds at a moment's caprice. That rough school master war has taught, so far, the superpowers self-restraint and moderation. The condition for peace and security is not arms and force by which men and nations can be compelled. It is the all-conquering power of good will. But good-will among the superpowers, as a restraining impulse, is a tenuous thing because America and Russia are centered in a different moral atmosphere.

Never in her two centuries has America confronted an adversary of comparable strength and ideological resolve on a permanent basis so antithetical to American values. Two great nations are caught in the casting net of destiny. The American confidence and will to endure as democracy, and the Soviet determination to give traditional Russian ambitions a theoretical formulation are pitted against the physical power to destroy each other.

The modern political cosmos pulses with potential tragedy because America's weakness of strength (parts I-II) is matched by Russia's strength of weakness (parts III-IV). Those who seek moral holiday in political thought or prefer small questions with precise answers are unlikely to find it in the Soviet-American confrontations over human rights. The nuclear age has locked together America and Russia like Dante's hapless lovers in Purgatory's miasmic swamp. This is the inescapable reality of our fin de siecle.

The humanist in me wishes to pardon the present for the sake of the future. But the student of ideas, essaying a comparative study of American and Russian political thought, must yield to evidence on the frailty of civilization, enrolled in the martial array gathered in the superpower rivalry.

This book represents a long-term investment and my intellectual debts to many people have been mounting, with interest compounded daily. The following scholars have been generous with their advise and criticisms: Herman Pritchett, John Chapman, Graeme Auton, Peter Merkl, and Gordon Baker. To all these scholars I owe a deep gratitude.

Coming at the formative stages of the project, my Research Fellowship at Harvard University's Russian Research Center in the summer of 1980 provided a uniquely supportive and stimulating intellectual environment. .ly work has undoubtedly benefited from that environment in many ways that I have never recognized or have forgotten. The works of three eminent scholars, Leszek Kolakowski, Adam B. Ulam, a.id Richard Pipes, unknown to them, shaped my engagement with Russian reality.

My approach to American political thought was influenced by such masters of democratic ideas as the late Ray Billington, friend and tutor of this book, Henry Steele Commager, J. Rolland Pennock, Bernard Bailyn, Joseph Cropsey, Sheldon Wolin, and Alpheus T. Mason.

During the research and writing stages of this study, I received invaluable financial support from the University of Puget Sound. To its Board of Trustees goes my sincere gratitude for making the via dolorosa easier, even enjoyable. To my family and immediate circle of friends, for their forebearance and Job-like patience during spells of often obsessive work, I offer one consolation: all scholars are mortal.

Finally, nothing gives me greater pleasure than to record my gratitude to the president of my iniversity, Philip M. Phibbs, un homme d'espirit if ever there was one.

Nothing is unchangeable but the inherent
and unalienable rights of man.

                    -Jefferson

We expressly declare the great rights of mankind.

                    -Madison

                 Part One

        HUMAN RIGHTS IN AMERICAN THOUGHT

1. Origins and Antecedents

     In the year 1776, when the 13 American colonies
gave to the world their famous Declaration of Independence, America has served a note that a Novus ordo
seclorum--a new order of things--begins in the political destiny of nations. Thomas Paine captured the
spirit of America when he declared, "We have it in our
power to begin the world anew."[1]

     To understand what Paine meant or Locke, who
stated, "In the beginning all the world was America,"[2]
one has to understand what Jefferson and his fellow
revolutionaries understood by the noun "rights"
contained in the Declaration of Independence. Drafted
mainly by Thomas Jefferson, to capture what he called
the "American mind," and adopted by the Continental
Congress of the rebel American colonies on July 4, 1776,
this document is probably the most famous and best
known statement on the rights of man. Here the rights
are defined as life, liberty, and the pursuit of
happiness. The American nation's birth certificate
states:

     "We hold these truths to be self-evident,
     that all men are created equal, that they are
     endowed by their Creator with certain unalien-
     able Rights, that among these are Life, Liberty
     and the pursuit of Happiness. That to secure
     these rights, Governments are instituted among
     Men, deriving their just powers from the
     consent of the governed, That whenever any
     Form of Government becomes destructive of
     these ends, it is the Right of the People to
     alter or to abolish it, and to institute new
     Government, laying its foundations on such
     principles and organizing its powers in such

                     1

form, as to them shall seem most likely to effect
their Safety and Happiness."

This revolutionary Declaration highlights two
principal assumptions in American political thought.
First, government is to serve and secure rights and,
second, free men form a compact with government whose
just powers derive from consent. The textbook
version of government by consent is familiar to most
American schoolchildren. In the fetid, and smelly
cabin of the Mayflower, the Pilgrims drew up a parchment which declared:[3]

> "We whose names are underwritten. . . . Do by
> these presents solemly and mutually, in the
> presence of God, and one another, Covenant
> and Combine ourselves together into a Civil
> Body Politick. . . ."

The difference between a political system based on
consent and government without consent is the difference between the American and Russian concept of
politics. Power is the irreducible element of
political existence. But whereas Americans brought
power under constitutional limitation and forged a
union between power and moral purpose, Russian thought
imposes no limitation on political power. In Russian
body politic the citizen submits rather than consents
to government. Americans talk about government in
terms of "rights" and Russians are taught to think
of their "duties" toward government.

But to return to the Delcaration, American
thinkers distinguished between physical power and
moral power. The distinction between power obedient
to physical force and power obedient to natural law
originates with Samuel Pufendorf[4] (1632-1694) who
contributed to building up the classic version of the
natural-law theory of the state. The moral approval
of power, as distinct from its efficient or physical
cause, means that power, to be just, must be based on
right rather than force. The conceptual separation
of power and right means that physical quality of
power is not sufficient ground for authority. A power
based on right includes a relation to agreeableness
to a rule, that is, power must be based on consent.

By designing power in conformity with, and not
in violation of, natural law, the American Fathers
placed power within a moral sphere. The constitutional

2

framing of ethics and politics became the charter
principle of American politics. Thus the Declaration
of Independence conceives political life in terms of
rights to which all men are naturally entitled.
To appreciate the American constitutional design
that seeks to reconcile ethics and politics and,
most significant, to make it a universal truth
relevant to all regimes, it is instructive to sketch
its relevant antecedents in Western political thought.
The narrowing of the legitimate scope of government
by making general moral values obligatory on the
political conduct of power constitutes the moral
foundation of the American Republic. But the moral
basis of politics, or, the framing of power according
to rights, antedates the American constitutional system.
Let's briefly trace, then, some antecedent alignments
of ethics and politics.

2. Antigone and Natural Rights.

Looking down the corridor of time, Machiavelli or Hobbes see but a restless desire for power in all men that, in Hobbes's celebrated axiom, "ceaseth only in death."[1] Thus Monitour, feeding upon interest and power, is an enduring image of politics. And yet even Max Weber, fascinated as he was with the bureaucratic, charismatic, and legal configuration of modern politics, drew attention to the normative or teleological aspects of natural law. As Weber stated,[2]

> "Natural law is the sum total of those norms which are valid independently of, and superior to, any positive law and which owe their dignity not to arbitrary enactment but, on the contrary, provide the very legitimation for the binding force of positive law."

Though acknowledging that all politics tend toward realism by maintaining the external and internal distribution of power, Weber noted that natural law norms have not only legitimized a revolution created order in America but remained the "specific and only consistent type of legitimacy of a legal order",[3] consequent to the loss of religious revelation and sacredness of tradition as its basis.

The legitimation of legal order has received its dramatic expression in Sophocles's tragedy, Antigone. Sophocles captured the inherent psychology of power to establish law and order, even when it violates the higher laws of the moral universe. Antigone invokes the divine or "higher" laws of the universe against Creon's tyrannical power. Faith in a higher law, in effect, is a form of prayer against the man-made yet naked power. Without natural rights, the mighty rule and the weak suffer and hope. In Sophocles's drama, Antigone appeals to conscience in disobeying Creon's positive law, the king's ukaz, that she must leave unburied her brother, an enemy of the state killed in a battle. She asserts defiantly man's right to burial, even when the powers that be decree otherwise.

Against state authority, she sets the unwritten laws of heavens. She chooses the divine command over the human-political compulsion. Sophocles's tragedy embodies a profound vision of the human condition which summons man to the task of reconciling his

political being with his transcendental bond. The
conflict between civic duties and transpolitical
idealism compel us to consider, now and then, life
at the limits, vita in extremis, and ask, "What
is Man?" In Sophoclean tragedy the human condition
is driven by the conflicting claims of politics and
conscience. Antigone opposes the "decrees"
(kerygmata) of Creon to the "laws" (nomina) of
the gods. Sophocles dramatically captures what
constitutes "law" (nomos).

She challenges human or man-made law with
the absolute which she backs up with the resolute
and defiant resolve of her own death. Her self-
sacrifice in support of moral idealism is the fullest
assertion of heroic individualism natural law norms
exact. If one has doubts on the recurrent conflict
of state authority and individual conscience,
one should read Antigone. The humanist, Joseph
Wood Krutch, said man is the only creature whose
nature leads him to dispose the cadavers of its
species "in some traditional and ritual fashion."[4]

Antigone, in clear violation of Creon's edict,
sees the right to burial as the immutable law
of heavens. She obeys, in short, this right of
the human species. Buries her brother's corpse
and is arrested and taken to Creon.

"Do you know the law?" the King demands.
"Yes," she replies.
"Then why did you break it?"

Answering the King, Antigone invokes conscience
as the law of ultimate justice.[5]

Your edict, King, was strong
But all your strength is weakness itself against
The immortal unrecorded laws of God.
They are not merely now; they were, and shall be,
Operative for ever, beyond man utterly.

Called into power during a crisis, Creon is resolved
to be tough and rule strongly. As a ruler, he
defines the justice of man solely in relation to
the polis, and identifies justice in private life
with that in public life. Unyielding in his authority,
he understands nothing about the limits on human

6

power and control Sophocles gives us a masterly
characterization of tyrant in Creon who subordinates
the human world to the ruler's political expediencies.
Creon even invokes Zeus to his view that the state
comes before the individual.

Creon personifies what Kant called the
"political moralist" as distinct from the "moral
politician."[6] The political moralist subordinates
principles to his end and, as Kant argues, treates
the problems of political and human rights as mere
technical tasks. To the moral politician, on the
other hand, the reconciliation of politics with
the morality is, first and foremost, a moral task
and never a technical one. Equating his might
with right, Creon's authoritarian willfulness devalues
things and demeans the sanctity of love, marriage,
and person. Creon fails to honor the moral progress
inherent in civilization when he decrees that
Polyneices's corpse be exposed. Creon's resolve
to leave the corpse exposed to the elements not
only violates moral sanctions, but reveals what
uncontrollable forces lurk in unchecked power.
The exposed body would not only pollute society
but threaten man's moral progress attained by
civilization.

Sophocles's drama captures twofold truth
relevant to our concern. First, the polity is
part of a larger sphere of moral values. Second,
and most important, the degradation of man to accord
with political expediency is a transgression against
the moral order of things. The Soviet regime's
periodic assault on dissent and the internal exile
of Andrei Sakharov, the Nobel laureate and leading
human rights advocate to Gorky, are Communist
variants of the degradation of man.

The Sophoclean drama leads us to the paradigm
case of politics. In his celebrated ode to man,
Sophocles laments,[7]

> O fate of man, working both good and evil!
> When the laws are kept, how proudly his
> city stands!
> When the laws are broken, what of his city
> then?

Antigone dared to defy the positive law or Creon's

decree. Not surprisingly, Creon responds to Antigone's defiant challenge with the voice of the state. Traitors must be punished and the ruler obeyed in all things, just and unjust alike. Otherwise, if individual conscience has its sway, it unties the political order and creates anarchy. By invoking the immutable and unwritten laws of heaven, Antigone discredits the positive, or man-made law Creon foresworn to uphold. Her inborn moral conscience challenges the political order kings swear to enforce. Sophocles's much admired ode to man's ability to act creatively upon his environment, utilizing reason and science, is veined by the tragic awareness that in creating a polity, together with law and justice, man remains deficient.

In plain language, success in the area of justice and moral limitation on power are more difficult to attain than the control and transformation of society by technology. The Soviets may probe deep into space and decipher its secrets, but they have failed to conquer and legislate away the independence of the human soul. Acts of moral conscience like that of Sophocles's Antigone is a commonplace heroism in Soviet society. Sophocles's drama vividly reminds us of the recurrent conflict of individual conscience and political power. The Soviet government's relentless pressure on dissent helps us to verify Sophocles's claim that our effort at understanding the human condition has occurred, and continues to occur, amid the violence of unchecked power.

Moral conscience, invoked and steadfast, has the potential to check the spread and scope of political power. Sophocles's _Antigone_ expresses the universal belief that man has a moral character, or at least the makings of one. And this does not merely allow us to hope for human improvement in the conduct of political power, but Antigone's action is already a form of improvement in itself. Sophocles's drama reveals itself in public and, as such, it is a drama of great political change that came about in Sophocles's generation. There is little question that Sophocles's ode, enumerating civilized man's achievements, also includes the discovery of "statecraft." In Sophocles's time, the Sophistic view of man's ability to work creatively upon the human environment and the Protagorean notion that the _polis_, along with law and justice, is a human creation is one of the most significant political developments in antiquity.

As tyrant, Creon embodies regressive tendencies in statecraft in polluting the body politics with a mouldering corpse. Creon disvalues politics and ultimately himself in his attempt to make even death another instrument of political control. He denies that the state must approach death and the dignity of man as the necessary condition of just rule. As a king he "used" death. As a result of Creon's state-centered view of man the Sophoclean drama reveals the inadequacy of a political rule which reduces the individual to a mere social unit.

In Antigone's heroic humanism of refusing to yield to Creon's decree, we see the double center of the gravity of politics: individual conscience and state authority. The tragic conflict of Creon and Antigone, the two protagonists of the Sophoclean drama, though totally opposed in their views, are nevertheless almost demonically bound to each other. To use Hegel's famous analysis, the "rights" of Creon and those of Antigone are even-balanced.[8] Hegel assumed not only that in such conflicts, Creon enforcing the right of the state and Antigone committing herself to the value and dignity of the individual irrespective of the social order, some good was to be found on both sides but also that both sides were equally justified.

Sophocles's _Antigone_ captures the tragic collision when two rights meet without yielding or giving an inch of compromise. Antigone's moral judgment is an integral part of a larger process of action designed by the term conduct. Her defiant stand on moral rights, to the point of self-sacrifice, may appear strange, if not foolhardly, to a modern mind educated to the virtues of compromise and reconciliation. Nonetheless, Antigone's ethical appeal is timeless because it comes out of a universe of discourse, autonomous and self-justifying.

We in the twentieth century bear witness, time and again, to the recurrence of universal discourse of moral judgment which, on a scale unimaginable to Sophocles, Soviet dissidents use against despotic power. The intellectual and moral gulf that separates Russia's prisoners of conscience from political orthodoxy is expressed in the Russian word, _blazhenny_. Russians

refer to their dissidents as <u>blazhenny</u>. The term
denotes both sainthood and divine madness. In
Aristotle's celebrated dictum, only gods and beasts
can dispense with the state. Ironically yet
revealingly, the Soviet dissidents' moral privilege
is to secede from a state that is neither rightful
nor morally good. Andrei Sakharov's admirers and
friends recognize this when they refer to him as
Andrei Blazhenny. The Greek word <u>etheos</u> - a good
within - conveys enthusiasm and also implies divine
madness. The Russian language captures both
meanings in the work, <u>blazhenny</u>. It takes divine
madness, indeed, on the part of Sakharov to engage
in a death-defiant hunger strike to persuade
the Kremlin to let his stepson's fiance emigrate
to the United States. As a result of Sakharovs'
17 day hunger strike, the Kremlin relented and
granted Miss Alexeyeva the exit visa in December 1981.

Sakharov's moral courage to speak truth to
Soviet power underscores the personal and moral
drama that grips Soviet-American relations. The
unrivaled strength of Sakharov reposes in his
uncompromising integrity and unqualified refusal
to lie. The "divine madness" that sears Russia's
soul in playing Antigone to the Kremlin Creons
may appear somewhat Quixotic to convinced political
realists. Yet the example of Sakharov, as that
of Antigone, draws our attention to what stands in
the way of enlarging the Soviet rulers' power. The
inherent limit to Soviet power is the moral courage
of men like Sakharov. As Aeschylus put it,[9]

> The man who seeks what is right
> Of choice and free will, shall not be unblest;
> The seed of just man shall never perish.

3. Socrates and Aristotle

A famous etymology tells us that martyrs are "witnesses." Our age, noted for its ravenous appetite for material rewards and democratic man longing for comforts rather than lunging for the spiky fruits of the spirit, may not appear fit for martyrs. And yet our age, whose ideological conflicts are so sharp and arms so deadly as to engrave civilization with mortality, has introduced human rights into the context of international relations. The Soviet Union's persistent evasion from its responsibility, signed and sealed at Helsinki, to uphold and respect the rights of man continues to proliferate dissidents who bear witness to the irreducible dignity and humanity of man. From the standpoint of power politics of Hobbesian or Machiavellian variant, the human rights advocates' private sensibility bears no relation to the civic-political standards of behavior.

Yet the private sensibility of such unageing intellects as that of Antigone or Socrates, who died for ideals without dishonoring humanity, reminds political orders, be it oligarchic ancien regime or totalitarian in Soviet cast, of mea res agitur. In his classic essay On Liberty, Mill said, "Mankind cannot be too often reminded that there was once a man named Socrates."[1] Inserting Socrates into our analysis of natural rights in American political thought may appear incongruent with the much acclaimed common sense style of American thought. In his keynote address on American civilization, George Steiner noted America's bias for "pragmatic bricolage"[2] as distinct from the ontological centrality and metaphysical discourse on values that characterizes Western thought, in Steiner's words, from the pre-Socratics to the present. Much can be said for Steiner's thesis that American thought is derivative and rather thin when compared with classical and European achievement. Yet I would contend, contra Steiner, the Socratic conviction that a community of men, to borrow his own terms, is one pervaded by explicit philosophical argument is central to Jefferson's philosophical attempt to bring government before the bar of reason and bid it to secure natural rights for the benefit of public good.

That in America, more than in any nation before or after, political power must plead its case before the bar of individual conscience has something to do with a man named Socrates and later the sage of Monticello.[3] As a nation, America is truly a living Socrates. Socrates was born into a democracy and died by its verdict. He told his jurors that the "unexamined" life is not worth living. When we cut through Socrates's tendentious arguments--for he was a Greek in love with all existence and surrendering no part of it undiscussed--there emerges a man who preferred getting beyond parties and classes to the study of ethical principles that are the measure of all politics.

So as a nation, America persists with the Socratic quest, "What we are and what we stand for" in establishing justice and securing the blessings of liberty to ourselves and our posterity. America also inherited one character trait from Socrates, self-display through profligate and prodigous self-examination, which other nations judge as hubris, arrogance of a Socratic nation. The Soviet Union is just as intent to demonstrate to the world that the American ideals cannot master force as were Socrates's jurors determined to assault the loftiest intellect in Athens.

As beneficiaries of Socrates's stand on private conscience, we can excuse his un-inhibited self-display. Nor can we regret that Socrates was not humble. A humble Socrates would be as absurd as the United States not mastering the courage of its ideals and affirm its identity with human rights at home and abroad. Yet the Socratic quality of America, the national pursuit of Know Thyself among the family of nations, is not an unqualified blessing in an international setting where nations preach persuasive moral sermons while pursuing power politics. There is what may be called the morality of Americans--a very real and influential thing--which allows departure from its principles in confrontation with an adversary presumed to be ruthless.

Our libertarian tradition, religious and Jeffersonian, makes us reticent and wary to pursue power politics that would demand, to be successful, the reconstitution of American society. When John Adams wrote that happiness of society is the end of government and "the happiness of the individual is the end of Man,"[4] he intimates why Americans seek solution to problems by reason and not be force.

Among Marx's many gifts to mankind, set forth in a quaint if not starchy philosophical language, is the conviction that "contradictions of capitalism" will usher in a socialist future. The irony of this maxim is that the billion or so people who live in various forms of socialism are not the result of the contradictions of capitalism. Even more subtle irony is that Communism, claiming linear descendency from contradictory capitalism, presents elaborate historical and moral grounds why "contradiction" will disappear in the happy future.

The rights of man were established because, despite the highest ethics men are capable of, conflict between man and state on matters of values and interest is unlikely to diminish. The strength of American civilization derives from the recognition that, in spite of Marx, the conflict of Antigone and Creon is not historical. Take the Bill of Rights in the Constitution. It summons critical minds to examine the political order and its principles. Hence what Marxists would label as "contradiction" constitutes the double majesty of America: a great political design scrutinized by so many Socrates from generation to generation.

But America's double majesty, creating a political order by inviting individual conscience to consent to it, cannot be understood apart from the First Amendment to the Constitution. The declaration that "Congress shall not make law . . . abridging the freedom of speech, or of the press," fixes a certain point to halt the government abruptly with a "thus far and no farther."

The First Amendment, wrote Alexander Meiklejohn, "could not have been written without Socrates."[5] Because there was once a "man called Socrates," who sacrificed his life for the right to individual conscience, democratic Athens set an antecedent to the First Amendment. As Meiklejohn put it, "It could be argued that if the Apology had not been written, the First Amendment would not have been written. The relation there is one of trunk and branch."[6]

The Socratic quality of America, summoning citizens to the right of conscience, cannot be subsumed in the daily management of conflicts and reconciliation of interests in a pluralistic polity. To interrogate

13

its political values and ideals is the most ambitious
undertaking that can command the attention of any
nation. But none more than that of the United States.
The invasion of democracy by pluralistic opinion and
individual conscience is so much taken for granted by
Americans that we overlook what distinctive role
American citizens play both in their private and public
capacities.

One of the great paradoxes of American democracy
is that its Bill of Rights invite criticism and yet
survive in spite of the active, critical, and Socratic
selfhood of some 240 million citizens. The first
American settlers found not only a new continent but
created a new condition of the mind, the intellectual
version of mundus novus promised by St. John. The
liberty of seeking and questioning reduces itself to
the proposition that the Republic is imperfect.
"America is imperfect," wrote Emerson to Thomas Carlyle.[7] The latter was somewhat skeptical of the
American "cousins'" attempt to create a democracy.
Emerson, however, expressed faith in this "wild
democracy" where, he wrote, "the swing of natural laws
is shared by the population as it is not--or not as
much--in your feudal Europe."[8]

One of the distinctive features of American
democracy is its ability to accomodate power to the
asocial sociality of men. In mundane terms, American
political thought disjoints the regime from the
people. Government by the people legitimizes the conflict of competing interests. But there is something
more. There is the dignity of thought, spelled
"We, the People." To enlarge its meaning, consider
the following incident as reported by Marshall Goldman
who, as a Fulbright exchange professor, taught at the
Moscow University. During one of his lectures--
attended by carefully screened students ~ Goldman
criticized the U.S. economy. Afterwards, some students
asked him,[9]

> "Mr. Goldman, are you a Communist? The rumor is
> that you are. Several of our classmates assume
> that if an American criticizes his economy,
> he must be a Communist."

The query highlights the paradise lost of an
authoritarian regime. To train free citizens to exercise judgment on behalf of a self-governed community

14

is the art and science of constitutional democracy. This science of politics is beyond the moral calculability of Communism.

There are inherent philosophical difficulties, to be discussed later, in the natural or human rights. But these problems can be overlooked when we consider the political benefits that derive from tying the destiny of the American Republic to a Bill of Rights. The latter are truly revolutionary in the annals of politics. Not only are the rights "natural" and "inalienable," but, and herein lies the novel aspect of the American Bill of Rights, the Founding Fathers unequivocally asserted the "right to conscience." This is how Madison understood it. The amendments to the Constitution should provide, he wrote, for the "rights of Conscience in the fullest latitude."[10]

Though much can be said for the parallel between Socrates's stand on individual conscience and the First Amendment, the Founding Fathers were, by and large, rather critical of Greek political thought. John Adams boldly asserted that America exemplifies the first instance of governments erected on the "simple principles of nature."[11] Antecedents for the "simple" principles of nature, coding norms for political order, can be found in Greek thought. The notion that there is a "law of nature," eternal amid the endless qualifications and innovations of human circumstances, pre-dates Platonic political theory. When Euripides asserted that man's "law of nature is equality" he expressed the rather common ethical belief that man's nature, as well as inanimate nature, can provide intelligible value-statements independent of the ever changing particulars of conventions and customs. That there are things irrevocably "natural" to man, or a permanent principle among the flux and variety of human conventions, has been broiling in the caldron of political philosophy for at least two millenia.

Indisputably, of all the political conceptions, the "natural," as the solvent of the complex universe man's reality and aspirations present, is the most difficult and ambiguous. Yet the idea persists because it affirms that freedom and moral choices are not incompatible with the existence of objective values, resident in man and his society. For these reasons, natural law concept is a powerful alternative to

15

relativist skepticism, legal positivism, and Machiavellian power politics.

It should be said at once that natural rights, as understood by Locke and his followers, would have been incomprehensible to Aristotle. The Greek political dream was an intrusive one. It left no moral-ethical sphere "private" from which the state was excluded. Liberty to the Greeks meant the citizen's liberty to be sovereign. Aeschylus boasted that the Greeks are "slaves to no lord, they own no kingly power,"[12] Indeed, Greek political theorists keyed citizenship so high that it effaced all antithesis between political society and the individual. The sovereignty of law-confirming citizen elicited the admiring lines of Euripides,[13]

> Free is our city, here the people rule,
> Rich man and poor are held equal by law.

But this equality before the law did not presume natural rights that received classical expression in American political theory. Socrates's trial by a democratic jury provides a revealing instance that Greek concept of right precluded the right to dissent from the normative values of the polis. Bestowing upon the citizen his moral essence, the polis was the measure of all things. Not unlike Calvin's Church, the Athenian polis, which tried Socrates, exercised holy discipline on Socrates.

Neither Plato nor Aristotle have conceded that individuals can dissent from the moral perfection of the state. Consequently, in Greek thought the Socratic stand on individual conscience could not fall under the protective clauses of minority rights. Aristotle gave the fullest expression of the organic view of the state.

> "The proof that the state is the creation of nature and prior to the individual is that the individual, when isolated, is not self-sufficient; and therefore he is like a part in relation to the whole."[14]

Like Greek thinkers in general, Aristotle saw in law prescriptive norms binding on individuals. The law had not only compulsory power but was a rational ordinance proceeding from a kind of "prudence of reason."[15] The relevance of this argument is that some American political theorists have alleged a certain parallel between Jefferson's conception of the "pursuit of happiness" and Aristotle's conception of "good."[16] In so many words, to Jefferson "happiness" and to Aristotle "good" are the primary ends of politics. Aristotle does argue that happiness is the chief good men always seek "for its own sake and never for the sake of something else."[17]

But Aristotle drew a rather different, or, rather un-Jeffersonian conclusion from the concept of "good" as evident from his position on suicide. Since suicide is hardly congruent with the dicta that individuals seek happiness, Aristotle is compelled to say that the law does not expressly permit suicide. Consequently, a man who takes his own life acts unjustly. Suicide is unjust not so much toward one's own concept of happiness as "towards the state"[18] because, in Aristotle's view,[19]

"A certain loss of civil rights attaches to the man who destroys himself, on the ground that he is treating the state unjustly."

That a state should promote morality is hardly an issue here. But Aristotle failed to realize that to promote morality by state-command is the end of moral autonomy. Though the end of the state is the happiness of all, Aristotle, unlike Jefferson, grants no individual rights for an effective pursuit of happiness. Aristotle's concept of happiness, inherent in his eudaimonistic ethics, does not belong to the genus of natural rights as understood and developed by Jefferson.

The Aristotelian concept of nature contains no norms for the universal equality of men. Nature does not always succeed, stated Aristotle, "in achieving a clear distinction between men born to be masters and men born to be slaves."[20] He confuses the descriptive and potential meaning of the term "natural" when he interprets it as original, innate, and inherited impulses prior to training. At the same time, he also equates "natural" with the ideal, teleological, or ultimate end.

More useful, in sketching the antecedents for natural rights, is Aristotle's definition of two kinds

17

of laws; the particular and the universal. By the
particular, he means the social conventions a given
community lays down and applies them to its own
members. Creon's edict, forbidding the burial of
Antigone's brother, was a customary law of Thebians.
Above the customary law, based on conventions peculiar
to society, stands the "higher" or universal "law of
nature" that Antigone invokes against Creon's positive
law. Aristotle affirmed that there really is "a
natural justice and injustice that is binding on all
men, even on those who have no association or covenant
with each other."[21] This "natural justice" is identical with the eternal law of "heaven" Antigone appeals
to in confronting Creon. If there is conflict between
conscience and the written law, Aristotle recommends
"we must appeal to the universal law, and insist on
its greater equity and justice."[22] The principles of
equity are permanent and universal because they are
the "laws of nature, whereas written laws often do
change."[23]

4. Stoicism and Natural Law

The concept of natural law receives its strongest expression, prior to the eighteenth century, in Stoic thought. The Stoics were heirs to the dissolution of the Greek city-states. As the political scale expands from polis into cosmopolis, from city to empire, political thought relocates its concern from reason to cosmology. With the demise of the polis, individuals are released from the compact city-state and become so many solitary atoms, filling the vast space of empires. The Stoics adjusted political thinking to the spatial expansion of politics. It bears analogy of the Founding Father's attempt to design a Republican form of government on a continental scale.

The principal doctrine of the Stoics, germane to natural law, can be stated as follows. The universe is endowed with divine purpose, discernable in laws that can be understood by reason. To Stoics, man is citizen of the universe, and humanity denotes a concordia of human hearts. "In its general aspect justice," declared Epicurus, "is the same for all, for it is a kind of mutual advantage in the dealings of men with one another."[1] Natural justice was conceived as a norm for the happiness of all men. The egalitarian ecumenism of the Stoics endows the individual with dignity and compassion. In the expanding brotherhood of man, Nature, not law, is the supreme legislator. The Stoics did not reject customary or positive law as nonexistent. Rather, they subordinated it to the "blessed and immortal" nature that knows no "trouble itself nor causes trouble to any other."[2]

Cicero, the leading exponent and transmitter of Stoic ideas, equated natural law with right reason. Right reason, he said,[3]

"applies to all men, and is unchangeable and eternal . . . To invalidate this law by human legislation is never morally right, nor is it permissible ever to restrict its operation, and to annul it wholly is impossible."

To Cicero, men are by nature plural, rational, and social. Man possesses an inner authority based on his individuality. Human nature yields a permanent concept of justice that transcends the expediency of

19

kings and republics. By this logic, positive law must embody justice to found support in human conscience. The claims to the invisible empire of human conscience, however, belong more properly to the Christian concept of rights.

God's people were and ought to be non-conformists.

-Roger Williams, 1664

5. Protestant-Puritan Contribution to Rights

Commonplace truth holds that the Bible and the
Puritans, who dared the "desarts of America," laid
the religious foundations of the American tradition.
Authoritarian theocracy and democratic dissent coexisted
in colonial America. The vast continent, open to experimentation by religious dissenters, produced not only
the ideals of Bible Commonwealth, but a righteous government whose spirit lives on in our secular age. In
his Magnalia Christi Americana (1702), Cotton Mather
ventured to prophesy:[1]

> "Tis possible, that our Lord Jesus Christ carried
> some thousands of Reformers into the retirements
> of an American desart, on purpose that, with an
> opportunity granted unto many of his faithful
> servants, to enjoy the precious liberty of their
> ministry . . . ."

As a result of the Protestant and Puritan religious
movements, individual conscience emerges as the primary
unit of religious and political thinking. It is sufficient to indicate that St. Augustine's City of God had
inspired the Puritan concept of holy commonwealth or
righteous government that received its fullest expression in New England. The Puritans, not surprisingly,
strenuously objected to Hobbes's Leviathan, the "mortal
God," whose legitimacy is relieved of any spiritual or
ecclesiastical disabilities. The Puritans insisted on a
righteous government, to be maintained in the interest
of the City of God. After all, vision of a holy commonwealth was less of an irrelevant dream in the wilderness
of New England than in Cromwell's England of the 1660's.

The most important development in the English Puritans's political theory originates, somewhat ironically,
in Luther's Reformation. Specifically, the notion of
individual conscience, as the seat of authority, leads
to the Puritan enlargement of the psychology of individual self. Whatever theological contribution Luther made
to religion, it was his intense preoccupation with
Christian righteousness or liberty that had a major impact on political thought. It is of course a commonplace truth that with the Reformation, we enter a world
where God speaks to the soul. He communicates his word
and spirit "from above" rather than through priest or

21

ecclesia. God, then, communicates directly and without intermediaries--solus cum solo. The voice in the heart, and in the heart alone, gives authority to religious faith. Christian man needs no elaborate church hierarchy to teach him duties and rights. The Bible and individual conscience, Luther never tires repeating, are sufficient guides.

The next formative stage in the evolution of Lutheran political theory was the rejection of Roman Law and suspending the authority of Canon Law. In the process, Luther not only re-defines natural law's relation to the Church but reinterprets natural law itself. He argues that, unlike the Greeks and Romans, who lacked an understanding of the true natural law, the Persians and Tartars observed it far better.[2] What Luther seems to be suggesting is that the prince ought to be regarded as legibus solutus, "free from the operation of the law." This did not mean that political principles, as understood by Lutheran thinkers, were not subject to the inherent limitation binding on all earthly powers. But it is also true that, as the leading student of Lutheran political theory put it, "had there been no Luther there could never have been a Louis XIV."[3]

It was Luther who, more than any other protestant thinker, by redesigning a new relationship between ecclesiastical and political power, blurred the traditional Thomist distinction between the law of nature and particular laws of local societies. Aquinas claimed that the law of nature provides the moral basis for the positive laws.[4] Replacing Aquinas's vision of a universe ruled by a hierarchy of laws, from the divine law to the law of nature, which God implants in men in order that they can understand his design, with the simplistic imperative, Luther's political theory attains authoritarian perspective. In fact, by glorifying authority and recommending rational submission to dominant authority, Luther's thinking invites some comparison with that of Machiavelli.[5]

But Luther, unlike Machiavelli, endows the state with devine character and imputes it transhuman reason. He sees the state's primary function as the preservation of external discipline and order. Yet, consistent with Augustinian view, as an institution, the state was a divinely ordained remedy, if not necessity, against man's sin or fall from grace. In Puritan

22

thought, then, we see the re-appearance, via Luther, of the Augustinian view of the state as an institution of fallen humanity. The interesting aspect of Luther's political theory is that his conservative concept of natural law coexists with an individualistic, religiously super-idealistic conviction, based on the infallibility of Scripture.

Luther's idealism derives from his simplistic imperative that man's true vocation is to prepare himself for God's free gift of grace. This leads to a purely inward sense of individualism which, for all practical purposes, is beyond human authority. Luther's fervent belief that "the word of God, which teaches full freedom, should not and must not be fettered,"[6] had a lasting impact on Western political thought. By disengaging the political element from its religious modes of thought, Luther shatters belief in authority by restoring the authority of belief. He frees man from outward or formal religiosity in order to sanction the religiosity of the inward man.

Differently put, Luther's Protestant doctrine frees the body from institutional fetters--Church--only to put the heart in spiritual fetters--Reformation. Luther gave symbolic expression to his revolt against institutionalized religion by burning at the town dump of Wittenberg copies of canon law. As the parchment of canon laws curled up in the flames, Luther and his followers chanted Te Deum, Laudamus and De Profondus.

To Luther, natural law was a correlate of men being under God's universal demand for justice and his sanction against wickedness. Though he recognized that natural rights and obligations have a universal basis and scope, nonetheless only in a fellowship of faith can rights have a positive effect. He eloquently defended the sanctity of individual conscience as long as it was contained by political quietism. Though he shared, as indicated, Machiavelli's exaltation of political absolutism, Luther refused to emancipate the secular ruler from the dictates of natural law. Yet in the end, he put more faith into the goodness and wisdom of rulers than into the promulgated natural law.

By contrast, Anglican Reformation, to round up the religious antecedents of American Puritanism, was more inclined and disposed to natural law. To the "judicious" Richard Hooker (1554-1600), who affirmed

23

the threefold cord not quickly broken--Bible, church,
and reason--all men everywhere have some sense of moral
obligation and right. He stated unequivocally there
is "some manifest root or fountain thereof common to
all."[7] Following the Thomist line of argument, Hooker
saw in natural law, or God's own nature, the reason for
doing good things. The fundamental rule of reason, so
crucial to Locke and Jefferson in verifying natural
law, he believed "nature herself must have taught"[8]
because it was lodged in the general assent of mankind.

Next to Hooker, no Protestant contribution to
natural law could be complete without at least cursory
comments on Hugo Grotius (1583-1643). Horrified by
the "hideous spectacle" of religious wars, Grotius
attempted to base a just society on the common rever-
ence for the Creator, rather than on theocratic ethics.
To Grotius, men share a divinely implanted universal
need for community, organized according to man's
measure of intelligence and sociableness. A social
order, allied with human intelligence, is the source
of natural law. The latter, according to Grotius,
dictates to man the right reason whose judgment on
human moral baseness is independent of God. Grotius
appears to have placed natural law on utilitarian,
rather than transcendental, considerations.

Grotius, of course, can hardly be considered
as belonging to the English school of natural law.
Nonetheless, his removal of religious sanctions from
natural law, and his demonstrative system of law
and politics, puts him close to English empiricists
who contributed significantly to the development
of Puritan thought. Like Protestant thinkers in
general, Grotius also expressed "doubts" about received
authority. Skeptical towards political power,
Protestant writers not only managed to wrench the
individual faith from the discipline of established
church, but in the process legitimized the habit of
dissent. The certainties that once belonged to God and
society, shepherded over by God's vicar and warded
over by the Church, were transferred to the Bible-
reading individual. From this perspective, it is not
difficult to see why Protestantism played such a historical role in the evolution of democratic thought.[9]
Already in Hooker we can detect that politics is trust
and stewardship.

There is no place or need to enlarge on the political consequences of Protestantism. Suffice to say,

Puritanism and Americanism are a textbook version of how Lutheran doctrines--sola scriptura and congregatio fidelium--laid the foundation of a political society in the New World.

The Puritans talked a lot about covenant of grace, of church, and the civil covenant. Theocracy was, paradoxical as it may sound, an assertion of liberty and democracy, at least for the elect. When the grave farmers of New England elected and ordained their ministers, they also exercised liberty and democracy. It was, needless to add, liberty and democracy of the elect and only later did the halo of righteous government extend to the unregenerate majority. But it cannot be overemphasized that the defense of democracy in the churches by Puritan thinkers, like John Wise, was based on ideas borrowed from Pufendorf's De Jure Naturae at Gentium. Wise asserted the natural equality of men. The end of government, he said, was to "promote the happiness of all, and the good of every man in all his rights."[10] This is but one instance of the slow, yet incremental secularization of American democracy. After all, the ideals of Puritan theology and those of the Declaration of Independence are really not that distant in spirit.

The American settlers represented what certainly was the hardiest and most assertive element among those who had an individualistic approach to creed and ideas. They discarded those aspects of political Anglicanism which, in Tudor England at least, sanctioned royal authority and conformist religion. All that was democratic in seventeenth century English politics and Protestant in her religion, the settlers carried across the Atlantic in a pronounced form. In Europe, the Protestant and Puritan movement redesigned the state and church relationship. In America, the religious dissenters prepared the revolution in civil and political liberties. Due to its Puritan origin, by 1776 the American mind is satisfied with no less than self-government under republican form. Thus the Revolution was a vindication of the liberties inherited and possessed by the early dissenters. In a large sense, the 1776 was also a conservative revolution because the Puritan spirit, born in the Old World, finally settled into a republican mould in the New World.

That dissenting conscience and radical individualism would create such an enduring political order in

the New World may, indeed, appear providential and
explain much of America's evangelism at home and abroad.
But it was Locke who, in his Valedictory Speech (1664),
reveals the uniqueness of the American political
experiment. When mankind begun to thirst for happiness,
he said, "the world was then very young."11

In the Beginning of the world was America.

-Locke, 1689

All bourgeois literature testifies to the
rising hatred of America.

-Lenin, 1918

6. The Eighteenth Century Thesis of Natural Rights.

We have sketched the main Protestant contribution,
relevant to our concern, to individualism and the
concept of private conscience as the starting point of
political analysis. Modern democratic theory, as
Rolland Pennock put it, "got its start as an individualistic doctrine."[1] Historically, at least, democratic
theory is associated with individualistic theory. Many
proponents of the rights of man rest their case upon
the belief in the supreme value of the individual.
Deriving support from such diverse sources as ancient
Greco-Roman Stoicism and the Judeo-Christian concept of
the dignity and sacredness of the self, the doctrine
of individualism holds that all human beings are
precious and that each person possesses an unforeseeable
potential for good. The prime goal of societies, then,
should be to permit and encourage the growth of each
person. Mortimer Adler postulated that society is good
or bad to the degree it interferes with the "pursuit of
happiness for all or for more of its members."[2]

He judges, in essence, modern political systems by
the criteria of whether they encourage or inhibit the
individual pursuit of happiness. In defining man's
basic right as the right to the pursuit of happiness,
Adler subsumes it under the so-called "teleological
ethics." It states:[3]

"We have in these natural rights the objective
and transhistorical standard for measuring the
justice of government, and the justice of
economic and social institutions as well."

By this criteria, one society is better than another
in proportion as its socio-economic, institutional, and
value systems promote good life for larger percentage
of its human beings.

Adler's teleological theory of rights presupposes
that all societies equate the "pursuit of happiness"
with the dominant end of political system. Though aware

that the postulated unity of private and public interest, taken for granted by Locke and Jefferson, produces
an ethnocentric predicament, nonetheless, Adler maintains that the validity of our own value system,
read American democracy, still enables us to judge
other political systems. In his view, the right to
happiness can be conceived as "goods",[4] common to all
humans irrespective of socio-cultural circumstances
under which they live.

In the contemporary world, however, liberal individualism and pluralistic democracy are under relentless
attack by those who espouse "collectivism" or "holism."
For instance, in his widely acclaimed work, A Theory of
Justice, John Rawls raises several objections to the
notion that "happiness" is the dominant end of society.
He contends that since a person pursues many aims,
"happiness" can hardly constitute the principal standard
of judgment. The so-called "indeterminacy of judgment"[5]
inhibits the use of happiness as dominant-end theory.
Human goods are heterogeneous because the aims of the
person are heterogeneous. The pursuit of happiness as
the primary right can only be rational and legitimate,
historically and politically, in the American political
context.

As Rawls points out, to Aquinas the dominant end
of man is to serve God.[6] Since Rawls's concept of
"social justice" is designed to replace the desire for
liberty as the common ground of various communities, we
shall recur to Rawls's argument in analyzing the Marxist
concept of "social justice." Though there is merit to
Rawls's assertion that the panoply of Lockean natural
rights cannot be decided in advance until the "basic
wants of the individual are fulfilled,"[7] nonetheless,
it cannot disqualify the historical connection
between human dignity and autonomy of person and democracy, nor derogate the close relation between
individualism and popular government. John Dewey insisted, rightly we think, that democracy is the net
consequence of a vast multitude of responsive adjust-
ments to a vast number of situations. He drew attention
to the historical appeal of some "inalienable sacred
authority resident in the protesting individuals"[8] as
contributors to the evolution of democracy. The birth
of individualism is not germane to our concern. Yet the
revolt of the individual against established authority
and institutions, designed earlier under the concept of
"civic consciousness," contributing to the limitation
of authority by consent, has inherent justification
in the very structure of the individual. [9]

Political thinkers who appealed to the dignity
and autonomy of person, from Milton to Locke and
Jefferson, all share the conviction that the liberty
to express his talents, and his right to be governed
by a power to which he consented were fundamental. The
justificatory theory of liberal, constitutional
government, in Austin Ranney's epigram, is that the
"People are the measure of all things."[10]

7. Civic Consciousness

Though product of the eighteenth century, the transatlantic Republic's Lockean-Jeffersonian premises must be understood against what Alfred North Whitehead called the "genius of the seventeenth century."[1] The political expression of this "genius" is the emerging civic consciousness in seventeenth century English thought. The term, civic consciousness, refers to the elementary perception that there is a public or social order whose problems and purposes are the proper concern of political authority. This recognition becomes, in due course, the focal point of Locke's natural rights-based government. The civic frame of reference, anchoring power to consent, restructures society and radically alters the political vision of men.

We can only refer to those features of civic consciousness which, in some way or other, set the stage for the American experiment in self government. In England, civic consciousness was the product of spiritual and constitutional controversy spanning the decades from 1640 to 1688. By analogy, the American Revolution, as it ran its course from 1764 to 1776, and down to the Constitutional design of an extended and compound federal Republic, was inspired by the "doctrines of the natural law."[2] Tracing the importation of natural law to colonial America, Cornelia Boutillier wrote:[3]

> "Our American forefathers were not concerned to deduce by the powers of reason a 'higher law.' Rather, they were concerned to trace and clarify and claim and use that fundamental law they sought to transplant to the American continent, free from its entanglements with king and Parliament beyond the sea, so that it might bear fruits as well for America."

It was in America, rather than in England, that the natural law doctrines attained their fullest significance. In England, at least since the Glorious Revolution of 1688, the supremacy of Parliament limited the scope of natural rights. But in America, more than any force, natural rights exploded the authority of the English Parliament and discredited its enslaving power in the colonies.

The core meaning of America's constitutional conflict with England is that certain rights and legal

31

trust in individual conscience--singular as it may
be--are beyond the legitimate reach of power. The
combined authority of intellect and conscience, embodied in Locke and the Protestant sects respectively,
produce the compelling argument that justice cannot be
bound by political time and social space. Despite
its metaphysical language and Deistic overtones,
natural rights to most Americans denoted a right, or
what Jefferson declared as "self-evident" truth,
timeless and "natural."

It is hardly an exaggeration that America begins
her constitutional history by re-enacting the great
seventeenth century English struggle against government
by royal fiat and prerogative. Paradoxical as it may
seem, the constitutional history of the American colonies is but a splendid, well thumbed page torn from
Stuart England's constitutional controversies. The
colonial charters and statutes expressly conceded
that the English common law is part of the legal
heritage carried across the Atlantic.

Already in 1630's there is unmistakable evidence
that the American colonies had initiated and codified
statutory protection, based on English precedent, for
individual rights and liberties. The notion that
individual liberties depended, in the last resort,
upon the courts was truly unprecedented in seventeenth
century. To appreciate its historical and political
significance for the development of American democracy,
one need only to recall--see Chapter 3--that a protective judicial space enveloping the individual is an
unknown and alien concept in Russian as well as in
Soviet political culture.

But already in the 1680's the charters and liberties granted to the American colonies embrace the
principle of government by law. Its antecedents date
back to Aristotle and, closer to modern thought,
James Harrington (1611-1677) who defined government as
"the empire of laws, and not of men."[4] His republican
faith is nowhere more evident than in his unequivocal
statement that the laws must be made according to the
interest and rights of the governed. As illustrated
in Table 1, with the exception of the right of petition
and right to bear arms (not listed in Table 1), all
the Bill of Rights concepts are specifically American
in origin.

TABLE 1

History of Bill of Rights

Bill of Rights Guarantees	First Document Protecting	First American Guaranty	First Constitutional Guaranty
Establishment of Religion	Rights of the Colonists (Boston)	Same	N.J. Constitution Art. XIX
Free Exercise of Religion	Md. Act Concerning Religion	Same	Va. Declaration of Rights, S. 16
Free Speech	Mass. Body of Liberties, S. 12	Same	Pa. Declaration of Rights, Art. XII
Free Press	Address to the Inhabitants of Quebec	Same	Va. Declaration of Rights, S. 12
Petition	Bill of Rights (1689)	Declaration of Rights and Grievances (1765). S. XIII	Pa. Declaration of Rights, Art. XVI
Due Process	Magna Carta, c. 39	Md. Act for Liberties of the People	Va. Declaration of Rights, S. 8

TABLE 1. - cont.

Bill of Rights Guarantees	First Document Protecting	First American Guaranty	First Constitutional Guaranty
Jury Trial	Magna Carta, c. 39	Mass. Body of Liberties S. 29	Va. Declaration of Rights, S. 8
Witnesses	Pa. Charter of Privileges, Art. V	Same	N.J. Constitution Art. XVI
Counsel	Mass. Body of Liberties, S. 29	Same	N.J. Constitution Art. XVI
Rights Retained By People	Va. Convention Proposed Amend. 17	Same	Ninth Amendment
Reserved Powers	Mass. Declaration of Rights, Art. IV	Same	Same

Nothing underscores more the revolutionary importance of the inclusion of the Bill of Rights in the
American Constitution than Locke's ineffectual advise
that when individual and public policy clash, the
individual can appeal "to Heaven" and wait for enlightenment. The Bill of Rights, limiting political power
in relation to individual rights, fill the yawning
hiatus in Locke's political theory. This is not to
deny the importance of Locke for inspiring the constitutional design of the Founders. It was Locke, not
Hobbes, who reconstructed the concept of political
authority to accord with consent and rights. To be
sure, the relation between consent and power, though
crucial to Locke, is not generic to democracy. David
Hume had shrewdly observed that every system of rule
requires at least tacit consent of some body of men,
even if they be but a handful of "mamelukes."[5] The
need for at least tacit consent, rather than explicit
or popular, leads to what Charles Merriam defined as
the "poverty of power."[6]

The poverty of power is evident in the great
seventeenth century English constitutional controversies that shaped, to a measurable degree, Locke's
thought. Under the influence of Locke, the Founding
Fathers translated the principles of natural rights
into working institutions of a constitutional government. The American political enlightenment revolves
around three basic concepts: reason, experience,
and progress. It must be stressed, particularly in
contrast to Russian political thought, that the colonial debaters went beyond Locke to English precedents
to untangle the relation between natural rights and
parliamentary sovereignty. Reflecting on the American
experiment in constitutional thinking, John Adams
said, "we began to dance"[7] to the political choreo-
graphy besigned by Scottish, English, and French
thinkers.

Dispensing with the Scottish and French influence,
we can concentrate on the English sources of American
constitutional thinking. It is hardly coincidental
that John Fortescue (1385-1479), Chief Justice under
Henry VI, is so frequently quoted by American colonial
debaters. Fortescue distinguished between a political
and despotic government. Though it is still disputed
whether his famous phrase, dominium politicum et
regale, really denotes "constitutional monarchy,"

35

nonetheless, Fortescue stated explicitly that the king "may not rule his people by other laws than such as they assented unto."[8] By placing the king's rule under law, Fortescue revived Aquinas's famous dictum[9] that a regime is political when the ruler's power is constituted by the laws. Laws are not only binding on sovereign power but they are the sinews of legitimate authority. Most important from the natural law perspective, Fortescue derives some laws from the concept of natural law whose function is to dispose man to virtue. The concept of constitutional government, then, has foundation in natural law which, like divine law, is immutable.

As Fortescue makes it rather plain, all other laws are, so to speak, the servants of natural law and pay deference to it. He also contests the king's right to change the laws of the state, particularly natural law to which the civil or human laws ought to conform. Natural laws, in essence, comprise an ethical norm, binding on man and government. To Fortescue, the assent of the whole realm is required for just laws lest they be injurious to the people. He puts laws in the service of justice and not justice in the service of the laws. The necessity of testing the validity of positive laws by referring them to normative natural laws becomes, despite some setbacks and critical reservations, an influential teaching in Western political thought.

According to natural law theory, moral obligation is the most important basis for social unity. Moral values, resident in natural rights, are prescriptive values determining political action. And rights and duties tend to overshadow interests and preferences, both as standards and as referents of behavior. In Fortescue's writings there is an implicit, if not explicit, awareness that constitutional power is to be predominantly shaped by beliefs in rights and, significantly, in moral values. That such maximizing concept of rights becomes a prominent feature in the American political logic, producing a constitutional government, hardly needs elaboration.[10]

8. Locke and Jefferson

Among classical theorists, the maximizing concept of natural rights is most eloquently, if not persuasively, stated by Locke and Jefferson. Both have their detractors. It has often been objected that "inalienable rights" are about as concrete as a big pie in the sky. Such skepticism misjudges the nature and history of natural rights. Already Fortescue recognized that the rule of nature and custom, quaranteeing the rights of king and his subjects, might be changed into constitution through a formal promulgation, provided such an act receives the consent of the king's subjects. Promulgation, however, did not imply that either the king or his subjects might redefine, abridge, or obstruct a right belonging to the other. In sum, natural rights, though transcendental in nature, have an unmistakable utility.

In relying upon natural law, natural rights, and consent, Locke stresses moral obligation without which a polity cannot sustain itself. According to the celebrated thesis, Locke is the primary source of the Jeffersonian philosophy of rights and self-evident truths. In his turn, Locke traced natural rights to the Creator's metaphysical and divine design. Jefferson's intellectual borrowings and the endless search of who got what from whom is a knotty problem worthy of resolute academic concern. Tracing the sources of the Jeffersonian "self-evident" truth, "inalienable rights", and the "nature of man" cannot detain us here[1]. Our concern is that Jefferson's relation to Locke has been seriously questioned of late.[2] The orthodox view that Jefferson is an intellectual descendent of Locke has been challenged time and again. Richard Hofstadter[3] was one of the first to suggest Hobbes, not Locke, as the true guiding spirit of the Founding Fathers. The primary evidence for this line of argument is that the Hobbesian Covenant, where desires and passions of men, such as the aggressive pursuit of riches, glory, and dominion are overcome by those other "passions" that incline men to peace, became "operational" in today's jargon in post-revolutionary America. Hobbes's single-minded insistence on man "as he really is" has allegedly influenced Madison's constitutional thinking. Hobbes's political theory is anchored to the proposition that[4],

37

"I put forth a general inclination of mankind,
a perpetual and restless desire for Power after
power, that ceaseth only in death."

The Federalist theory of politics, propounded by
Madison, is to create a constitutional system where
liberty and factional interests can co-exist. To
retain liberty and yet utilize the dynamism of
factionalism and self-interest, Madison proposed that
it can be accomplished by enlarging the society to be
so governed. The larger the society, hence the spatial
aspects of politics, the greater the "variety of
parties and interests"[5] and the less likely that any
faction can or will congeal and become destructive of
the Republican polity. In sum, conflict management is
integral to Madison's constitutional theory. In
Hobbesian terms, the founding of a state must be so
constituted that the problem created by passionate and
selfish men can be curbed and cured once and for all.
A strong, centralized power is Hobbes's countervailing strategy to tame human passions and desires.
The grand political result of Hobbes's countervailing
strategy is a legal despot whose virtues and virtuosity
are delineated in the Leviathan.

In contrast to Jefferson's idealism, the Madison-
ian concept of government, if its lineaments are traced
to Hobbes, is not an instrument for the realization
of men's higher ideals or a nation's broader interests.

Summarizing, Madison's constitutional thinking
created what Hofstadter called a harmonious system of
mutual frustration. Hofstadter contended that the
American constitutional government, thanks to Madison,
the father of the Constitution, was based on "umpired
strife."[6]

The attempt to link Madison's constitutional thinking to Hobbes, rather than to Locke, is important because it depreciates the natural law foundation of the
American thought. Frank Coleman[7], for instance,
declared that Hobbes is the "true ancestor" of
American constitutionalism. Coleman has questioned the
transmission of natural law doctrines, via Locke and
Paine, to America. In his view, "the revolutionary
character of Locke's thought truly consists in his
political dissemination of the modern philosophy of
constitutionalism provided by Hobbes."[8]

38

Coleman's *ipsissima verba* assertion that Hobbes's constitutionalism is the source of Locke's thought is inconsistent with the generally held view that Locke rejected Hobbesian absolutism on many grounds.[9] Locke and Hobbes begin with the individual. But to Locke man is a moral agent whereas to Hobbes he is not. We do not question Hobbes's rightful place among the masters of political thought. But such defence of Hobbes is beside the point when he is seen as the precursor of American constitutional philosophy. The theory of Hobbes is a theory of unadulterated despotism, or it is nothing. Freedom to him is a wild horse to be broken and chained. As for Hobbes' theory of the state, the "society" called together by the "covenant", upon closer examination, is no society at all. All life is gathered into the one man, Leviathan, at the head of society. The rest of the body is a dead weight, a mere aggregate or mob huddled together by sheer terror, not that organized body which alone can be called the state.

Reproaching Hobbes for denying even the modicum of civic life to community is not intended to overlook the deficiencies in Lockean thought. From our perspective, the law of nature is the key component in the Lockean design for civil government. This law of nature exists prior to and in complete independence of any positive law that a given political society may subsequently enact, and by which all such positive laws are to be interpreted and judged. This law not only commands man to "love his neighbor" in general, but it also contains a detailed code of specific duties covering the whole spectrum of conduct in society. The problem is that Locke moralizes the law by endowing it with purpose of making men both obedient and virtuous. Such concept of law squares neither with the facts of experience and history, nor even with other elements of Lockean political theory.

As a result, the Jeffersonian natural rights philosophy, expressing the rational and co-operative character of *homo sapiens diurnus*, also lacks any positive concept of community and an explicit definition of what moral ends are to be served by government. Investing the Creator with a moral economy that can sanction the indefinitely enumerable "rights," Jefferson, in essence, reduces the government to a list of rights. He prescribes what the government cannot do, without suggesting what it ought to do.

And since the Creator has only rights and no duties, Jefferson cannot say what the Republic should do in extending the "unalienable rights" to the negroes.

The Jeffersonian paradox of rights derives, in large measure, from Locke's postulate that natural law is an expression of God's will, rather than originating from the general consent of men. We emphasize this because, despite the ambiguity in Locke's concept of natural law, it cannot be said that the Lockean natural rights philosophy is Hobbesian by intent or implication. Nor is Locke sympathetic to Grotius and Pufendorf's suggestion that man's inherent sociability and rationality is the source of natural law. In essence, Locke's natural law theory rests on two assumptions. First, reason can discern moral truths which, invariably, refer back to natural law. Second, to Locke, the moral standards ascertained by reason are rational. Both assumptions reflect Locke's conviction that a moral-rational purpose is written into the created universe from which, via rights, issue binding commands and prohibitions on government.

Undeniably, Locke's verification of the first assumption contains a tautology. In attempting to prove that reason is the inherent quality of humanity, Locke argues that reason affirms it. To sort out what Locke means by the binding moral force of natural rights, we must keep in mind the relationship he sets up between God, natural law, and human nature. To begin with, natural law is the expression of God's will and the created man is endowed with reason. Finally, natural law is consonant with human nature. This is another way of saying that God's will is in conformity with what he has created. Thus Locke imposes a twofold obligation on man: to follow God's will on the one hand and man's own nature on the other. But both obligations are the same since both constitute and are subsumed in the law of nature.

It appears that Locke, after all, shared Grotius' view that even if God did not exist, natural law would remain valid.[10] This can be construed from Locke's position that God's will will not only expresses natural law, but, as Locke clearly implies, there is a conformity between rational human nature and natural law. To demonstrate the latter, asserts Locke, is like demonstrating the truth of geometrical theorem. He makes no concession to the claim that men's general consent can

establish natural rights. Locke predicates general
consent on God whose divine economy creates homogeneous
knowledge. Consequently, Locke denies the possibility
for a normative standard or "rule of life" in society
where deities grew up "in garden, where a harvest of
gods was to be expected every year, and where ox and
dog received divine honors."[11]

Locke is explicit that neither utility nor self-
interest can serve as the base of natural rights. This,
more than anything else, sets him off from Hobbes.
To Locke, the rightness of an action is independent of
its utility. Utility, in sum, is the result of an
action's rightness. As Locke put it, if utility is the
standard of what is right then Hercules deserves a
"felon's cross rather than a place in heaven."[12]

What gave the Lockean concept of natural law
power and vigor, inspiring the modern theory of natural
rights via the Jeffersonian philosophy, is the connection it draws between law and freedom. In Locke's
own words,[13]

> "The end of the law is, not to abolish or
> restrain, but to preserve and enlarge freedom.
> For in all states of created beings capable
> of laws, where there is no law, there is no
> freedom. For liberty is to be free from re-
> straint and violence from others which cannot
> be, where there is no law: But freedom is not,
> as we are told, a liberty for every man to do
> what he likes."

To validate the interdependency of natural freedom
and man's knowledge of natural law, Locke was also
relying on the laws of England. The freedom of an
Englishman, he said, consists in his "liberty to
dispose of his actions and possessions"[14] according to
the laws of England.

It should be noted that the American colonists
saw a close association between natural rights and the
"fundamental law" as it developed in seventeenth
century England. Being anchored to the common law
tradition, English thought endorsed emphatically the
law of the land. But the colonists, who revolted not
so much against George III's vest-coated "idiocy" as
against the sovereignty of his corrupt Parliament,

relied on and invoked the law of nature. By a shrewd, masterly insight, Americans had postulated an extra-parliamentary body of constitutional law, discovered in natural law. The broad moral principles of the latter, significantly enough, became the super-constitution to which the American colonists appealed in justifying their cause. The American position was stated eloquently by John Adams. "You have rights," he wrote, "antecedent to all earthy government; rights cannot be repealed or restrained by laws; rights derived from the great legislator of the universe."[15]

Rights antecedent to all earthy government provide the clearest, if not epigrammic, expression of the American concept of natural rights. In asserting the supremacy of natural rights, Americans, and herein lies the conserving element of the American Revolution, rely on the common law tradition. In his Commentaries on the Laws of England, Blackstone speaks of "ethics or natural law" as interchangeable and treats natural law as the ultimate measure of obligation by which legal precepts must be tried, and from which they derive their force and authority. Though Blackstone upheld the Parliament's absolute sovereignty--abhorrent to Americans--he assigned a superiority to natural law because it was dictated by God himself. Natural law, said Blackstone, "is binding over all the globe, in all countries and at all times."[16]

The conflict of authorities, namely, the constitutional struggle between England and America, became the breeding ground for the growth of legal individualism. The latter concept, elaborated in more detail in Ch. 3, is completely unknown to Russian political thought. Analyzing the antecedents of the American Revolution, Charles McIlwain wrote, "Stripped of its constitutional non-essentials, the American Revolution seems to have been the outcome of a collision of two mutually imcompatible interpretations of the British constitution."[17] It was, in so many words, the asserted omnipotence of Parliament in her colonies that drove Americans, in addition to Jefferson's admission that in 1776 "all eyes opened, or opening to the rights of man,"[18] to burst their chains and assume the blessings and security of self-government.

Summarizing the American commitment, at the seed-time of the Republic, to natural rights, it is well to quote Marvin Mayer's conclusion:[19]

42

"Let it be remembered finally that it has ever
been the pride and boast of America that the
right for which she contended were the rights
of human nature."

Whatever the shortcomings of Jefferson's political
theory, so brilliant in metaphysical subleties that
they refuse any institutional mould, he laid the foundation of this nation on the "unchangeable but the
inherent and inalienable rights of man."[20]   Julian P.
Boyd, the doyen of Jeffersonian philosophy, expressed
best what Jefferson embodies in American thought.
"The salient fact that we have long overlooked,"
wrote Boyd, "is that the cardinal principle of Jefferson's life was his uncompromising devotion to the union
because of its identity with human rights."[21]

NOTES

Part One

1. Origins and Antecedents

1. Thomas Paine, Common Sense (Penguin Books, 1976), p. 120.

2. Locke, Two Treatise of Government, ed. Peter Laslett (New York: Mentor Book, 1965), p. 343.

3. The Mayflower Compact (Worcester, Mass.: A. J. St. Onge, 1970), p. 3.

4. Pufendorf, Elementorum Jurisprudentiae Universalis, trs. W. A. Oldfather, in Classics of International Law (Oxford University Press, 1931), p. 168.

2. Antigone and Natural Rights

1. Hobbes, Leviathan, ed. Michael Oakeshott (New York: Collier, 1978), p. 80.

2. Max Weber, Economy and Society, eds. G. Roth & C Wittich, 2 vols. (New York: Bedminister, 1968), 1:867.

3. Ibid.

4. J. W. Krutch, Human Nature and Human Condition (New York: Random House, 1959), p. 203.

5. Sophocles, Antigone, trs. Robert Fitzgerald (New York: Harcourt Brace Jovanovich, 1977), p. 203.

6. Kant's Political Writings, ed. Hans Reiss (Cambridge University Press, 1977), p. 122.

7. Sophocles, Antigone, p. 199

8. Hegel, The Phenomenology of Mind, trs. J. B. Baillie (New York: Harper Torchbooks, 1967), p. 452.

9. Aeschylus, Eumenides, trs. George Thomson, in The Portable Greek Reader, ed. W. H. Auden, (New York: Viking Press, 1973), p. 358.

3. Socrates and Aristotle

1. Mill, On Liberty (Baltimore: Penguin Books, 1974), p. 84.

2. George Steiner, "The Archives of Eden," Salmagundi (Fall 1980-Winter 1981), pp. 57-89.

3. For the continuity of classical heritage in Jefferson, see Merrill D. Peterson, Thomas Jefferson and the New Nation (Oxford University Press, 1970), esp. pp. 922-1004.

4. John Adams, The Works of John Adams, ed. Charles F. Adams (Boston: Little, Brown, 1850-56), 4:193.

5. Alexander Meiklejohn, Free Speech (New York: Harper & Row, 1948), p. 20.

6. Ibid.

7. The Correspondence of Emerson and Carlyle, ed. Joseph Slater (New York: Columbia University Press, 1964), p. 547.

8. Ibid.

9. The New York Times, 25 January 1978, Op. Ed. Section.

10. James Madison, The Writings of James Madison, ed. Gaillard Hunt (New York: Putnam's Sons, 1900-1910), 5:319-20.

11. Alpheus T. Mason, Free Government in the Making, 3rd ed. (New York: Oxford University Press, 1965), p. 173.

12. Aeschylus, The Persians, in The Complete Greek Drama, ed. Whitney J. Oates, 2 vols. (New York: Random House, 1938), 1:58, lines 241-42.

13. Euripides, The Suppliants, in Complete Works, ed and trs. Gilbert Murray (Oxford University Press, 1902-13), 2:403.

14. Aristotle, _Ethics_, in _Basic Works of Aristotle_, ed. Richard McKeon (New York: Random House, 1941), bk. 1, ch. 2.

15. Aristotle, _Ethics_, 1180 a 21.

16. Mortimer Adler, _The Time of Our Lives_ (New York: Holt, Rinehart, and Winston, 1970), p. 123.

17. Aristotle, _Ethics_, 1097a37-1097b6.

18. _Ibid._, Bk. V, ch. 1.

19. _Ibid._, 1138a 8-10.

20. Aristotle, _Politics_, I, 5. 1255.

21. Aristotle, _Rhetoric_, I, 13, 1373.

22. _Ibid._, I, 15.

23. _Ibid._, I, 15, 1475a 25-30.

4. Stoicism and Natural Law

1. Whitney J. Oates, _The Stoic and Epicurean Philosophers_ (New York: Modern Library, 1940), p. 38.

2. _Ibid._, p. 35.

3. Cicero, _On the Commonwealth_, trs. Georg Sabine and S. B. Smith (Columbus: Ohio State University Press, 1929), III. 22.

5. Protestant Contribution to Rights

1. Cotton Mather, _Magnalia Christi Americana_, 2 vols. (Hartford: Silas Andrus & Sons, 1853), 1:27.

2. Quoted by Ernst Troeltsch, _The Social Teaching of the Christian Churches_, trs. Olive Wyon, 2 vols. (New York: Harper Torchbook, 1960), 2:532.

3. J. N. Figgis, Studies of Political Thought from Gerson to Grotius 1414-1625 (New York: Harper, 1960), p. 81.

4. Aquinas, Summa Theologiae, (New York: McGraw Hill, 1964-1976), 28: question 94, article 2.

5. Figgis, Studies of Political Thought, pp. 55-61.

6. Bertram B. Lee Woolf, ed., Reformation Writings of Martin Luther, 2 vols. (London: Lutterworth, 1952), 1:345.

7. Richard Hooker, The Works of Richard Hooker, ed. John Keble (Oxford: Clarendon Press, 1888), 1:233.

8. Hooker, Ecclesiastical Polity, ed. George Eden, 2 vols. (Cambridge: Belknap Press, 1977), 1:84.

9. Summing up the Protestant contribution to democracy, Troeltsch noted that the "really permanent attainment of individualism was due to religion, and not to a secular movement, to the Reformation and not the Renaissance." Quoted by R. H. Murray, The Individual and the State (London, n.d.), p. 81.

10. John Wise, A Vindication of the Government of the New England Churches (1717) (Gainseville, Flo.: Scholars Fascimile & Reprints, 1958), p. 61.

11. Locke, Essays on the Law of Nature, ed. W. von Leyden (Oxford University Press, 1954), p. 225.

6. Eighteenth Century Thesis

1. Rolland Pennock, Democratic Political Theory (Princeton, N.J.: Princeton University Press, 1979), p. 62.

2. Adler, Time of Our Lives, p. 123.

3. Ibid., p. 204.

4. Ibid., p. 103,143.

5. John Rawls, A Theory of Justice (Cambridge: Harvard University Press, 1971), p. 201, 361f.

6. Ibid., p. 554.

7. Ibid., p. 543.

8. John Dewey, The Public and Its Problems (Chicago: The Swallow Press, 1976), p. 86.

9. Ibid., p. 87.

10. Austin Ranney, The Governing of Men, 4th ed. (New York: Dryden Press, 1975), p. 526.

7. Civic Consciousness

1. Alfred North Whitehead, Science and the Modern World (New York: Macmillan, 1962), p. 57.

2. Otto Gierke, Natural Law and the Theory of Society, ed. & trs. Ernest Barker (Cambridge: Harvard University Press, 1950), p. XLVI; see also, F. F. Wright, Jr , American Interpretation of Natural Law (Cambridge: Harvard University Press, 1931), esp. ch. 3.

3. Cornellia G. L. Boutillier, American Democracy and Natural Law (New York: Columbia University Press, 1950), p. 152.

4. James Harrington, The Oceana and Other Works (London: A. Millar, 1747), p. 37.

5. David Hume, The Philosophical Works of David Hume, 10 vols. (Boston: Little, Brown, 1854), 3:28.

6. Charles Merriam, Political Power (Chicago: University of Chicago Press, 1934), p. 159.

7. See C. Vann Woodward, ed., The Comparative Approach to American History (New York: Basic Books, 1968), p. 42.

8. Fortescue, The Governance of England, ed. Charles Plummer (Oxford University Press, 1926), p. 109. Concerning the dispute over the meaning of dominium, see Charles H. McIlwain, Constitutional

8. <u>ism</u> (Ithaca, N.Y.: Great Seal Books, 1958),
    pp. 88-90.

9. Aquinas, <u>Summa Theologica</u>, 1-2, question 105,
    answer 1.

10. On the relationship of American constitutional
    tradition and Revolution, see Michael Lienesch,
    "The Constitutional Tradition," <u>The Journal of
    Politics</u> 42, no. 1 (Feb. 1980), pp. 2-30;
    and comments by G. W. Carey, <u>Ibid.</u>, pp. 36-46.

            8. Locke and Jefferson

1. See Carl L. Becker, <u>The Heavenly City of the
    Eighteenth Century Philosophers</u> (New Haven:
    Yale University Press, 1932).

2. Garry Wills, <u>Inventing America</u> (New York:
    Vintage Books, 1978), interprets Jefferson as
    almost "anti-Lockean" (p. 235).

3. Richard Hofstadter, <u>The American Political
    Tradition</u> (New York: Vintage Books, 1948),
    p. 16.

4. Hobbes, <u>Leviathan</u>, ch. 11.

5. Federalist Papers, #10. Madison's famous axiom
    that passions and interests can be harnessed
    by making them work toward the general welfare
    is traceable to Bacon. "For as in the govern-
    ment of states it is sometimes necessary to
    bridle one faction with another, so it is in the
    government within." cf. Bacon, <u>Works</u>, ed.
    James Spedding, 15 vols. (Boston: Brown &
    Taggard, 1862), 3:338. For similar argument,
    see also Spinoza's assertion that no "effect"
    can be removed unless by "an opposed and stronger
    effect." cf. Spinoza, <u>The Ethics</u>, trs. W. H.
    White (Oxford University Press, 1927), part IV,
    prop. 7 & 14.

6. Hofstadter, <u>Op. Cit.</u>

7. Frank M. Coleman, <u>Hobbes and America</u> (Toronto:
    University of Toronto Press, 1977), p 54.

8. <u>Ibid</u>., p. 68.

9. See Peter Laslett's essay, "Locke and Hobbes,"
   in Locke, <u>Two Treatise of Government</u>; by contrast,
   ʼOakeshott see Hobbes as a theorist of <u>Rechtsstaat</u>
   from whomₗ next to Aristotle and Hegel,
   "we have the most to learn" on jurisprudence.
   cf. Oakeshott, <u>On Human Conduct</u> (Oxford University Press, 1975), p. 109.

10. Grotius, <u>The Law of War and Peace</u>, trs. F. W.
    Kelsey (Indianapolis: Bobbs-Merrill, 1962),
    Proleg. #11.

11. Locke, <u>Essays on the Law of Nature</u>, p. 175.

12. <u>Ibid</u>., p. 209

13. Locke, <u>Two Treatise of Government</u>, #57.

14. <u>Ibid</u>., #59, #63.

15. John Adams, <u>Works</u>, 4:449.

16. William Blackstone, <u>Commentaries on the Laws of
    England</u>, 5th ed. (Oxford University Press, 1778),
    1:41.

17. Charles McIlwain, <u>The American Revolution:
    A Constitutional Interpretation</u> (New York:
    Macmillan, 1923), p. 5.

18. Jefferson, <u>Writings of Thomas Jefferson</u>, ed.
    A. E. Bergh, 20 vols. (Washington, D.C., 1907),
    16:181.

19. Marvin Meyers, <u>The Mind of the Founder: James
    Madison</u> (New York: Bobbs-Merrill, 1973), p. 32.

20. Jefferson, <u>Writings,</u> 16:48

21. Mason, <u>Free Government</u>, p. 371.

Fire burns both in Hellas and Persia
but men's ideas of right and wrong vary
from place to place.

-Aristotle

What Fitness have the United States . . . to
become the secular arm of Reason in checking
the unreason of the world?

-Santayana

Part Two

HUMAN RIGHTS: A CRITICAL PERSPECTIVE

Tracing the historical antecedents of natural
rights and their formative role in America's political design, we emphasized that human rights constitute
the moral foundation of the American Republic.
America's self-regeneration through identification
with moral ideals predisposes it to introduce
virtue into a Hobbesian international world.
"The idea of right," wrote Tocqueville in his brilliant reflections on Democracy in America, "is simply
that of virtue introduced into the political world."[1]
The Carter Administration's crusade for human rights
and placing it at the core of American foreign policy,
re-affirmed by the Reagan Administration, reveal as
much about this nation's commitment to the morality
of politics as it raises critical questions about its
wisdom and policy-effectiveness in the nuclear age.
To put forward moral precepts as universally normative
in a heterogeneous, nuclear world is not without its
inherent problems and dangers. In this chapter
our concern is to present theoretical objections to
human rights. The question whether human rights
should be made more or less salient by the U.S. in
a world where she functions as a state can be better
answered after the conceptual objections to rights are
laid bare.

Before embarking on an overview of the skeptics
and detractors of human rights, let's recap the two
key assumptions in American political thought. Not
surprisingly, both derive from Madison. He made the
principle of consent the axiom of American politics.
He proposed to the First Congress that "there be

51

prefixed to the Constitution a declaration, that all power is originally vested in, and consequently derived from, the people."[2] Second, Madison declared it a perversion of the natural order of things "to make power the primary and central object of the social system, and Liberty but its satellite."[3] It is against this American idealism, embodied, paradoxically, in Madison's political realism, that David Hume's skeptical realism can be outlined.

The science of politics affords few rules which
will not admit of some exception.

-David Hume

1. David Hume

One of the most notable refutation of human rights
is advanced by Hume. In his Treatise on Human Nature,
Hume makes a sharp point,[4]

"Men cannot live without society, and cannot be
associated without government. Government makes
a distinction of property, and establishes the
different ranks among men. This produces industry,
traffic, manufactures, lawsuits, war, leagues,
alliances, voyages, travels, cities . . . and
all those other actions and objects which cause
such a diversity, and at the same time maintain
such a uniformity of human life."

Celebrated for his cool skepticism, Hume recommends the
use of experimental method of reasoning in approaching
moral subjects. In his view, the concept of Nature
cannot be the cause of natural rights. All human
reasoning, said Hume, concerning causes and effects
derive from custom. A belief in natural rights is
more properly an act of the sensitive, rather than
cognitive, part of human nature. As for the particu-
larity and uniformity of values in nations, they are
to be verified by observation rather than attributed
to some rational metaphysics.

According to Hume, values depend upon human pro-
pensities for action. Reason, therefore, cannot
create any obligation in morals or in politics. The
alleged conjunction between universal Nature and
rational man may be true of a particular time in a
particular age. But, as Hume contends, the frequent
conjunction of A and B gives no sufficient reason for
expecting them to be conjoined in the future.
Historically speaking, though Nature and Reason were
used interchangeably by the Stoics and later on by
Locke and Jefferson, it does not necessarily follow
that it will be true in the future.

To Hume, the fundamental "laws of nature," based
on the Lockean postulate that natural rights are

53

antecedent to the state, are entirely artificial and product of human intention. He is hard pressed to accept the Lockean principle that "property and right, and obligation, admit not of degree."[5] It is hardly coincidental that Macpherson, in contending that Western democracies have lost their "monopoly of civilization or world leadership,"[6] updates Hume's position on human rights. Arguing that the Soviet conception of a vanguard state and democracies of the underdeveloped nations "share" the world with Western democracies, Macpherson concludes, somewhat ingeniously, all that remains of Western superiority is its vaunted political, civil liberties. Western democracies' advantage will diminish in the coming decades because, in Macpherson's cheerful prognosis[7],

> "In the scale of political and civil liberties, the Communist nations have nowhere to go but up, while the demands of the welfare state can easily push Western nations down. The West will therefore, I think, be reduced to competing morally."

In Humean fashion, Macpherson invalidates the Western "advantage" on grounds that the "democratic" vision is not the common vision of mankind. Hume also sought to invalidate the universality of rights on grounds that absolute governments, refusing even to pay lipservice to consent and rights, are more common than free governments.

Nor is Hume alone in reminding us that nondemocratic form of governments are the norm in today's heterogeneous world. Ernest B. Haas[8] has compiled data on the political configuration of some 140 states. Of these only 41 states are democratic, or 36%, while the rest comprise the "nondemocratic" nations. Expressing his "worried skepticism" over America's commitment to human rights as a revitalized "global evangelism," Haas underscores the nondemocratic heterogeniety of the world. According to his data, only 36% of the nations today accept human rights as constitutionally binding, i.e. the individual has an enforceable constitutional right to oppose the government. In democratic polities dissidents are not suppressed, and there are regular and free elections. He lists some 31 states where dissent is possible only among a selective elite or within a ruling circle. And there are 20 states, belonging to the "totalitarian" category, where monopolized political power allows no scope for dissent. Not surprisingly, nearly 95% of the human rights violations, as reported by the Amnesty International, occur in non-democratic countries which, using Haas's figure, means 56% of the states in the world.

But to return to Hume. His study of political history convinced him that individuals in "absolute governments," which outnumber "free government," rarely question their rights. He concedes, however, that this might not be true when tyranny becomes too oppressive or unbearable. In Lockean terms, Hume approves opposition to tyrannical government if the latter's "long train of actings"[9] violate the law and discredit the trust reposited in the government.

Despite Hume's Lockean concessions concerning the right to rebel against an oppressive government, his philosophical skepticism cuts the very roots of natural law. Hume argues that natural law, encompassing God and man, cannot be verified empirically. Experimental method, in short, cannot establish a metaphysical, transcendental entity--God, and its rational agent--man. In contrast to the contractual and natural law theorists, Hume finds no social utility in the state of nature. Justice is solely a human device in the interest of society. More important, society means a sociological aggregate of rational creatures rather than autonomous ethical units.

Positing interest, rather than nature, as the sufficient ground for the formation of society, Hume presents an exclusively sociological concept of society and its rules. Predicating society on interest is Hume's most compelling argument for social evolution vis-a-vis the natural law theorists. Justice and morality are products of social evolution rather than originating in a deistic or metaphysical design, as alleged by Locke and Jefferson. In Hume's political philosophy there is an explicit recognition that justice and morality have a social evolution. The nature and scope of justice, he contends, are a matter of social progress.

The incontrovertible claim of Hume's political theory is that good life is dependent on economic progress.[10] And to secure the conditions of economic progress, subsumed in social progress, in an advancing society is the proper concern of government. But to Hume there is no progress without liberty. However, by

making economic progress the proper duty of government, Hume no longer calls for the maintenance of
personal rights. This concept, to be analyzed later,
is key to the Soviet approach to human rights.

Not unlike the Marxist thinkers, Hume sees
society as a "natural unit" and says man is so helpless
by himself that only society can "supply his defects."[11]
Men are so closely knit together in a system of mutual
interdependence that an independent action by any
one of them is virtually inconceivable.[12] Unlike in
the natural law arguments, the Humean individuality
is not "given" but is grounded in experience, social
and historical. Even human sympathy, which he judges
a "powerful principle in human nature,"[13] Hume doesn't
attach to individuality itself but treats it, significantly enough, as a means of human communication. The
concept of sympathy not only demonstrates Hume's
sociological imagination, but is the key component of
his moral theory. In fact, it is impossible to understand Hume's political theory without considering
the role sympathy plays in his moral theory. As Hume
put it.[14]

"So close and intimate is the correspondence
of human souls, that no sooner any person
approaches me than he diffuses on me all his
opinions, and draws along my judgment in a
greater or lesser degree."

The consequences of the Humean notion of moral
sentiment or sympathy is that to him there cannot be
a clean slate in politics. Consequently, it follows
that the true life of every community, as Hume understood it, the true springs of every action are to be
discovered not by the application of any abstract
formula - the rights of man or Lockean natural laws -
but by a watchful study of all that is inherited from
the past. The upshot of Hume's doctrine of sympathy
is that utility, not natural rights, is the key to men's
moral sentiments and judgments. As Hume says in the
Enquiry Concerning the Principles of Morals, men
judge an action or personal quality good insofar as it
is good for something.[15] Consequently, to Hume human
thoughts and actions are largely determined by the pre-
vailing opinions and standards of the group. "Our
opinions of all kinds," he wrote, "are strongly
affected by society and sympathy."[16] As the social
circumstances of men differ, different views of utility
prevail in different societies, and, conversely what

is generally approved or disapproved will be different. Applying Hume's general observation to the Soviet-American conflict on human rights, it can be said that Russian history and culture alter the usefulness and merit of the individualistic human rights that developed in the historical setting of Anglo-American civilization.

Hume's argument for the variety of mankind is grounded in the sociological assertion that men's ways and thinking are to a great extend moulded by those of the group to which they belong. This social plasticity of human nature, imprinted with social values, is the basic Humean thrust against the universality of human rights. The inference one can draw from Hume, germane to our concern, is that man values those things upon which society sets high value. And since Russian society had never set high values on individual rights, the suppression of individual conscience cannot elicit as much opposition in Russia as it does in America. To Hume, the ground of moral judgment is utility, not prescriptive human rights.

To recap the salient conflict between the Lockean-Jeffersonian human rights and Hume's disclaimer against them, to Locke the political order to be legitimate must rest on right and not on force. Logically, Locke defines tyranny as "the exercise of power beyond right."[17] To Locke, the government must guarantee the harmonious coexistence of authority and liberty. By contrast, Hume contends that in all governments there is a perpetual "intenstine struggle, open or secret, between Authority and Liberty, and neither of them can ever absolutely prevail in the contest."[18]

Hume's position is that by necessity individual liberty must make "great sacrifice" in every government, even though there might be a constitutional limitation on the exercise of political authority. Though the individual may prefer liberty, in the contest between liberty and authority the government may "challenge the preference."[19] Hume is equally skeptical about consent as the base of popular government. In his view,[20]

"Were you to preach, in most parts of the world, that political connections are founded altogether on voluntary consent or a mutual promise, the magistrate would soon imprison you as seditious for loosening the ties of obedience. . . ."

Leonid Brezhnev, needless to say, would understand
well this reasoning. According to Hume, not moral
consent but "fear and necessity" is the base of
government. Whereas to Locke and Jefferson natural
rights constitute a moral claim against the government,
to Hume nothing is more erroneous than to assume that
government ought to be based on consent. Natural
rights based power, in Hume's view, leads to paradoxes
"repugnant to the common sentiments of mankind and to
the practice and opinion of all nations in all ages."[21]

It is not individuals who have rights but states.

-Indira Gandhi, 1975

2. Legal Positivism

Legal positivism assails liberalism and its concept of individual liberty on two accounts. Dispositionally and historically, liberalism is a form of individualism.[1] Liberal thinkers seek to understand society, state, and economy as an expression of individual actions. Central to the liberal creed is the emphasis on individual's freedom, which subsumes individual dignity, moral autonomy, and opportunity for self-development. In Isaiah Berlin's felicious phrase, "To be free to choose and not to be chosen for is an inalienable ingredient in what makes human beings human."[2] In sum, freedom is the necessary condition of translating one's worth, as a moral and rational agent, into reality, to actualize one's potentialities as a person. Freedom, then, is a good "if anything is."[3]

It is against the liberal concept of liberty that legal positivism makes its disclaimers. As the term "positive" indicates (derived from the Latin positus, i.e. set down), legal positivism conceives the concept of law as the product of human will, in contrast to what has not been invented but had arisen by nature. Second, legal positivism is critical of individualism in which repose rights against the government. As the leading exponent of legal positivism put it, "rights are made by recognition."[4]

Though not a legal positivist, Margaret Macdonald, in her much quoted classical essay, "Natural Rights,"[5] argues it is a tautology to claim "men have natural rights." Reminiscent of Hume, she argues human nature fails to measure up to the transcendental demand that the individual ought to realize himself in reason or moral purpose. Noting the absence of a generally agreed upon definition of man, she concludes that the ethical assertions inherent in natural rights arguments are merely value expressions. Differently put, statements about natural rights are analogous to personal preference in art. Consequently, making claims to natural rights is similar to expressing aesthetic preferences. Aesthetic judgments, inherently personal and subjective, can impress and even convince some. But, as a general theory of art, they do not prove anything.

In another essay, "Ethics and the Ceremonial Use of Language,"[6] Macdonald argues that moral judgments display those characteristic uses of language that expediate action, or the larger process of action designated as conduct. Relying on the findings of the anthropologist Bronislaw Malinowski, she suggests a certain parallel between the ceremonial-ritualistic use of language and moral discourse. Malinowski, indeed, saw in the ceremonial language of primitive society that publicity and normative authority we commonly associate with moral discourse. In primitive societies, ceremonial acts congeal around the rites of birth, marriage, war, and hunting. Ceremonial rites impart communal importance to otherwise individual events or acts. Even in an authoritarian state, she wrote,

> "the leader must distinguish, by some formalities, laws from other personal decisions. So the authority of law itself is inexplicable without the ceremonies conducted by their characteristic modes of utterance, which attend its introduction."[7]

To Macdonald, as to Hume, the moral standards embodied in natural law derive their authority from the social-ized disposition of the members of the community, rather than from the presumed reason or moral value of "natural man."

We need to stress that Margaret Macdonald, though not a positivist, shares Hume's skepticism concerning the metaphysically presumptive, individualistic natural rights. Paradoxical as it may sound, many protagonists of natural rights subscribe to different forms of individualism, though not the Lockean-Jeffersonian variant. In fact, human rights could be classified into three models in terms of what roles and values are assigned to the individual. Table 2 sketches three models of human rights which, for our purposes, are provisional and heuristic.

The social rights model, box two in the Table, indicates that representative thinkers of public interest, or social good, are individualist. They

TABLE 2

Models of Human Rights

	Key Concept	Key Value	Representative Thinker	Model	
1	Individual	Reason, Nature Deity	Locke, Jefferson Dworkin	Natural Rights	1
2	Public Interest	Social (good) Society	Hume, Dewey, Rawls	Social Justice	2
3	Collective	History Communist Society "Real" democracy	Hegel, Marx	Collective Rights	3

deny, like Dewey, that individuals are the ultimate constituents of the social world, or that key values can derive from pre-political "right." Consider the position of Dewey who rejected the traditional duality of individual and society. Since the known and the knowable are in constant interaction with each other in society, no individual mind can be completely known when separated from society. To Dewey, the "social" is the most inclusive and important aspect of thought, and, in effect, of his own thinking.[8] Dewey subsumes the universal human relations in the category of "social" and declares that government is set up to serve the public interest. The state, he wrote, is a "public articulated and operating through representative officers."[9]

Dewey's central concern was to demonstrate that the habits of the mind, values, and beliefs are mediated and sifted through the medium of social environment. The encompassing social medium, he claims, like democracy itself, has a long evolutionary history. Consequently, it is a more transparent, if not congenial, medium for expressing individual moral tendencies than, for instance, Kant's moral imperative, which states that the individual must always be treated as an end and never as a means.

Unlike Locke or Jefferson, Dewey assigns priority to the community rather than to the individual. Only by considering "community" as a fact, states Dewey, can we develop a non-idealistic concept of democracy. Though praising the values of "fraternally" shared experience, to Dewey, "Fraternity, liberty and equality isolated from communal life are hopeless abstractions."[10] It is not without paradox that Dewey could express preferences for communal values and also lavish praise on Jefferson with all his devotion to Lockean natural rights. After all, the Lockean reason, the "one eyed reason"[11] as Whitehead called it, is not known for its social vision. But there cannot be doubt about Dewey's preference of social over individual value. He explicitly recommented the substitution of "moral rights" for "natural rights."[12]

To sum up, Dewey, representative figure of the social rights model, is critical of Locke's concept of natural rights. To Locke and Jefferson man is a moral agent whose ends are, ultimately, determined by God, the Creator. To Dewey, public good and government are

the product of a socialized man's rational and cooper-
ative effort. In Lockean philosophy, on the other
hand, the government as well as the social order
derive their value from the created universe. In
short, the natural rights model of government is
predicated on a transcendental, extra-human order of
values. Nothing distinguishes the natural rights
model more sharply from the Marxist model of human
rights than the extra-human authority Locke invokes
for liberalism. Though the contrast is developed
in the next chapter, Locke deserves here a full quote.[13]

> "A dependent intelligent being is under the power
> and direction and dominion of him on whom he
> depends and must be for the ends appointed him
> by that superior being. If man were independent
> he could have no law but his own will, no end
> but himself. He would be a god to himself
> and the satisfaction of his own will the sole
> measure and end of all his actions."

3. Hegel's Concept of Natural Right

The seminal importance of Hegel's political philosophy and concept of natural right is that they lay the
foundation of Marx's critique of natural rights. Marx
himself admitted that "The great thing in Hegel's
Phenomenology. . . is simply that Hegel grasps the
self development of man as a process. . . that he
grasps the nature of work and comprehends objective
man. . . ."[1]

To illustrate how Hegel prepared the ground for
Marx's attack on the rights of man, we must analyze
briefly the distinction Hegel drew between the laws of
nature and the laws of right. The first are immutable.
The latter, the so-called positive laws, are subject
to change. The Hegelian distinction between the laws
of nature and that of normative laws is, in effect,
the contrast of nature and spirit. To Hegel, whereas
right proceed from the Spirit, Nature possesses no
laws of right. Consequently, Nature and Spirit
stand opposed to each other.

The Hegelian concept of Nature carries the imprint
of God. But this Nature is modified by human labour
and, as such, is the product of human will. The
importance of the two concepts of Nature; the physical
Nature independent of the human will and Nature modified
by and dependent on human will, is that Hegel ascribes
higher priority to humanized Nature. Not surprisingly,
the Hegelian concept of natural law recalls Hobbes
whose all-embracing state power derives its legitimacy
from the psychological impulses of human nature. The
Hobbesian man behaves in accordance with his own brute
naturalness, rather than the precepts of morality of
the created Nature. As the Lockean quote indicates,
(p.63), man is under the dominion of the superior
being-Creator.

Hegel breaks radically with the liberal notion of
rights by displacing God, key to Locke and Jefferson's
political theory, with an absolute will. Putting will
in place of God is the decisive step toward the Hegelian
concept of right.[2]

"The will that wills itself is the basis of all
right and of all obligation, hence of all positive
laws, moral duties, and imposed obligations."

By releasing the ego from all transcendental limitations, Hegelian concept of "rights" stand squarely on Hobbesian grounds of natural rights. In the Hegelian system, it is not the individual who is free but his will. All man's values, the spiritual actuality he possesses, are realized through the state alone. In Hegel's hyperbolic dictum, man's spiritual and ethical value depend on the state. When Hegel argues that the state is the actualization of human freedom and embodies man's moral-ethical dimension, he doesn't mean the deciding and doing man. He means the concentrated inwardness or the internal center--will--of man. As he put it, "Will without freedom is an empty word, just as freedom is only real as well, as thinking subject."[3]

The Hegelian will refers to itself rather than to something outside the will. In Hegel's own words, the spirit is "self-contained being, and this precisely is freedom."[4] The crucial assumption in the Hegelian philosophy of right is that the necessity of the state, though reminiscent of Hobbes, rests upon that law which freedom prescribes to itself. The contrast then between Hegelian and Lockean concept of "rights" can be stated as follows. To Locke, natural law principles prescribe a limited government. To Hegel, the absolute ethical (sittliche) totality, embodied and expressed through the state, is not confined by natural rights.

Hegel abandons the traditional view that the telelogical order of nature transcends the individual and civil society. Though the Hegelian philosophy of the state, as indicated, starts from the liberal concept of the individual, his philosophy of right is primarily concerned with the state. And the latter, expressing the common good which emerges from the individual will, is not the guarantor of individual rights and liberties.

The salient feature of Hegelian political thought is to minimize and remove the fatal antagonism between state and individual, which from the days of Hobbes had divided Europe into two hostile camps. The state, Hegel urges, is not formed by a grant of certain arbitrarily selected powers from the individual, but by taking up into itself a whole spectrum of individual life. Hegel struck a fatal blow at the theory that individual conscience, which Locke, Jefferson, and Kant held an absolute law unto itself, allegedly owes its determined form to the rights that repose in nature or common sense. It is Hegel's insistence on the impossibility of a purely individual morality draining the state of all vitality, moral and intellectual, that we recognize as his chief contribution to political thought.

In the Hegelian state individuals no longer pursue their private aims unless they contribute, directly and immediately, to the public interest. The restoration of classical model of community-polis-as an alternative to the liberal model influenced Marx's thinking in assigning primacy to the community over the individual. In Hegelian philosophy, the individual striving for happiness or good is contingent upon taking into account the common good. In case of conflict, the welfare of all takes precedent over individual rights.

That Hegel deifies the state is commonplace truth. It invited Kierkegaard's ridicule[5] and Schopenhaur's scurrilous remark about Hegel "this Caliban of the spirit."[6] The Hegelian state was to remedy the liberal defects of the state. Hegel believed that the individual's "destiny" is to lead a "public life." But the latter, placed by Hegel within the realm of "spirit," is predicated on the unity of particular and general. In plain language, individual subjectivity can be suppressed, or overcome, in favor of substantiality, i.e the community.

Unlike the liberal model of the state, the Hegelian state contains ethical-spiritual values. In Hegel's daring locution, the state is that spirit which marches through the world with God's steps. Hegel sketches a spirit-glutted ethical state, beyond individual control and consent. This state has nothing in common with the state the American Fathers framed and ratified to promote, among others, "general welfare," and "secure the blessings of liberty." Nor is the minimal state, bound by rights and anchored to consent, Hegel's philosophical prescription. As Hegel expressed it,[7]

"It is false to maintain that the foundation of the state is something at the option of all its members. It is nearer the truth to say that it is absolutely necessary for every individual to be a citizen."

In the polis the individual was educated and
trained to be a citizen, first and foremost. Belonging to such a community qualified for what Hegel
defined as the "absolute ethical life" (absolute
Sittlichkeit). It tells us something about American
values that Thoreau, summing up the political creed
of transcendental individualism, preferred the
experience of huckleberrying because there was
"no state in sight among the berry bushes."[8]
Raised on the eighteenth century liberal ideas,
Thoreau, who also idealized the Greeks, offers a
revealing contrast to Hegel's ethical state.
"I would remind my countrymen," Thoreau wrote,
"that they are to be men first, and Americans only
at a late and convenient hour. . . ."[9]

No student of politics can fail to detect in
Hegel a brilliant attempt to utilize natural law
doctrines for the justification of the individual's
conscious identification with the state. Subsuming
the individual in the citizen, Hegel transforms the
science of politics into a science of the state. To
be sure, he endorsed the principles of 1789 and, in
fact, had never forgiven the passivity of Germans
while the French Revolution evolved toward a republic.
Yet Hegel is not part of liberal thought, despite
some recent attempts to put him next to Paine, Locke,
and Montesquieu.[10] Hegel goes so far as to argue
that the individual must show readiness to die for
the community.

Hegel's critical view of natural rights can be
inferred from his searching analysis of Sophocles's
great drama Antigone. He sees Antigone, who appeals
to conscience, as an example of the individualistic,
Kantian ethics which legislates unconditionally
and universally. Antigone defends the so-called
"higher laws." But as Hegel interpreted it, private
conscience cannot constitute an alternative to the
state's social norms. Creon's law, Hegel argued,
is the ethical equivalent of Antigone's law of
private conscience. The supreme tragedy then is that
two ethically valid laws collide without hope of
reconciliation. Hegel leaves no doubt that Creon's
civil act is more related to Geist than Antigone's
personal courage. In the drama of ethical values,
Hegel sides with Creon and, therefore, against
natural rights.[11]

It is not without relevance to note that Hegel's major work, <u>Philosophy of Right</u>, is actually titled <u>Natural Law and Political Science</u>. Though the book contains natural right arguments, Hegel's vision is Platonic not only because it idealizes the ethical life of classical Greece but because he describes a series of meditations necessary for individual consciousness to identify with the ethical state. And in his major essay, <u>The Scientific Treatment of Natural Law</u>, Hegel assaults the whole tradition of natural law thinking.

Assigning a central role to the state in his philosophy of history, Hegel, in effect, suspends natural law doctrines as prescriptive for politics. The Hegelian system is characterized by the reciprocity of the individual and society. The majestic, sweeping and solemn Hegelian cycles of history, inexorable and irreversible, are silent about individual rights. Contrast it with liberal thinkers like Locke, Mill, and Tocqueville. To them, the irreducible essence of good government is that the organs of the sovereign people--free speech, press, and right to conscience--enjoy an autonomy within body politics. In other words, these organs of the people cannot and must not become the organs of the state. But they do become the organs of the state in Hegel's ethical state.

It is hardly surprising that Hegel referred to the ruled as "crowd" or "heap." In the popular representative body, he saw but an invitation to political turmoil, associated with the destructive phases of the French Revolution. As he expressed it,

> ". . . what can one begin to do with such a rabble (<u>Pobel</u>). . . which does not lead a public life and which has not been educated to the consciousness of the common will and to action in the spirit of the whole."[12]

Obsessed with unity and order, all bound up with final causes, Hegel could not allow individual conscience to intrude into the totality of an ethical state. According to Hegel, it must be firmly grasped that there is[13]

"only one spirit, one principle, which leaves
its impress on all political situations as well
as manifesting itself in religion, art, ethics,
sociability, commerce and industry, so that the
different forms are branches of one trunk."

The notion that man is but an "empty singleness,"[14]
without attachment to the universal trunk, is contrary
to the whole spirit of human rights

The Hegelian philosophy of rights suffers from
the worst case of the fallacy of misplaced concrete-
ness. Namely, he conceives every aspect of human
reality as an expression of a single, unitary
Weltgeist. The uniqueness of the person, or what
Hegel calls the "atomic personalities," loses its
concrete validity in his general analytical scheme.
He was explicit that the "Government is the universal
supervisor; the individual is mired in the particular."[15] To counter Hegel with Shakespeare, the
so-called honest physicians of the state--Plato's
favored image--degenerate into quacks, administering
the "poppy and mandragola"[16] of oblivion to individuals.

We have underscored Hegel's use of natural law
as a means to social-political cohesion, leading to
an absolutist state. In his own way, Hegel's
philosophy of right typifies the pervasive eighteenth
century German tendency to reconstruct man's shattered
unity, under the impact of modernity, and project
an alternative to the "atomic personalities" of
liberal thought. Hegel's expressivist anthropology
had a major impact on Marx's thinking.

Nor is it coincidental that it was Hegel who,
conceiving the law as an instrument of the state
and associating the latter with "objective freedom,"
became something of a philosophical hero in mid-
nineteenth century Russia.[17] The reasons for this
are not difficult to see. Leading members of the
Russian intelligentsia were suspicious, if not outright hostile, of liberal-democratic trends in
Western thought. It should never be lost sight of
that Hegel's Rechtsphilosophie marks the final and
conscious break with the individualist theory which,
under one form or another, had shaped European
thought at least since the Renaissance and definitely
since the Reformation. It is generally accepted that
Hegel, in many respects, followed Kant's footsteps.[18]
But Hegel also made systematic attempts to refute
Kant's categorical imperative that man, as a moral

agent, must treat humanity in himself as in others as an end, never as a means.

Hegel's anti-Kantian stand to demonstrate the impossibility of purely individual morality also reveals Hegel's own instinctual dislike of the uncertainty and insecurity he associated with individualism. In Hegelian thinking, the individual has no rights against the state, and a fortiori never any duty to resist it. Undeniably, there are problems in the Kantian categorical imperative, premised on the conviction that purely rational procedures can show us what we ought to do to escape from determinism and to achieve freedom and autonomy. Yet Kant's insistence that man ought to set moral example to others is more acceptable that Hegel's view that freedom can only be realized in the state and citizens have an "interested obligation" to obey the state. To conclude on a note how Hegelian philosophy leads to the poverty of morality in Marxism, the Hegelian attempt to overcome Kant's individualistic morality paves the way for the Marxist replacement of the individual moral agent with the historical man.[19]

Marx and Engels did not even appreciate political
proclamations of human rights.

-Thomas Masaryk

4. Marxism and Human Rights

The leading Marxist thinker of this century,
Georg Lukacs argued that Hegel and Marx parted company
over the concept of "reality." According to Lukacs,
Hegel failed to understand that "Society becomes the
reality for man."[1]

In his Critique of Hegel's Philosophy of Right,
Marx defined the special role of the proletariat as
follows.

"When the proletariat announces the dissolution
of the existing social order, it only declares
the secret of its own existence, for it is the
effective dissolution of this order."[2]

The Marxian impulse to dissolve the world-order, one may
add, also includes the dissolution of natural law tradition. To Marx, Communism is not merely an ideal,
but an "actual movement" destined to sweep away
"the present state of things."[3]

Convinced that Communism heralds the final "human"
solution to class-ridden social existence, Marx scorned
the rights of man. Congruent with his scornful view
that the so-called eternal metaphysical values have
an economic substratum, Marx held that the content of
legal institutions is not legal but always political and
economic. In his own words,[4]

"Thus none of the so-called rights of man go beyond
egostic man, as he is in civil society, namely
the individual withdrawn behind his private
interests and whims and separated from the
community."

To Marx it was axiomatic that the real basis for
the development of law is the ever changing power relations between the classes. Consequently, since the
dominant class imposes the conqueror's law on the
weaker, the capitalist legal system, in Marx's opinion,
could never be neutral. Furthermore, if man's social
existence determines his conscience and not conscience
his social existence, then law is caused by the social

73

condition of man. But the Marxist genesis of law is
not without its own serious problems. The postulate
concerning the human mind's inability to reflect accurately the social reality leads Marx to the costly fallacy to subsume law itself in the category of ideology.
Differently put, Marx's own philosophy compels him to
deny, despite commonsense evidence, any autonomous
development and function to the legal system in society.
Lenin put the issue with his customary bluntness. He
concluded that law and the state are not two distinct
phenomena, but are, in essence, the two sides of the
same phenomena, namely "class dominance."

Compare this with Locke's theory that natural
rights are antecedent to political society and, as
such, binding on the government men consent to live
under and obey. The Marxist view that neither the
state nor the law transcend the material substratum
of society has far reaching consequence. To Marx the
law has no validity apart from the class structure
of society at a given historical period. In this
Marx may have been influenced by Bentham who leveled
the severest blow at those who saw law as consonant
with antecedent moral principles and rights.
"Property and Law," said Bentham acidly, "were born
and die together."[5]

Engels expressed forcefully the Marxist view
of law. "The jurist imagines," he wrote, "that he
is operating from a priori principle, whereas they
are really only economic reflexes."[6] The Marxist
claim that law has no history of its own apart
from the economic development and interest of the
ruling class merits some comments. There is some
kernel of truth in this. Justice Holmes wrote,
the life of the law has been shaped by the "felt
necessities of the times, the prevalent moral and
political theories, institutions and public policy
. . . ."[7]

Incontestably, the concept of law has changed
as society has undergone economic changes. But
Marxism goes much further than this commonplace
truth. The claim that economics begets the law fails
to indicate whether changes in law are variables of
the changing economic order, or, most important, men's
changing perception of what is "right" transforms
the economic order. Marxism cannot explain why,
for instance, the taught tradition of law, expressed

in judicial decisions in the United States, did and does oppose class interest. In the Anglo-American law, at least since the fifteenth century, judges handed down decisions inimical to dominant class interests.

If we insist with Marx that the law cannot be anything but the reflex of economic relations, how are we to explain such permanent principles of the law as Habeas Corpus. If there are no stabilities in law, transcending the material substratum, how are we to account for the Bill of Rights? When a prominent Soviet jurist in the 1930s declared that, "We refuse to see in the law an idea useful for the working class,"[8] he was true heir to Marx's tragic misunderstanding of the concept of law.

To argue with Marx that the law, particularly in bourgeois society, is a great sham is to ignore centuries of struggle in which the poor and the dis-possessed--whose cause he championed--attempted to fill the law with a humane and compassionate content. Ironically, class struggle itself was mediated through the forms of law. Even a cursory study of the evolution of law in eighteenth century England cannot fail to establish the extraordinary psychic power of the law. Among other things, it was the evolution of procedural formalism which enabled the pauper criminal to escape from the gallows as well as leading to the occasional conviction of a nobleman.

In addition, the mercy and pardon power of the law also reached the poor, even if not so frequently as Marx may have wished. Pardons, after all, were presented as acts of grace rather than as favors granted to class interests. The legal process in the West, despite Marx's argument that law is a mere epiphenomenon, was one of the primary forms of social practice through which the actual relationships, embodying class interest, were created and articulated. Most important, it was the subordinate classes in the eighteenth century who argued that a "just price" in the sale of grain had a moral base.

The highly schematic and reductionist Marxist view that law is but another mask for class rule cannot be supported by historical research. Even such a sympathetic student of Marxism as E. P. Thompson, the leading authority on the English working class, rejects the Marxist view that law was a pliant "medium to be twisted this way and that by whichever interests already possess effective power."[9] Thompson's conclusion on the question whether law denotes class power deserves full quote.[10]

> "I have shown in this study a political oligarchy inventing callous and oppressive laws to serve its own interests. . . . Indeed, I think that this study has shown that for many England's governing elite the rules of law were a nuisance, to be manipulated and bent in what ways they could. . . . But I do not conclude from this that the rule of law itself was humbug. On the contrary, the inhibitions upon power imposed by law seem to me a legacy as substantial as any handed down from the struggles of the seventeenth century to the eighteenth, and a true and important cultural achievement of the agrarian and mercantile bourgeoisie. . . ."

We concur with Thompson. The Marxists consistently and systematically overlook the "difference between arbitrary power and the rule of law." Though one ought to expose the shams and inequalities concealed beneath the law, yet Thompson unequivocally affirms that the "rule of law" itself is an "unqualified human good."[11] To deny or belittle the latter, as Marxists do, is, in Thompson's own words, "to disarm ourselves before power." The tragic record of Soviet Communism, with its sordid tale of arbitrary rule and Stalinist reversion to a Hobbesian state of nature, is hauntingly captured by Thompson. To deny the rule of law, Thompson wrote, is

> "to throw away a whole inheritance of struggle about law, and within the forms of law, whose continuity can never be fractured without bringing men and women into immediate danger."[12]

Marx's reductionist argument about law as a class rule is evident in the Soviet treatment of law as an instrument of rulership, rather than as the guardian of right. For Marx, Isaiah Berlin reminds us,[13]

"the conceptions of natural rights, and of
conscience as belonging to every man
irrespective of his position in the class
struggle, are rejected as liberal illusions."

What a subtly tragic irony that Marx, so passionate for pure truth, unqualified good, who wanted above
all to liberate man from the invisible tyranny of
God and the visible tyranny of class, disdained
civil liberties and human rights. Granted that it
is still in the lap of gods whether a society can
succeed by adhering to civil liberties and human
rights. But the Marxist alternative to civil
liberties, that appeared so far in Communist
societies, have been immeasureably worse. Marx
has convinced himself that the metaphysical illusions
of man, the intolerable labor of thought man continues
to undertake in order to overhaul existing assumptions,
must be torn to shreds before a social existence,
devoid of any hiatus irrationalis can be realized.
While Marx declared war on irrationalism, he fell
victim to his own myth that the "essence of man does
not possess any true reality."[14]

The final irony is that Marx, who came to
Communism in the interest of freedom, ends up
defining liberty as the necessity of labor. On
historical grounds, one can readily see why Marx
opposes the principles of freedom and rule of law.
Examples could be multiplied at random of Marx's
critical comments on the rights of man. Just to
cite a few examples. "We have no liking for 'freedom,'"
he wrote, "that only holds good in the plural."[15]
Evaluating the history of rights in England, he
concludes that habeas corpus is the "privilege of the
rich" and trial by jury is a "political and not a
legal institution."[16]

To be sure, William Pitt and his ruling elite
had suspended the habeas corpus in 1794 when they
perceived the danger that the Jacobin clubs, organized
in Birmingham and Manchester, might subvert the
"rights of free-born Englishmen." Jacobin radicals
were arrested on warrants from the Secretary of State
and confined without indictment or trial at his
"Majesty's pleasure." But once again it is only
half of the story. Despite Pitt and Walpole's
abuse of habeas corpus, in the end the ruling class
of England surrendered to the rule of law rather

than repudiate the constitutional legality of political power. By contrast, the Soviet ruling elite, many of whom are accomplices of the Gulag Archipelago, have yet to submit their political power to the rule of law.

Nor is the Soviet ruling elite's arbitrary power without doctrinal support. Marx not only declared the law as political in scope and substance, but poured ridicule on the whole notion of impartial juryman or impartial judge. He dismissed both as consummation of "juridicial mendacity and immorality." More to the point, Marx stigmatized the "sanctity of the defendent," i.e. the principle that one is innocent until proven guilty. In light of the Soviet judicial history, Marx's statement hardly needs elaboration. Vladimir Bukovsky, who spent twelve of his thirty-five years -- over half of his adult life -- in Soviet prisons and labor camps, left this account of his trial:[17]

> "The fate of the accused had been decided in advance--the ideological state could not afford to have a civil-rights point of view imposed upon it. . . . The charges, the court, and official propaganda insisted on their own ideological prescriptions, whereas the defendants, their defense lawyers, and the witnesses invoked their legal rights."

And Engels, himself a keen student of English history, could write, "The whole English Constitution and the whole constitutional public opinion is nothing but a big lie."[18] In similar vein, Marx swept aside the Christian idea of freedom as an "illusion." As to the claim that each born human being is entitled to freedom and dignity, Marx adds the acid comment:[19]

> "An Irish peasant, e.g. he can only choose to eat potatoes or starve, and he is not always free to make even this choice."

Paradoxical as it may seem, Marx condemns capitalism not because it is unjust or violates man's natural rights, but because it denies the individual's basic needs. Though Marx constantly speaks of "exploitation" of the workers and the wretchedness of their condition, he never expressed indignation over capitalism being an unjust system.

It may sound strange, indeed, that Marx took
a critical view of the judicial aspects of politics.
The whole legal process and appeal to courts to
secure and redress rights and liberties Marx
found quite "ridiculous." Throughout his voluminous
writings, there is no evidence that he ever considered
that rights can constitute and add up to the
"power of man." The following schema illustrates
Marx's reasoning on the rights of man.

1. The right of man ~ ~ ~ ~ ~ ~ -my right

2. Human rights ~ ~ ~ ~ ~ ~ -egoistic right

In Western political thought the concept of rights
and justice play a formative role. Marx, by contrast,
finds the whole judicial approach to man as irrelevant,
if not an outright sham.

In the Epilogue to his three volume work, Main
Currents of Marxism, Kolakowski wrote, "Marxism
has been the greatest fantasy of our century."[20]
Kolakowski associates this "fantasy" with Marx's
attempt to create a "society of perfect unity."
From our perspective, the key to this fantasy is
Marx's determined effort to alter the standpoint
from which society is judged. In so many words,
Marx recasts Western political thought by shifting
from legal-ethical to socio-economic evaluation of
the human order. To him the concept of law and
rights, to name only two elements of the superstructure, are metaphysical constructs, incompatible
with the "objective reality" of social existence.
Marx insists that values and principles are the
product of historical man whose essence is inseparable
from the "economic structure" of society. This
does not mean that the political is merely a mechan-
istic reflection of the economic. But it does mean
that the standpoint from which Marx judges society
has shifted from the legal-ethical to the socio-
economic perspective. This shift, offering a
new dimension on society, recalls, in terms of its
far reaching consequences, Kant's so-called Coper-
nician Revolution.

Ranking Marx next to Kant in philosophical
importance does not imply identity. Far from it.
Marx was critical of Kant for separating principle
from history. As Marx put it,[21]

"When we ask ourselves why a particular principle was manifested in the eleventh or in the
eighteenth century rather than in any other,
we are necessarily forced to examine minutely
what men were like in the eleventh century,
what they were like in the eighteenth,
what were their respective needs, their productive forces, their mode of production and
their raw materials. . . ."

It is this real or "profane history" of men that was
to replace those "eternal principles" Marx so resol-
utely opposed.

It is appropriate here to note that Marx
rejected the generic role of justice in politics
in favor of the value of labor. He sacrificed, in
his political philosophy, rights in the name of the
normative role of labor. But this is not without
some paradox. On the one hand, as we saw, Marx
had no use for the autonomous sphere of judicial
decisions based on generic principles of justice
and rights, which he viewed as relative to a given
society's structure. On the other hand, and herein
lies the paradox, Marx suspended his own historical
relativism when appealing to "rights" in arguing
for the necessity of the disorganized proletariat
to form a cohesive unit.

Differently put, the proletariat could appeal
to "rights" in order to transform itself into a
cohesive, revolutionary mass. Marx consistently
argued that the ruling class utilizes the law, including natural rights, to oppress, under the pre-
text of universal reason and principles, the ruled.
Yet the oppressed proletariat appeals to the same
principles and rights in seeking a redress what they,
rightly, consider a legal wrong. But for Marx to
appeal to rights on behalf of the proletariat
presupposes that the concept of law is generic and
contains normative principles not assimilated into
the state apparatus of the ruling class.

Marx, however, contradicts his own general
theory that legal standards disguise class oppression
when he describes how the rising middle class appeals
to natural rights in its historical struggle with
the landed aristocracy. Conversely, and consistent
with Marx's philosophy of history, in bourgeois

society, coinciding with the American Declaration
of Independence and the French Declaration of the
Rights of Man, the proletariat appeals to natural
rights in seeking to forge an effective unity against
its oppressors. In short, Marx treats both the
concept of law and natural rights as the means of
legislative enactment of an ascending class.

There is a final paradox in Marx's insistence
that legal relations arise from economic ones. In
his attempt to give a "scientific" and not legal-
moral basis of society, Marx forgets his own dicta
when invoking one concept of justice in condemning
the proletariat's decreasing proportionate share
in the socially created values. To argue that the
proletariat receives a diminishing sum of total values
presupposes a norm or principle whereby a more just
distribution of values is possible. But one can
search in vain Marx's writings, including the Capital,
for any explicit appeal to conscience or moral principle. In fact, Marx does not indict capitalism for
its injustice or violation of man's natural rights.
He explicitly dismissed "natural justice" as "nonsense."[22]

Furthermore, commenting on his own reflections
on the Hegelian philosophy of law, Marx said it
convinced him that,[23]

"juridicial relations, like forms of the state
are to be grasped neither through themselves
nor through the so-called universal development of the human spirit, but rather are rooted
in the material relations of life, whose totality Hegel . . . comprehended under the term
of 'civil society.'"

Though Marx was correct to underly the socio-
economic variants of concepts like the law, justice,
and freedom, he failed to understand that the core
of justice, for instance, must be beyond the force of
political power and economic interest. In the light
of Marx's critical view of rights, it is surprising
to read Thorstein Veblen's assertion that Marx
"does not take a critical attitude toward the underlying principles of natural rights."[24] According to
Veblen, not even Hegel's preconceptions of natural
law disposed Marx toward "questioning the fundamental
principles of that system."[25]

Veblen's perception of Marx as part of natural rights tradition is untenable on at least two grounds. First, Marx, unlike natural rights thinkers, placed the primary emphasis on society, which he defined as a productive system of collective activity. And in clear departure from Locke and Jefferson, Marx assigned to man self-creative powers that belonged to a designing Creator. In the Jeffersonian universe, no less than in Locke's, God as supreme maker had all the skills of a craftsman, a Workman. It is this power of the Creator that saved Jefferson from the Marxian error of declaring man his own creator, the full implication of which will be analysed.

Second, and most important, Marx interpreted the judicial activity as an ideological aspect of the productive relations. The result was that natural rights were treated as dependent on society's organizational set up and modes of production. Engels was explicit on this. Commenting on the practice whereby different legal systems are compared by the standard of "natural right," Engels said the concept of "natural right" is just as an abstract expression as is "eternal justice."[26]

Marx saw no efficacy for human rights beyond their historical instrumentality of assuring the ascendency of one class over the other. Why should a member of civil society, asked Marx, be called "man" and his rights labeled as the "rights of man?" He answered that liberal philosophy creates a fictitious being who not only possesses universal rights, but they are secured by a partisan state. The great rights of man, rooted in man's individuality and sanctity, Marx considered destructive to the proletariat's ascribed historical mission. _Tantae molis erat_, declared Marx at the end of his account of the growth of capitalism.[27]

Analyzing the French declaration of the Rights of Man, Marx argued not all rights possess equal importance. Though the right to property is not mentioned in the French declaration, Marx contends that an implicit hierarchy of rights derives from and is founded upon the genus of all rights--the right of property.[28] To be sure, the French Constitution of 1793 stated that the right of private property allows each citizen the enjoyment and dis-position of ". . . as he will of his goods and revenues, of the fruits of his work and industry."[29]

In Marx's interpretation, however, the phrase "as he will" forces man to view his fellow beings as an enemy, or as a means to property. The right to property posits, according to Marx, materialistic goals as the end of man. To use Marxian logic, if A refuses, for any reasons, to pursue materialistic goals as an end, he will be reduced to the means of B, who accepts and pursues materialistic goals. Consequently, the bourgeois concept of human rights are subservient to the genus of right--the right to property. Hence the so-called equality before the law means no more and no less than, in Marx's view, the protection of property right.

From Marxian standpoint a human being, like the proletariat, who is denied of property is also denied the protection of the law. Significantly, to Marx. the equality of right preordains a de facto inequality of right. The argument assumes there cannot be legal equality between individuals possessing unequal properties. Unequals in property cannot be made equal before the law. Marx here broke with Aristotle who denied that private or unequal distribution of property has an adverse effect on the claims to political rights. Aristotle, in effect, underscores the difference. "The distribution of property," he wrote, "works in the opposite way from the distribution of office"[30] or political power. To Aristotle, unlike to Marx, economic inequality does not preclude equality before the law, which Aristotle defined as "reason free from all passion."[31] From the sociological premise of the bourgeois and the proletariat as unequal classes, Marx concludes that any general proposition about the quality of right is "a right of inequality in its content, like every right."[32] Hence the Lockean-liberal right to property is judged incompatible with a de facto equality of right for all individuals. For man to regain his "essence" or what Marx called "authentic" being, the Lockean freedom to property must be transformed, via the "revolutionary dictatorship of the proletariat",[33] into freedom from property.

It was, however, Georg Lukacs (1885-1971) who expressed with merciless logic the dispensability of law for Marxism.[34]

> "The law and its calculable consequences are of
> no greater (if also of no smaller) importance
> than any other external fact of life with which
> it is necessary to reckon when deciding upon
> any definite course of action. The risk of
> breaking the law should not be regarded any
> differently than the risk of missing a train
> connection on an important journey."

Analyzing the Marxian prerequisites of revolution,
Lukacs adds this revealing comment. As long as the
revolutionary considers the law as a universal norm,
rather than a mere power factor, his "genuine,
inner emancipation has not yet occurred."[35] For
the Communist Party, Lukacs argued, the question of
legality or illegality is a "mere question of tactics."
It is not difficult to see why Communism's moral
and juridicial bankruptcy are rooted in the dictum
that Communism must be guided by "immediate expediency."
It is not without irony that Lukacs, the leading
philosopher of Communism, drove the last nail into
the Marxist coffin of human rights when he wrote:[36]

> "In this (Communism) wholly unprincipled solu-
> tion lies the only possible practical and
> principled rejection of the bourgeois legal
> system. Such tactics are essential for
> Communism and not just on grounds of expe-
> diency. They are needed not just because it
> is only in this way that their tactics will
> acquire a genuine flexibility and adaptibility
> to the exigencies of the particular moment,
> (but) such tactics are necessary in order to
> complete the revolutionary self-education of
> the proletariat. For the proletariat can
> only be liberated from its dependency upon
> the life-forms created by capitalism when it
> has learned to act without these life-forms
> inwardly influencing its actions."

In summary, to Marx the law and natural rights
denote a life-form incompatable with the "life-
form" of communist society. In place of the individual,
the depository of rights, Marx places the "species-
being" who dispense, once communism is attained,
with laws, authority, and discipline. Not unlike
Spinoza, whom he admired, Marx convinced himself that
freedom means to "act according to the laws of
one's own nature."[37] But human behavior, as Hume

warned, is not always coterminus with human essence. The Marxist solution to the Humean problem was to turn the legislator into a "scientist." In Marx's opinion,[38]

"The legislator must regard himself as a scientist. He does not make laws, he does not invent them, he only formulates them, he enunciates the inner laws of spiritual relationships as conscious positive laws."

Compare Marx's "scientist" legislator with the American concept of government by law. The Marxian legislator is not subject to any higher "authority" other than his own demiurgic genius. While in the American polity no power is above constitional limitations, Marx rejects any notion of freedom in law or through law. To compound the problem, the Marxian human essence, as predicate of freedom, is not empirically given. Its possibility lies in the yet to be realized future-Communism. In the meanwhile, of course, somebody must guide man toward his own essence. This "somebody", Marx's surrogate philosopher-king, is the Communist Party. At this point, we should introduce and expand on Marx's latent Romanticism and Promethean-complex.

5. Romanticism and Marxism

The basic argument here is that Marx's critique
of natural rights reflects the Romantic aspects
of his thought. The relationship of Romanticism
and Marxism is a complex issue, layered with many
implications. We cannot untangle or trace the
rational core of the dialectical imagination in
Marxism. Our concern is that Marxism, product of
the post-Kantian generation in Germany, is a variant
of the Romantic imagination. In German cultural
context, Romanticism held that the inherited
paradigms of evil and suffering can be overcome by
man's return to unity and goodness.

If one key phrase expresses Marx's latent
romantic imagination it is his statement that
"the worker's religion is Godless because it seeks
to restore the divinity of man."[1] Though the
claim that Marxism owes more to German Romanticism
than to the rational French Enlightenment is not
without controversies[2], we see an elective affinity,
supported by Lukacs's oeuvre, between Marxism and
some dominant concerns in German Romanticism. The
concept of alienation as the constitutive element of
reality, the quest for perfect society, and belief
in a latently perfect human nature, all are common
to Romantic and Marxist thought.

Nor is it accidental that Lukacs's road to
Marx is marked by an intense search for God or its
secular surrogate.[3] But more relevant to our analysis,
in Christian thought, God is not only part of the
created universe, but he invites and encourages
individual values and goals. By contrast, Marx's
latent Romanticism predisposed him toward an integra-
tive metaphysics-so striking in Lukacs's early writings-
whose values are not only accessible to but binding
on all. Not surprisingly, Marx is unequivocal that
the primal unity of man, he once possessed and now
lost, will be regained. This insistence on coherent
and integrated values is, from political perspective,
one of the most grievous errors of Marxism. It
makes socialism the younger brother of an almost
decrepit despotism. To regain and reinforce the
unity of man demands a state power as only despotism
has possessed. Ironically, Marxism outdoes all the
past in that it aims at complete annihilation of
diverse individualism. To borrow Nietzsche's

insight[4], Marxism considers the individual an
unauthorized luxury of nature, which is to be improved by making it into an appropriate organ of the
general community.

The additional irony is that the Marxist
concept of progress also calls for a restoration of
man's lost unity. This is but a variant of the Hegelian claim that "the true is the whole."[5] But the
principal architect of man's quest for wholeness or
totality, the acclaimed journey from alienation to
essence, is Schiller. In his famed work, _Aesthetic
Letters_, laying dormant, in Carl Jung's words,
"like a Sleeping Beauty of literature,"[6] Schiller
delienates the Romantic roots of the Hegelian-
Marxist concept of alienation, the most elusively
influential idea in Marxism. To cut through the
metaphysical verbage surrounding alienation, it
is well to remember that alienation is premised on
Marx's metaphysical anthropology that man, not God,
is the creator of the human universe.

Marx's thesis that man exists on his own accord
and progresses by his own effort, un-aided by God
or Heavens, counters the theory of creation. It
is man who produces, and he alone understands himself
without recourse to God or his design. In so many
words, man's productive activity is inseparable
from the historical becoming of human nature. By
the same logic, freedom to Marx coincides with the
necessity of man attaining his integrity or wholeness
in Communism. The immortality of the soul is but
a metaphysical fiction that bears no relation, in
Marx's view, to the genesis of real man.

By alienation then Marx understands that man,
prior to Communism, is confronted with the task of
restoring, if not creating, his own integrated self.
Marx's emancipatory vision on the "essence" of man,
unfortunately, is nothing but vision and, as such,
not accessible to empirical verification. Yet Marx
was convinced that,[7]

"The premises from which we begin are not
arbitrary ones, not dogmas, but real premises
from which abstraction can only be made in
the imagination. . . . These premises can
thus be verified in a purely empirical way."

To presume at any point in history that a

87

qualitatively better rule is possible because it is
within man to be solidarist-participatory is either
laden with fideism or, at best, is insanely utopian.
When all is said, the plain fact is, the Marxian man
as self-creator, endowed with magical potency and
power, carries neither moral nor practical plausabil-
ity. The vision of a global species community is at
odds with Marx's own socio-economic realism. More to
the point, the Marxist construction of human essence
in reconstituted reality is beyond empirical validity.
Differently put, the riddle of man cannot be overcome
historically, let alone through credulous fideism.
The crucial weakness in Marxism, leading to the pro-
scription of rights, is its metaphysical premise about
human essence and the assertion that Communism marks
the reconquest of man's species-being.

Since Communism means the future, Marx, ex hy-
pothesi, is critical of Romanticism which, by idealiz-
ing the past, must be superceded. Romanticism, to be
sure, makes little philosophical draft on the future.
Though Marx denounced Romanticism for its egotistic
individualism, he himself had a Romantic expectation,
typified by Schiller's aesthetic demand for an integrated being. In his Aesthetic Letters, Schiller calls
upon man to achieve a balance of form and feeling. An
idealist in the age of German Idealism, Schiller was
irrestistably drawn toward aesthetics as paradigm
of the formative activity of human personality. The
whole question of the relation between art and politics
and constructing a bridge between the two, manifest in
Hegelian-Marxist thought, can be traced back to Schiller. As Stuart Hampshire pointed out[8], Schiller provides
the first, and still unsurpassed attempt, to devise
a theory of relationship between art and politics
since Plato raised it. Without Schiller, the whole
Hegelian-Marxist aesthetics, so crucial to Lukacs's
oeuvre, can hardly stand up to analytical rigour.

Schiller saw modern man as fragmented and alienated
from his essence, defined in aesthetic terms. Thus
he placed culture, society, and his aesthetic state,
under the admonition of the whole man. Modern man,
then, rather than stamping his humanity on things,
becomes the imprint of his occupation and specializa-
tion.

Schiller's aesthetic modulation of modern man,
a brute matter in need of form and feeling, presages

Marx's alienated man. To Schiller, man is but a mono-
tonous round of economic and utilitarian ends. Man,
in fact, is a self-seeking entity without a Self.
Modern civilization has inflicted, Schiller believed,
a deep wound on man. The separation of ranks and occu-
pations, the division and fragmentation of labor and
life have fractured the "inner unity of human nature."[9]
When Schiller concludes that the split within man cannot
be healed politically, we are àt the source of Marx's
theory that only "human emancipation" can restore man's
lost unity.

Both Schiller and Hegel saw alienation, by and
large, in aesthetic-metaphysical terms. For Marx,
on the other hand, alienation denotes alienated labor
that is to be terminated with the final liberation of
man. Though it is the proletariat, not man in general,
that embodies alienated humanity, Marx mythopoetizes
the proletariat. It represents what Marx called the
"complete loss of man and can only regain itself,
therefore, by the complete resurrection of man."[10]

From the perspective of political theory, the
Marxian resurrection of man has far reaching consequences. If for no other reason than it places the
social order beyond any constitutional and legal
arrangements. Resurrected man is not only wrapped
in messianic metaphysics, but he is parasitic upon
Marx's Romantic imagination. The advocacy of man's
wholeness involves what one might call the technique
of negative definition. The whole man is never defined
positively by Marx or his followers. Rather, he is
inferred from what he is not. The proponents of
man's alleged wholeness are more explicit on what they
dislike in actual man than concretizing alternatives
to the errant, bourgeois man.

The attempt to ground the social order in the
species being provides a revealing contrast to the
political order set forth in the Declaration of
Independence. The Marxist social model dispenses
with legal codes, natural rights, and legislative
power. Marx's latent Romanticism is evident in his
expectation that bourgeois class-society will give way
to an "association" where the free development of
"each individual is the condition of the free development of all."[11] In Marx's vision a soaring humanism
and reckless irony are strongly mixed. The preordained
terminus or essence for man reveals more about Marx's
elective affinity with Romanticism than about his

political realism.

Human rights are designed, from philosophical perspective, to correct man's falling short of what Christians define as "perfection" and Marx chose to call "essence." But whereas Christian thinkers, like Aquinas and Luther, subscribe to variants of natural rights, Marxism is consistently hostile to the very concept. It is not the moral and political rights of citizens, but the resurrected species being that, in Marx's view, will correct the tyrannical inclination and human omission of political power.

We have stressed that Marx, like German Romantics in general, idealized the earthly reality of man. German Romantics injected a discordant voice about modern man's values in industrial setting. Schiller, as we saw, placed culture and society under the admonition of the whole man who, for all practical purposes, leaped off the Grecian urn. And Marx, like Schiller and Hegel, saw the Greeks as incarnations of the Apollonian element. The German mind, unhappy with the technical-economic aspects of modernity, consciously domiciled itself in Hellas, the very antinomy of modern society. Marx was full of a nostalgia about Hellas where mankind had its "natural childhood" and obtained its "most beautiful" development.

It is not difficult to see what Marx found so attractive in Greek antiquity. Classical political thought, though it acknowledged the individual, refused to legitimize the antithesis between individual rights and political order. Plato and Aristotle have made moral perfection the end of good government. The moral end of society took precedent over individual rights in Greek political thought. And we have seen why Marx found natural rights incompatible with the moral end of Communism. To this day Communism has yet to learn to distinguish its concept of law from organized brutality. A government that refuses to take the concept of law seriously cannot take human rights seriously either.

It is instructive to compare the Marxist revolutionary model of society with the American political design. The American Fathers were bound by the constitutional system they created and later ratified. By contrast, Marx understood Communism to mean an unlimited fulfillment of human hopes, including the nth dimension of freedom. Communism was to transfer man from the realm of necessity into the realm of freedom. Equating Communism with the "realm of freedom," Marx could easily dispense with the recurrent democratic problem of reconciling rights with political order.

Marxism disdains democracy for its daily demonstration that men can have rights and dignity without submerging their individuality in the monochrome species being. Through long historical trials and errors, democracy has learned to harness the conflicting human passions and interests and yet maintain social order. Democracy is the political apotheosis of the poetic line that,[12]

> On life's vast ocean diversely we sail,
> Reason's the cord, but Passion is the gale.

Marx, however, was determined to remove the causes of social conflict and class interest. Engels merely summed up Marx's position in defining the state as a transient feature of civilization. Engels said the state will join the museum of antiquities, next to the spinning-wheel and the "bronze-axe."

Though Marx abolishes state power, the historical agent of dominance, he leaves intact the proletariat's philosophical sovereignty whereby it can achieve hegemony on "broader basis" than the bourgeois class.[13] The proletariat, by creating society "anew", known as a classless society, no longer needs any constitutional organs. Metaphorically put, democracy secures the individual's inalienable rights, Marxism endows the proletariat with an inalienable right to Communism.

In many respects, the Marxist constitutional thinking is but a variant of Schiller's view,[14]

> "We have to begin, therefore, by creating the citizens for a Constitution, before we can give a Constitution to the citizens."

As a Romantic, Schiller failed to draw any distinction between an artist creating and the legislator at work. The medium of art, be it marble or canvas, need not consent to the artist's intent. But in politics, as the American Constitutional Fathers attest, statecraft and constitution-making must take into account human aspirations and ideals. The invariant

principles of body politics are human reason and consent, not man's "essence" or species being

When Kolakowski said that Marx was a "German
philosopher"[15] he implied Marx's romantic perspective.
Romanticism is many things to many people. In a
strict sense, one should use Romanticisms to acknowledge the diverse strains of the movement. Nonetheless,
the generic meaning to Romanticism is expressed in
the "infinite striving"[16] for some indeterminable
moral or human ideal.

By absolutizing the proletariat as the redemptive
hope of mankind, Marx is true heir of German Romanticism. The latter converts the Kantian "finite being"
into an absolute ego whose conflict with external
reality unfolds the great drama of man's struggle to
realize his essence. In Kantian ethics, the categorical imperative only indicates an endless approximation
of the moral ideal, rather than its perfect realization.
The Romantics, however, have transformed the finite
being, striving for moral perfection, into a world-
historical being who realizes his totality by titanic
struggles against hostile reality. To Romantics,
and Marx is no exception, the concept of infinite
human possibility takes precedence over the prosaic,
finite, and determined being. Politically expressed,
the proletariat's titanic struggles to realize classless society is the motive force of the historical
process working toward Communism.

Revealingly, Rene Wellek not only included Hegel
among the Romantic thinkers, but claimed that Romanticism had penetrated "German political theory."[17]
Though Veblen misjudged Marx's affinity to natural
rights, he was correct to argue that Marx, as a
Hegelian, is a "romantic philosopher."[18]

6. Marx's Promethean Complex

It is a commonplace truth that Marx was fascinated by the mythical figure of Prometheus, the defiant, uncompromising hero of Aeschylus's <u>Prometheus Bound</u>. This tragedy captures the terrifying suffering man must endure by releasing the forces of progress. In Aeschylus's drama the immensity of human misery and sense of tragedy reaches an unmatched intensity. In Aeschylus's Prometheus, Marx has found an inspiring example of the will to endure pitted against the will to crush.

The story of Prometheus carries deep significance for Marxist conception of man and progress. Prometheus stole the secret of fire from the gods and gave it. to mankind. Utilizing fire, i.e. technology, mankind can now escape from its primitive past. In Marxian terms, technology hastens the process of sending an old form of life to "the grave." Differently put, the historical discovery of technological invention enlarges the human order through risk-taking. Literally and symbolically, Prometheus invents the future by changing the conditions of human existence. Bestowing the secret of technology upon man, Prometheus, the far-sighted philanthropist, imparts momentum to man's transit from nature to civilization.

Prometheus's daringly defiant act of stealing the secret of fire from the gods coincides with the creation of the technological womb of civilization. Technology enables man to satisfy not only his physiological needs but, most important from historical perspective, delineate civilized man's fate which the poet, T. S. Eliot[1], described as,

We shall not cease from exploration,
and the end of all our exploring
Will be to arrive where we started
And know the place for the first time.

To Marx, Prometheus symbolized the technological conquest of the world by and for man. Above all, he was taken by Prometheus's defiance of naked force and threats as he dissents from the oppressive rule of gods. Prometheus, indeed, broke with his own class of gods and makes common cause with the dispossessed mankind. Endowing mankind with knowledge and

technology, civilization emerges as the result of a
world-historical hero's rebellion against class
rule. Without technology, men were like ants crawling
in the crevices of earth. "They acted without plan
in all they sought,"[2] says Aeschylus about the
human-ants. What Marx admired in Prometheus is best
expressed by Goethe who, like Marx, admired Hellas.
Goethe's Prometheus's says,[3]

>Here I sit, kneading man
>In my image
>A race like myself
>Made to suffer, weep.

Such unbound faith in man's power as self-
creator, a will to outdo gods, is the key to Marx's
Promethean-complex. What is more, Marx transfigures
with near-divine ruthlessness the proletariat into
a collective Prometheus. Like the solitary and
mythological figure, the collective Prometheus,
i.e. proletariat, is not constrained by rights or
law. Since the Marxist proletariat embodies
the future, it can dispense with rights and the law
that redress the inconclusive political order.
Promethean figures, whether solitary or collective,
are cast into a mould that transcend the restraining
values of rights and law.

There is a striking parallel between Aeschylus's
mythopoetic creations and Marx's political imagination. Not unlike Aeschylus's poetic-dramas, Marx
wrote in prose one of the great political dramas
of human suffering and salvation in modern times.
In Aeschylus's <u>Prometheus Bound</u>, Prometheus corrects
a misrule by gods. The proletariat also corrects
a bourgeois misrule in Marx's political drama.
Though Marx renounced the bourgeois's misrule,
on economic and moral grounds, the Promethean aspect
of the proletariat precludes the possibility of
misrule in Communism.

In fairness to Marx, he neither lay the bound
nor built the roof of Soviet misrule . Nonetheless,
he lay the theoretical foundation for the Communist
regime's systematic disregard for the rule of law and
civil liberties. The dramatic construction of
Aeschylus's Prometheus is devoted to the welfare of
humanity. There is no reason to doubt that Marx
assigned the same Promethean mission to the historical
proletariat. But the analogy has tragic implication

for Marx's political theory. For as long as the proletariat, or, more specifically its surrogate, the Communist Party, continues to rule in Promethean fashion, Communism will flout human rights. In a revised Goethe, then, the Communist science of politics reads,

Here we rule, kneading men
In one image.

7. Summary.

At least since 1776 Americans have agreed that
the United States must be the beacon of human rights
to an unregenerate world. The unresolved question
that haunts America is how to execute its moral
mission in a Hobbesian world. John Quincy Adams,
commenting on America's choice, said that "wherever
the standard of freedom and independence has been or
shall be unfurled" there will America's "heart, her
benedictions and her prayers be." Adams went on to
say that America is the "well-wisher to the freedom
and independence of all."[1] In similar vein,
Albert Gallatin, last survivor of Jefferson's
revolutionary generation, said America's mission "was
to be a model for all other governments and for all
other less-favored nations. . . ."[2]

Created in the name of political ideals, the
American Republic continues to arraign at its moral
bar the nations of the earth. In additon to its
secular ideals, America's strong religious base
also contributes to this nation's idealism. The
Christian concept of man's origin, nature, and destiny,
observed Carl Becker, form the essence of the American
political tradition.[3] Tocqueville was the first to
see that in America religion bounds politics within
a moral sphere.

By contrast, Marxism enters the historical stage
with a sweeping attack not only on religion but on
ethical socialism. Cresting around the mid 1830s,
ethical socialism attempted to reconcile revolution
and individual rights. In Kantian thought, politics
is not only subordinate to morality, but rights not
utility or happiness, is the base of politics. In
Kantian philosophy, politics and law are designed
to serve morality and contribute to its realization.
Laws should not be construed, warned Kant, as accidental or arbitrary commands for expedient purposes.
Laws are necessary for the "achievement of universal
freedom,"[4] said Kant.

The law-protected sphere of freedom constitutes,
in Kantian thinking, the environment in which morality
can realize itself. The dignity of persons as
"ends in themselves" are the product of that moral
sphere which cannot be subordinate to politics. Hence
in Eternal Peace, Kant insists that "true politics

cannot take a single step without first paying homage to morals."[5] Without this moral sphere, antecedent to and autonomous from politics, men are manipulated and lorded over. But if "right" is to be the limiting condition of politics, then, as Kant unequivocally holds, morality and politics must be compatible and capable of co-existence.

The importance of Kantian concept of politics as an instrument of morality is that in the early 1920s there were important attempts by Georg Lukacs, Ernst Bloch, and Karl Korsch to revive Kantian ethics within Marxism. These neo-Kantians were quickly silenced or forced to repent by Soviet orthodoxy. The theoretical concern of neo-Kantian Marxists cannot detain us here. It is sufficient to indicate that they rejected the view that socialist law is coercive, and that the proletarian dictatorship denotes domination.

Not surprisingly, the theoretical attempt to ground Marxism in morality and law, Moscow proscribed as an ideological heresy. In a major essay, "Bolshevism as a Moral Problem," Lukacs stated categorically that without moral values communism is reduced to the question of power: the oppressed class becomes the ruling class. Lukacs said the "moral problem" of Communism revolves around the issue whether democracy is seen as a tactical weapon or accepted as integral to Communism. He left no doubt that Communism, in order to fulfill its ethical ideals, presupposes more than sociological necessity. The will-to-democracy, declared Lukacs, is the moral ideal of Communism. "Without this will-to-democracy," he wrote, "the whole edifice of Communism collapses."[6]

Prior to his conversion in 1918, Lukacs was convinced that Communism, notwithstanding its revolutionary ideals, cannot supercede the Kantian formula that politics is instrumental to morality. But Lukacs admitted that what makes Bolshevism attractive is its "metaphysical assumption" that good can come from evil and the road to freedom is through tyranny. In his own words,[7]

"Bolshevism is based on the metaphysical assumption that, as Razumihin expressed it in Crime and Punishment, we can lie our way to truth."

It is one of the tragic ironies of history that
Marx, determined to be the Promethean-liberator of
mankind, opened the road to a new form of domination.
Soviet-style Communism became a system dedicated
to the acquisition, consolidation, preservation and
extension of power. In his revulsion against the
inequities of his own time and his quest for just
society, Marx gave precedence to an emancipated,
collective humanity. Quite simply, by subordinating
the individual to an abstract collectivity, Marx
obliterates the protective moral sphere that human
rights place between the rulers and the ruled.

A system of governing that pits an abstract
collectivity against the individual establishes,
from the very start, an adversarial relationship
between the rulers and the ruled. Max Weber summed
up best the shortcomings of Marxism when he wrote,
"in the domain of the revolutionary theories of law,
natural law doctrine was destroyed by the revolutionary dogmatism of Marxism."[8]

As a final irony, Marx invoked natural rights
to aid the proletariat's "just" historical cause
against its oppressors. Within the Marxist framework
of class struggle, natural rights served the purpose
of legitimizing the proletariat's "revolutionary"
struggle. Yet once the Marxian freedom is realized
in classless society, Marx relegates natural rights
to the museum, next to the bronze-axe.

PART TWO

1. Tocqueville, _Democracy in America_, 2 vols. (New York: Schocken Books, 1970), 1:285.

2. Madison, _Writings_,5:376.

3. _Ibid._, 6:122.

4. Hume, _Works_, 2:152.

5. _Ibid._, p. 302.

6. C. B. Macpherson, _The Real World of Democracy_ (Oxford University Press, 1976), p. 56.

7. Macpherson, _Democratic Theory: Essays in Retrieval_ (Oxford University Press, 1973), p. 220.

8. Ernest B. Haas, _Global Evangelism Rides Again_ (Berkeley: Institute of International Studies, no. 5, 1978), pp. 16-17.

9. Locke, _Second Treatise_, #210.

10. Hume, _Works_, 2:152.

11. Hume, _Treatise of Human Nature_, ed. Selby Bigge (Oxford, Clarendon Press, 1888), p. 485.

12. Hume, _Enquiry Concerning Human Understanding_, ed. Selby Bigge (Oxford University Press, 1902) p. 89.

13. Hume, _Treatise_, p. 592.

14. _Ibid._

15. Hume, _Enquiry Concerning the Principles of Morals_, ed. Selby Bigge, 2nd ed (Oxford University Press, 1902), p. 336.

16. Hume, _Essays_, ed. T. H. Green, 2 vols. (London: Longmans, 1898), 2:152.

17. Locke, Second Treatise, #199.

18. Hume, Political Essays (New York: Bobbs-Merrill, 1953), p. 41.

19. Ibid., p. 42

20. Ibid.

21. Ibid., p. 61.

    2. Legal Positivism

1. For a comprehensive treatment of this, see Steven Lukes, Individualism (Oxford University Press, 1973).

2. Berlin, Four Essays on Liberty (Oxford University Press, 1970), IX.

3. J. R. Lucas, The Principles of Politics (Oxford: Clarendon Press, 1966), p. 144.

4. Hans Kelsen, General Theory of Law and State, trs. Anders Wedberg (New York: Russell & Russell, 1961), p. 228.

5. Margaret McDonald, "Natural Rights," in A. I. Melden, ed., Human Rights (Belmont, CA.: Wadsworth Publ. 1970), pp. 40-60.

6. MacDonald, "Ethics and the Ceremonial Use of Language," in Max Black, ed., Philosophical Analysis (Ithaca, N.Y.: Cornell University Press, 1950), pp. 211-29.

7. Ibid., p. 226

8. Dewey, Intelligence in the Modern World, ed. Joseph Ratner (New York: Modern Library, 1939), pp. 455-66.

9. Ibid., p. 379.

10. Dewey, The Public and Its Problems (Chicago: Gateway, 1946), p. 149.

11. Whitehead, Science and the Modern World, p. 60.

12. Dewey, <u>Freedom and Culture</u> (New York: Putnam & Sons, 1939), p. 156. See also, M R. Konvitz, "Dewey's Revision of Jefferson," in Sidney Hook, ed., <u>John Dewey</u>: <u>Philosopher of Science and Freedom: A Symposium</u> (New York: Barnes & Nobles, 1967), pp. 169-76

13. Quoted by John Dunn, <u>The Political Thought of John Locke</u> (Cambridge: Cambridge University Press, 1969), p. 1.

3. Hegel's Concept of Natural Right

1. Marx, <u>Writings of the Young Marx on Philosophy and Society</u>, eds. Easton and Guddat (New York: Doubleday, 1967), p. 321.

2. Hegel, <u>Verlesungen uber die Philosophie der Weltgeschichte</u>, ed. G. Lasson (Leipzig, 1917-1920) 4:921.

3. Hegel, <u>Philosophy of Right</u>, trs. T. M. Knox (Oxford University Press, 1967), p. 226.

4. Hegel, <u>Die Vernunft in der Geschichte</u>, ed. J. Hoffmeister, 5th ed. (Hamburg, 1955), p. 55.

5. For an authoritative analysis of Kierkegaard's attack on Hegel, see Gregor Malantschuk, <u>Kierkegaard's Thought</u>, ed. & trs. H. W. Hong & E. H. Hong (Princeton University Press, 1971), pp. 58-66.

6. Schopenhauer, <u>The World as Will and Representation</u>, trs. E.F.J. Payne, 2 vols. (New York: Dover Publications, Inc. 1966), 1:xxi.

7. Hegel, <u>Philosophy of Right</u>, p. 242.

8. Vernon L. Parrington, <u>Main Currents in American Thought</u>, 3 vols. (New York: Harcourt, Brace and Co., 1930), 3:409.

9. <u>Ibid.</u>, p. 411.

10. See Z. A. Pelczynski's introductory essay to Hegel's <u>Political Writings</u>, trs. T. M. Knox (Oxford University Press, 1964), p. 85.

11. Hegel, _Phenomenology of Mind_, p. 478f, 491f.

12. Hegel, _Gesämmelte Werke_ (Hamburg: F. Meiner, 1968-1980), 4:445.

13. Charles Taylor, _Hegel_ (Cambridge: Cambridge University Press, 1975), p. 510.

14. Hegel, _Phenomenology of Mind_, p. 504.

15. Hegel, _Jenenser Realphilosophie_, ed. J. Hoffmeister, in _Sammtliche Werke_, ed. G. Wason (Leipzig: F. Meiner, 1923-28), 19:233.

16. Shakespeare, _Othello_, III,iii, 331.

17. D. I. Chishevskii, _Gegel' v Rossii_ (Hegel in Russia) (Paris: Dom Knigi, 1939), partic. ch. 3 "Hegelian Circles."

18. Walter Kaufmann, _Discoveries of the Mind_ (New York: McGraw Hill, 1980), pp. 199-269.

19. For a perceptive analysis of how the "historical pathway to communism" disposed of the ethical impulse in Marxism, see Walter L. Adamson, _Hegemony and Revolution_ (Berkely/Los Angeles: University of California Press, 1980), pp. 229-46.

4. Marxism and Human Rights

1. Lukacs, _History and Class Consciousness_, trs. Rodney Livingstone (Cambridge: MIT Press, 1971) p. 19.

2. _Marx-Engels Reader_, ed. Robert Tucker (New York: W. W. Norton, 1978), p. 65.

3. Marx, _Selected Writings_, ed. David McLellan (Oxford University Press, 1977), p. 238.

4. _Ibid._, p. 54.

5. Bentham, _The Limits of Jurisprudence Defined_ (New York: Columbia University Press, 1945), p.84

6. Hans Kelsen, The Communist Theory of Law (New York: Praeger, 1955), p. 13.

7. Oliver Wendell Holmes, The Common Law (Boston: Little, Brown, 1881), p. 1.

8. Vladimir Gsovski, "The Soviet Concept of Law," Fordham Law Review 20, no. 76 (1938), p. 12.

9. E. P. Thompson, Whigs and Hunters (New York: Pantheon Books, 1975), p. 262.

10. Ibid., p. 265.

11. Ibid., p. 267.

12. Ibid., p. 266

13. Isaiah Berlin, Karl Marx (London: Oxford University Press, 1948), p. 9.

14. Marx, Critique of Hegel's Philosophy of Right, in Karl Marx: Early Writings, ed. T. B. Bottomore (New York: McGraw-Hill, 1963), p. 43.

15. Marx-Engels, Collected Works (New York: International Publishers, 1975), 1:178.

16. Ibid., 3:506

17. Vladimir Bukovsky, To Build a Castle - My Life as a Dissenter (New York: Viking, 1978), p.303.

18. Marx-Engels, Collected Works, 3:512.

19. Ibid., 3:305, 312.

20. Kolakowski, Main Currents of Marxism, 3 vols. (Oxford: Clarendon Press, 1978), 3:523.

21. Marx, Selected Writings, pp. 205-06.

22. Marx, Capital, 3 vols. (New York: International Publishers, 1967), 3:339-40.

23. Marx, Selected Writings, ed. V. Adoratsky, 2 vols. (New York: International Publisher, 1936-37), 1:328.

24. The Portable Veblen, ed. Max Lerner (New York: Viking Press, 1948), p. 277.

25. Ibid., p. 278.

26. Marx-Engels, Collected Works, 1:564.

27. Marx, Capital, 1:760.

28. Marx, Early Writings, p. 25

29. Ibid.

30. Aristotle, Politics, 1266 b 13-1267 a 10.

31. Ibid., 1287a

32. Marx, Critique of the Gotha Programme (New York: International Publishers, 1938), p. 9.

33. Ibid., p. 18.

34. Lukacs, History and Class Consciousness, p. 263.

35. Ibid., p. 264.

36. Ibid.

37. Spinoza, Ethics, p. 207

38. Eugene Kamenka, The Ethical Foundation of Marxism (New York: Praeger, 1962), p. 33.

5. Romanticism and Marxism

1. See Paul Ricoeur, Political and Social Essays, eds. David Steward and Joseph Bien (Athens: Ohio University Press, 1974), p. 218.

2. For Marx's relation to European Enlightenment, see Franco Venturi, Utopia and Reform in the Enlightenment (Cambridge: Cambridge University Press, 1971), p. 17ff; for Kantian influence on Marxist thought, see Hans Reiss, Kant's Political Writings (Cambridge: Cambridge University Press, 1970), p. 14ff; also, William A. Galston, Kant and the Problem of History (Chicago: University of Chicago Press, 1975).

3. For this, see Arpad Kadarkay, "George Lukacs's Road to Art and Marx," Polity 13, no. 2 (Winter 1980), pp. 230-60.

4. Nietzsche, Human, All-Too-Human, in Complete Works, ed. Oscar Levy (New York: Macmillan, 1924), 6:343-44.

5. M. H. Abrams, Natural Supernaturalism (New York: Norton, 1971), p. 187.

6. Carl Jung, The Integration of Personality, trs. S.M.Dell (London: Routledge & Kegan Paul, 1940), p. 124.

7. Marx-Engels Reader, p. 149.

8. Stuart Hampshire, "The Conflict between Art and Politics." The Listener 64, no. 1646 (13 October 1960):629-36.

9. Schiller, On the Aesthetic Education of Man, trs. E. M. Wilkinson & L. A. Willoughby (Oxford University Press, 1967), p. 33

10. Robert Tucker, Philosophy and Myth in Karl Marx (Cambridge: Cambridge University Press, 1961), p. 114.

11. Marx-Engels, Werke (Berlin: Dietz, 1956-65), 4:490.

12. Pope, Essay on Man, Epistle 11, 107-18.

13. Writings of the Young Marx, pp. 366-68.

14. Schiller, Des Dreissigjahrigen Kriegs, in Werke (Weimar: Hermann Bohlaus Nachfolger, 1976), 18:255.

15. Kolakowski, Marxism, 1:1.

16. Arthur O. Lovejoy, Essays in the History of Ideas (Baltimore: The John Hopkins Press, 1948), esp. ch. XII.

17. Rene Wellek, Confrontations (Princeton: Princeton University Press, 1965), p. 6.

18. Portable Veblen, p. 296. Interestingly, Marx

18. criticized Lasalle's tragedy, <u>Franz von Sickingen</u>, for "Schillerizing," i.e., his individuals were mouthpieces for the spirit of the age. cf. Marx to Lasalle, 19 April 1859, in Marx-Engels, <u>Werke</u>, 29:592.

6. Marx's Promethean Complex

1. T. S. Eliot, <u>Four Quartets</u> (London: Faber & Faber, 1944), p. 43.

2. Aeschylus, <u>Prometheus Bound</u>, trs. Philip Vellacott (Penguin Books, 1976), p. 34.

3. Goethe, <u>Werke</u> (Weimar: Harmann Bohlaus, 1900), 19:205, lines 243-46.

7. Summary

1. Walter LaFeber, ed., <u>John Quincy Adams and American Continental Empire: Letters, Speeches and Papers</u> (Chicago: Times Books, 1965), p. 45.

2. Albert Gellatin, <u>Peace with Mexico</u> (New York: Bartlett & Welford, 1847), Section vii.

3. Carl Becker, <u>Freedom and Responsibility in the American Way of Life</u> (New York: Vintage Books, 1955), p. 18.

4. Kant, <u>Philosophical Correspondence</u>, trs. & ed. A. Zwieg (Chicago: University of Chicago Press, 1967), p. 142.

5. Kant, <u>Eternal Peace</u>, in <u>The Philosophy of Kant</u>, ed. Carl Friedrich (New York: Modern Library, 1949), p. 469.

6. Lukacs, "Bolshevism as a Moral Problem," in <u>Történelem és Osztálytudat</u> [History and class consciousness] (Budapest: Magvető, 1971), p. 17.

7. <u>Ibid.</u>

8. Max Weber, <u>Economy and Society</u>, 2:784.

Man is tormented by no greater anxiety than
to find someone quickly to whom he can
hand over that gift of freedon with which
the ill-fated creature is born.

-Dostoevsky

The word freedom means one thing to us and
another thing to you. For example,
when in Russia they say 'It is necessary
to strengthen legality,' all Russia begins
to tremble.

-Ernst Neizvestny

Part Three

RIGHTS IN RUSSIAN POLITICAL THOUGHT

1. Introduction

This chapter does not attempt a comprehensive
or systematic analysis of Russian political theory.
Our aim is, first, to analyse what Montesquieu would
define as the "general spirit" of Russian political
thought. Second, to compare what roles rights play
in Russian and American political thought. Our method-
ological premise is that there is a continuity, despite
the discontinuity of 1917,in Russian political tradition.
We cannot subscribe to Solzhenitsyn's view that Russia
is an innocent and blameless victim, a captive maiden
kidnapped and seduced by Soviet Communism.

To Solzhenitsyn, Russia is to the Soviet Union
as a man is to the "disease" afflicting him. This
pathological approach is too imbalanced by a great
writer's personal experience with Societ reality he
suffered through. Disagreeing with Solzhenitsyn's
view of Communism does not invalidate his stature as
a writer. His luminous essence aspires to moral and
political heights which, understandably, appeals to
Americans who live blessed by the far-reaching dis-
pensation of their "Civil Fathers."1 Solzhenitsyn's
essence, as artist and visionary, is contained in his
writings like in some holy vessel. It is not
Solzhenitsyn's literary talent that is in dispute,
but his denounciatory vigilance towards Soviet Communism and apology for "eternal" Russia.

The U.S. and USSR, as superpowers, share a nuclear

world. As the adversary of Soviet power, the U.S. faces the insoluble dilemma that preserving freedom and security can bring about the end of civilization. The fearful trap into which the nuclear arms race has lead the world, though man-made, appears to be beyond human solution. Some, like George Kennan, urge us to accept the validity that

> "there is no issue at stake in our political relations with the Soviet Union-no hope, no fear, nothing to which we aspire, nothing we would like to avoid-which could conceivably be worth a nuclear war."[2]

Others would counter that the maintenance of democratic values take precedence over maintaining good relations with the Soviets.[3]

In contrast to Kennan, Richard Pipes, serving as a specialist on Communist affairs in the Reagan Administration's National Security Council staff, takes a hard line on Soviet-American relations. Kennan attributes the growing Soviet military power to Russia's deep-seated historical insecurity flowing from its relative weakness and vulnerability. To Pipes, on the other hand, militarism is inherent in Soviet Communism and the continuation of Russia's traditional expansionism. Consequently, the city, to adopt Augustine's image, the geopolitically priviliged transatlantic Republic, became a nuclear civitas by necessity and choice. This confronts the U.S. with the inescapable responsibility to maintain and defend democratic civilization, despite the suicidal danger that nuclear weaponry presents.

No one can ignore, of course, the serious deterioration in Soviet-American relations over arms, and, above all, ideas. Soviet Russia and American are two young, robust civilizations. George Kennan rightly called the Russians "another great people," and noted their long-sufferings and hardships through the centuries. The "great" people of Russia and America, and herein lies the problem, comprise two superpowers that, together, dance on the precarious feet of chance on the brink of abyss. Whether it is human rights or "fundamental" change in our outlook, Kennan calls for, that will deliver us from the nuclear bondage into a world where chance yields to purpose, is to fill Soviet-American relations with hope and faith.

Looking at Soviet-American relations from a
Kantian perspective, one could argue that ethical
principles are the ultimate solvent of political
problems. Kant also expressed hope that the spread
of "republican constitutions" would terminate wars.
If the citizens decide the question of war and peace,
argued Kant, then those who would have to make the
sacrifice would also hesitate to start the "evil game"
of war.[4]

Regrettably, Russian political thought is devoid
of the Kantian prerequisites of "perpetual peace"
among nations. Soviet-American relations more resemble
what Ambrose Bierce, in his Devil's Dictionary, called
"strife of interests masquerading as a contest of
principles." Practical reason informs of the necessity
of "eternal peace" among the two superpowers. Yet
perpetual peace, though a practical necessity, is not
within the reach of Russia and America who disagree
not only over the purpose of power and security, but
over moral values.

Differently put, the Soviet and American political
systems are not compossible. The doctrine of compossibility, borrowed from Bertrand Russell, holds that
among the values nation A and B adhere to, some values
can be realized on co-operative bases and others only
through conflict. Though Russia and America may share
an overriding need for peace, the nuclear equivalent
of Kant's foedus pacificum, they are not compossible
in terms of embodying irreconcilable political ideals
as the conflict over human rights demonstrates.

The Russie government is plaine tirannyical

-The English Merchant's Protest, 1591

2. The Russian State Tradition

Nearly a century and half ago Tocqueville pre-
dicted,[1]

> "There are two great nations in the world, which
> seem to tend towards the same end, although
> they started from different points: I allude
> to the Americans and the Russians. . . . The
> Anglo-American relies upon personal interest to
> accomplish his ends, and gives free scope to the
> unguided exertions and common sense of the
> citizens; The Russian centers all authority of
> society in a single arm. The principal instru-
> ment of the former is freedom; of the latter,
> servitude. Their starting point is different,
> and their courses are not the same; yet each
> of them seems to be marked out by the will of
> heaven to sway the destiny of half the globe."

Ever since Tocqueville, Russia and America were
subject to endless analysis, inspired by the question
whether nations converge or diverge in their develop-
mental pattern subsequent to revolutionary nation
building.

The Soviet Union and the United States are products of a deliberate political design whose ideals
are rooted in the revolutionary origin of the two
nations. The political tradition and practice of
America and Russia verifies Machiavelli's postulate
that great nations recur, time and again, to their
founding principles to renew their political legitimacy and self-identity. The founding ideals of the
American Republic have been analyzed and sketched.
It cannot be overemphasized enough that the American
constitutional design was laid, in Paine's felicious
phrase, "in freedom and justice." Put differently,
America was, in Tocqueville's phrase, une feuille
blanche, a blank page, upon which history waited to be
written.

Not surprisingly, the blank page called America
invited idealism and soaring imagination. Benjamin
Franklin said America was broad and strong enough to

113

support the "greatest political structure human wisdom ever yet erected."[2] Or as Leonard Bernstein put it,[3]

> "What Beethoven's Fidelio is about is really what
> America is about. It's about the right to speak
> the truth as you see it and not to be thrown
> into a dungeon. Fidelio should be the American
> national anthem."

Bernstein's image captures the exalted humanism and moral ideals of American democracy. By contrast, Russia's political beginning is less exalted. Even Hegel, by no means a friend of the United States, acknowledged that in America the individual is beholden to his private will. He noted, somewhat negatively, the "unbound license of imagination"[4] of Americans in religious matters. Marx himself recognized that America's political tone, though influenced by European past, is different. He associated America with religious disestablishment, extensive suffrage and, above all, an unfettered development of civil society. Compared to America's innocent past, unclattered by feudal legacies, Russia's past recalls Marx's image that the past weighs on the living generation like Mont Blanc.

The ominous burden of Russia's political past helps to explicate, paradoxical as it may sound, the continuity in discontinuity (1917) in Russian political thought. Or as Samuel Johnson put it, quoting from Pliny, in one of his Rambler essays (no. 86), "The burthen of government is increased upon princes by the virtues of their immediate predecessors."

Solzhenitsyn notwithstanding, the Russian concept and practice of political rule shows a fixed pattern of personal despotism. Even in the Age of Enlightenment, the government is inseparable from the charismatic, personal rulership of Peter the Great or Catherine. Though Russia is penetrated by European ideas under Peter and Catherine's autocratic reign, the dominant form of government remains, despite attempts at modernization and Western modeled reforms, a hybrid form of personal rule and patrimonialism. The historical coincidence of modernizing a backward country by autocratic fiat, expressing the political aspiration of rulers like Peter and Catherine, Lenin and Stalin, contributes to the uniquely Russian form of personal rulership.

The most durable component of the Russian state absolutism is the unbroken tradition, extending from the Petrine to Soviet Russia, that government is, in essence, the private affair of rulers or co-opting elites. Though autocratic rule is not necessarily incompatible with respect for laws, pace Prussian Rechtsstaat, Russian autocrats were not in the habit of being bound by any law, civil or natural. In Western political theory, the closest analogy to the Russian state absolutism is Hobbes's Leviathan. It has been often said that Russia had no eighteenth century. Broadly conceived, it refers to the absence of legal-rational legitimization of absolutism, and, most important, natural law thinking had neither penetrated Russia nor did it have any restraining effect on the government. Hobbes could at least quote with approval the old principle that the safety of the people is the supreme law. In Russia, by contrast, the safety and security of the state assumed both theoretical and practical priority.

It is instructive to analyze briefly how some Russian thinkers understood the concept of natural law. The leading proponent of Lockean ideas, Prince M. Shcherbatov (1773-1790), duly echoed the sentiment that all men are equal by nature. In the same breath, however, he adds that the hereditary nobility was born to rule. But natural law doctrines, as evident from Locke's Essay Concerning Human Understanding, disprove of hereditary rule. Consent based political authority, as understood by Locke, was predicated on the right of individual to search for knowledge and, inescapably, for a rational form of government. Natural law, among other things, was utilized by Locke and others to lay the rational foundations of a critical society of free men. Shcherbatov reads into Locke the conservative view that the "lower orders in Russia should not be educated since education might awaken in them the spirit of disobedience."[5]

The Lockean natural law, whose spirit informs Alexander Pope's couplet,[6]

Mark what unvary'd laws preserve each state,
Laws wise as Nature, and as fix'd as Fate

was a protest against arbitrary rule. But when Shcherbatov uses Locke to protest against Peter's arbitrary power, he protests against the tsar's

arbitrary decision to move the Russian capital from
Moscow to St. Petersburg--a remote, swampy place.
Peter's new capital, his famous "window" facing Europe,
was built, as the Russian saying has it, on "tears
and corpses." It is noteworthy that Shcherbatov
did not protest state absolutism, as did Locke, in the
name of popular sovereignty.

In Petrine Russia, popular sovereignty was not
even considered a theoretical possibility. Natural
law embraces not only the perfectibility of men, but
their equality before the law. More to the point,
natural law envisions universal values within each
individual. In Russia equality meant, first and foremost, that all social ranks, from peasants to nobles,
are equal in their servitude to the state. This is the
substance of Peter's famous reform to impose state
service on all social ranks. Ironically, civic
humanism in Petrine Russia denotes equal state servitude. The Russian state, embodied in the personal
will of the tsar, became the very "soul" of Russian
body politics. Thus emerges the Russian state, an
untamed Leviathan, whose will and caprice all must
serve.

Interestingly, when Jefferson was laying the
Lockean foundation of the Republic, Peter the Great
ordered the translation of Pufendorf's "On the Duties
of Man and Citizen." And the official apologia for
Peter's personal rule was The Justice of the Monarch's
Will--a Russian carbon copy of Hobbes's Leviathan.
Not surprisingly, the Russian poet, Lomonosov, referred
to Peter as "God-like man." Another Russian poet,
Derzhavin, queried,

> Was it not God
> Who in
> his person came down to earth.[7]

To be sure, the Russian development of statism
is a variant of European enlightened absolutism.
Whether Russian statism owes more to its native roots
than European influence is secondary, at best, to
our concern. The important thing is that, from comparative perspective, Western absolutism was never
"absolute," in legal or political terms, as it was in
Russia. The Russian tsars, no less than Soviet leaders,
ruled but never governed. This is the qualitative
difference between Russian and European absolutism.

Russia's rulers were, and still are, in Dante's timeless image, "the horseman of human wills."[8] The influence of Christianity in the West is directly felt on the concept of authority or sovereign power, none of which was legitimized as indivisible and total. The competing claims of temporal and spiritual authority, the power-struggles of imperium and ecclessia seldom, if ever, attained a harmony of interest. It is sufficient to recall St. Augustine's twin cities: the city of God and that of man. Though theocracy is explicit in Augustine's political theory, he counterweights it with the Ciceronian argument that the city of man, respublica, cannot stand without justice.

To Augustine, kingdoms without justice are nothing but organized force and gigantic robbery. If force is but human wills banded together in the pursuit of common goals, then the state can hardly be more than association for criminal ends. In Augustine's vivid image:[9]

> "In the absence of justice, what is sovereignty but organized brigandage? For, what are bands of brigands but petty kingdoms? They are also groups of men, under the rule of a leader, bound together by a common agreement, dividing their booty according to a settled principle."

Augustine argues that even robbers and pirates have a sense of ordo, an order based on agreement or contract to attain some ends. He relates how a captured pirate, upon being reproached for infesting the sea, responded to Alexander the Great, "I do my fighting on a tiny ship," said the pirate, "and they call me a pirate, you do yours with a large fleet, and they call you commander."

Western political theorists, even exponents of the divine right of kings, drew a distinction between absolute and arbitrary government. Jacquet Bossuet, for instance, insisted that royal power must be absolute in ecclesiastical and temporal affairs. Yet he also claimed, in Pauline fashion, that "every soul must be subject to the highest power, for all power is of God."[10] Even Robert Filmer,[11] staunch advocate of the "natural right of regal power," admitted that the King is required to observe the "upright laws" of the realm with discretion and mercy.

To the Christian Fathers like Thomas Aquinas,
what distinguished one state from another is the end
toward which its government strived. Like classical
thought in general, Christian thought is preoccupied
with the concept of the best regime (optima civitas).
In the optima civitas, said Aquinas, princes are not
"instituted to be a terror." Leading medieval thinkers
have distinguished between king and tyrant. According
to John of Salisbury (1115-1180), while the king rules
for the benefit of the ruled, the tyrant rules for
self-interest. In plain language, rule by law denotes
monarchy, and rule by force degenerates into tyranny.

Since the tyrant disarms the law, killing him is
not only lawful but justifiable. In Salisbury's
view, by killing a tyrant, justice arms itself against
the long-range danger of tyranny. In Western political
thought we have to wait until Locke to find such
an emphatic endorsement of the right to rebellion
against tyrannical power on legal and moral grounds.

In the West, unlike in Russia, the Church and the
constitutional ideas have challenged and confined
the absolutist states. The duality of power, the key
to Western political development, has been dramatically
captured by T. S. Eliot's play, Murder in the Cathedral.
The friendship and estrangement of Thomas Becket and
Henry II unfold the drama: the mortal conflict of
ecclesiastical and kingly power. Beckett dies as
martyr to the "eternal design" of God,

> To which my whole being gives entire consent.
> I give my life
> To the Law of God above the Law of Man[12]

The son of man, inhabiting the temporal civitas,
bears the eternal burden of having to suffer the consequences of his actions in defying the imperium.
Christian thought places man in a created universe
where he is envisaged as part of what the poet called
the "great chain of being." It is tempting to dismiss
all this as mythopoetic fancy. Yet the Christian concept of creation had a lasting impact on Western
thought. Judeo-Christian imagination sees man as link
in the created universe. Man is the ape that wants to
be a god. Man is unhappy in his skin and cannot shed
it. Reason enables man to strive consciously to
transcend himself. These statements underscore that
the greatest accomplishment of religion in the West

has been that it did not allow man to feel complacent and at home in the universe. In Christian imagination, man inhabits a universe that extends from the continuum of God's design to his creatures. Graphically sketched,

God	–	pure
Man	–	intellect/sense
Animals	–	sense
Plants	–	growth
Inanimate	–	mere unchanging existence/matter

As can be seen from the diagram, the maintenance of order in Creation depends upon the subordination of man, his social and sensual values, to the spiritual. This subordination, however, is a weak link in the great chain of being since man, acting as a "political animal," can turn his back on God and concentrate his fury upon the divine order. When man forgets his divine origin, he has nothing left but the Hobbesian brotherhood with the beast. In Eliot's own testimony,[13]

> I have seen
> Rings of light coiling downwards descending
> To the horror of the ape.

This poetic image points to the competing spheres of religion and politics. By contrast, the moral mediation of power, which medieval political thought envisioned as a triangle of

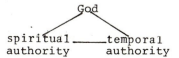

was alien to Russian political tradition. Dostoevsky claimed that the

> "constitution of Russia is the mutual love of the Monarch for the people and of the people for the Monarch. This principle of the Russian State, the principle of love not of strife . . is the greatest of all ideas."[14]

The principle of the Russian state, as defined by Dostoevsky, is incompatible with the dual spheres of authority. The Western spiritual and temporal spheres of authority presuppose a new concept of the

self, unknown to Russian political culture. This
self is personified by Beckett who, confronted with
Henry II's demand for "unified" power, declares,

> I give my life
> To the Law of God above the Law of Man.[15]

On this foundation rests the new concept of individuality whose relationship to God is beyond the control
of political authority.

Russian political thought was by-passed by the
formative influences that shaped Western thought.
Neither the supremacy of the law, from beggar to
king, nor the tradition that no succession to kingship
is legitimate without the election or recognition
of the community and, finally, that the people and
the ruler enter into a social contract of mutually
binding duties and rights played recognizable role
in Russian political theory and practice. On the
contrary, Russian political thought is insensitive
to the concept of government by law.

The political implications of it become apparent
when we juxtapose Russian statism and Western constitutionalism. Tracing the evolution of the latter,
Quentin Skinner[16] demonstrated convincingly that
the emperor was never legibus solutus. Monarchs
and kings, whatever their claims and pretenses may
have been, were bound by their coronation oath.
Above all, the continuation and legitimacy of royal
power was determined by discharging its sworn duties
and obligations. A lawful ruler, as recognized
by Aristotle and substantiated on Scriptural bases
by Augustine, is a servant, not master of the laws.

Compare to it paragraph 47 of the Russian
Fundamental Law (1832). It declared, among others,
that the "Russian Empire is ruled on the firm basis
of clearly defined laws which emanate from the
Autocratic Power." As Leonard Schapiro expressed it,[17]

> "The heart of the matter was that in Russia those
> factors and circumstances which in many countries
> of Europe either served to place fairly strict
> practical limits on the exercise of absolute
> power or made possible the evolution of institu-
> tions which eventually were to transform absolute
> rule into constitutional rule, were absent, or
> present only in very weak form."

When one studies Russian political thought from
the sixteenth to the twentieth century, one is struck
by the absence of any theoretical attempt to delineate
the concept of limited government. Paradoxical
as it may be, absolutism was not framed or defined
in theoretical terms until the nineteenth century
when, for the first time in Russian history, absolutism
was challenged by liberal and socialist thinkers.
As a leading Russian historian, Vasili Tatishchev
(1787-1850), wrote, "The autocratic system of
government is in Russia the most useful; all the
other are dangerous."[18]

In his massive, seven volume Russian history,
Tatishchev seeks to demonstrate Russia's greatness
corresponds to periods of strong autocratic rulers.
He spares no effort and examples to prove that state
monarchy is more efficacious in Russia than any
other form of government. Absolutism, he argues,
increases the state's power and glory, while other
political forms tend to diminish it.[19] Tatishchev's
works provide dramatic illustration that autocratic
government in Russia took the form of personal rule,
unrestrained by institutions or laws. Control of
the government from below, by basic laws and consent,
was not even a theoretical option in eighteenth
century Russian political thought. In Russia, as
Madam de Stael observed, the "moral character" of
the ruler was the sole source of an unwritten constitution. Complimenting Alexander I's reign
(1801-1825), Stael wrote: "Sire, your character is
a constitution of your empire, and your conscience
is its guarantee."[20] The problematic nature of
civil and political rights during Alexander I's
reign merit separate treatment.

3. Alexander I and Jefferson

Americans know Jefferson as the author of the immortal Declaration of Independence whose "self-evident" truths instruct us to think about politics in terms of universal priniciples. But few know about the Jefferson who corresponded with the Russian tsar, Alexander I, concerning human rights.

The story relevant to our analysis is this. Alexander I, seeking commercial ties with the United States, decided to establish a personal contact with Jefferson. The tsar wrote to a mutual acquaintance, the English scientist and cleric, Joseph Priestley (1733-1804), member of Jefferson's Circle. Alexander indicated to Priestley that he was interested in studying the American principles on freedom of the press, mass education, federalism, and humanitarian prison reforms. Priestley communicated these sentiments to Jefferson. He responded by suggesting that Alexander read the Federalist Papers, and Priestley's work, First Principles of Government, an eloquent defense of individual conscience and the rights of man. Jefferson concluded his letter by saying:[1]

> "Alexander will doubtless begin at the right end by taking means for diffusing instruction and a sense of their natural rights through the mass of his people, and for relieving them in the meantime from actual oppression."

The Russian autocrat, professing interest in constitutional principles and liberal ideas, was delighted with the reading list provided by Jefferson. He referred to Jefferson as cet eminent citoyen. Alexander was eager to close ranks with Jefferson as an enlightened monarch, embracing progressive European ideas. Later, when Jefferson had an occasion to thank Alexander for his assistance in freeing an American ship held captive in Tripoli, the Tsar wrote:[2]

> "I desire that this unmistakable token of my favorable disposition should serve to further the trade relations now being established between the two nations . . . I have always felt a great esteem for your nation, which knew how to make noble use of its independence by creating a free and wise Constitution assuring the well-being of each and all."

123

Jefferson responded to the overture by sending Alexander a four-volume biography of Washington and copy of the Constitution the tsar claimed to admire. In turn, Alexander sent Jefferson a marble bust of himself. Terrified by the outcome of the French Revolution, Alexander soon ended his brief flirtation with political and constitutional reforms. In fact, he became leader of the so-called Holy Alliance, a coalition of monarchies whose avowed purpose was to halt the spread of republicanism throughout Europe.

By 1821 Jefferson knew full well that Russia's "experimentation" with constitutional government was over. In a letter to Levett Harris, Jefferson wrote:[3]

"I am afraid our quondam favorite Alexander has swerved from the true faith. His becoming an accomplice of the soi disant (self-designed) Holy Alliance, the anti-national combination to chain mankind down eternally to oppression of the most barbarous ages, are clouds on his character not easily to be cleared away. But these are problems for younger heads than mine. You will see their solution and tell me of it in another world."

Jefferson sized-up well the Russian autocrat. Though Alexander had commissioned M. M. Speransky (1772-1839) to draft a liberal constitution for Russia, not much came of the project. Speransky submitted to the Emperor in 1809 a draft, entitled "Introduction to the Constitution of the Laws of the State," in which he attempted to lay the legal foundation of Russian monarchy. But nowhere in the draft is there a hint of an independent judiciary, the keystone of any constitutional government.

From Speransky's constitutional draft one can measure fairly accurately the deficiencies in Russian political thought.[4] Speransky defined (Art. 1) the autocratic power as unlimited (neogranichennyi) and associated obedience to sovereign power (verkhov-naia vlast) on Hobbesian and Filmerian grounds. In short, the subject obeys power out of fear and also by conscience as ordained by "God Himself." In theory, the monarch was limited by the principle of "legality" (zakonnost). But in practice, which continues to this day in the Soviet system, there was no distinction between "law" (zakon) and administrative decree (ukaz), implementing the law. The Russian tsar,

124

just like the Communist leader (vozhd), was above the
law. To make the whole Russian constitutional theory
a shamble, Article 70 expressly stated that an
Imperial decree supercedes any general law. The concept of "legality" remained inapplicable to Russian
political power, whether autocratic or Communist.
Whatever limitation was placed on power, it remained
personal and hence, from the perspective of Western
political thought, the exact opposite of constitutional
government.

Enlightenment thinking, particularly in America,
is predisposed to natural law doctrines, noted for its
prescription of constitutionalism. Under the influence
of Locke, American political thought develops a strong
reliance on individualism with its attendant civil and
moral rights. By contrast, in Russia it was Christian
Wolff's (1672-1725) interpretation of natural law,
not that of Locke, that attained ascendency. The
Prussian Wolff was particularly congenial to the
government and the educated classes of eighteenth
century Russia, just as Hegel was to mid-nineteenth
century Russian intelligentsia.

Wolff not only became scientific adviser to
Peter the Great (1716-1725), but played a key role
in founding the St. Petersburg Academy of Sciences.
As the major force in the development of rationalism
in German Enlightenment, Wolff assigned priority to
the community and the social institutions, not to the
autonomous individual as emphasized by English thinkers.
Above all, Wolff stressed obedience to political authority and appealed to man's rational faculty to prove
the efficacy of service-oriented society. Wolff in
particular wielded strong influence in Russia[5] by
his philosophical sanction of a goal-oriented, centralized, and active state administration Peter the Great
introduced. It should come as no surprise that German
Aufklärung ideas, rather than English natural law
doctrines, proved attractive to Russia   After all, to
German Aufklärers communal responsibility took precedence over individual rights.

It is instructive that Speransky, reflecting on
the absence of individual rights in Russia, wrote,
"The only free people in Russia are the beggars and
the philosophers."[6] His recommendation, concerning
the priority of political over civil freedoms in Russia,
is at variance with Western constitutional development

125

that civil liberties are antecedent to political
freedom. Though Speransky is sympathetic to equality
before the law, he qualifies it by saying it cannot
mean equality of rights. In his view, the separate
social ranks cannot be equal. Speransky's political
ideals are expression of his attempt to rationalize and
institutionalize political power. Yet despite such
sporadic reforms to introduce a Russian equivalent of
European Polizeistaat, the Russian government remained,
for all intents and purposes, personalized and arbitrary. Neither Speransky's reform proposals nor
Catherine's constitutional scheme contained even hints
of a limited concept of government. The self-limitation of autocratic power was recognized, even encouraged. Still, the Russian political soil was unable to
yield anything but a hybrid of oriental despotism
and enlightened European absolutism.

Speransky himself could not break away from the
Russian political tradition. He asserted that the
Emperor's assent was required before a law could be
passed. "It is from the sovereign power," he wrote,
"that the law and its enforcement eminates."[7] It
would be wrong to leave the impression that Alexander
I was in complete accord with Speransky's constitutional
draft. Where Speransky indicates that the proposed
constitution would improve Russian society by the
imposition of legal limits on the state, the Emperor's
marginal entry reads: "To a republic?"[8]

No sooner was Speransky's draft constitution
accessible to a small circle in the Imperial court,
it was attacked by N.M. Karamzin. He contended that
a "mixed" or "constitutional" monarchy is a historical
absurdity in Russia and violates the spirit of its
political tradition. Karamzin saw the law and state
as two incompatible, hostile forces. Joining state
and law in a constitutional system was, in his view,
like putting two "mighty lions in one cage, ready to
tear one another to pieces."[9] Misreading Montesquieu,
Karamzin argued that the autocrat's attributes and virtues, not the constitutional limitation of power, is
the true inheritance of Russian political tradition.
Commenting on Karamzin's political theory, Schapiro
wrote.[10] "This outlook, whether true or false, has
never died out in Russia in speculation on the nature
of government."

Interestingly, to refute Speransky's constitutional theories, Karamzin consistently invokes the Russian political tradition. Karamzin saw in the Russian past a compelling justification for an absolutist state. He understood autocracy to mean a system of government based on a personal rule, indivisible and unshearable. In paraphrased Shakespeare, then, the art of Russian government is to "find the government's construction in the ruler's face."[11] As for the contractual arrangement between the ruler and his subjects, common in medieval West, the Russian subjects had not rights other than those granted by the autocrat. Here we see the Russian historical pattern of personal rule. Karamzin's assidiuos study of Russian history lead him to conclude that civil rights can only be attained at the expense of political rights. Differently put, civil rights in Russia are predicated on the people's acceptance of an autocratic system of government.

Karamzin bolstered his arguments by misreading Montesquieu and by utilizing the Russian tradition. He wrote,[12]

"Autocracy has founded and resuscited Russia. Any change in her political constitution has led in the past and must lead in the future to her perdition. . . ."

Given Karamzin's reliance on Russian tradition, a few more quotes from his writings deserve consideration. He wrote, ". . . Russia had hitherto known only decrees, not laws. . . ."[13] As for the concept of rights, he said that "political rights in Russia are the rights of calling ourselves 'Russian.'"[14] As we shall see, this is basically the Soviet regime's rationale in suppressing dissidents. One final quote from Karamzin to underscore the continuity in Russian political tradition. Proclaiming the Russian sovereign the "living law," Karamzin added,[15] "Give people freedom and they cover you with mud--whisper a word in their ear and they lie at your feet." In the light of the Alexander-Jefferson exchange of letters, and Speransky's aborted constitutional proposal, one can concur with Richard Pipes that though in the eighteenth century no less than nine separate attempts were made to compile a new Russian legal code, all came to naught. The basic reason is that Russians failed to draw a distinction between general law (jus) and particular edicts (leges). All legal acts were issued in the name of the autocrat and thus possessed equal legal status.

To summarize, legalism in Russia was never conceived as a legitimate constraint on power. Nor was
it ever seriously considered that a constitution could
prescribe decencies and wise modalities of political
power. Russian political thought lends reality to
Homer's poetic dictum[16]

> It is not good to have many masters
> Let there be one master, one king,
> to whom Zeus has given the throne.

4. Enlightenment in Russia

To juxtapose the Enlightenment in America with
that in Russia is to underscore the vast difference
between two variants of Enlightenment. The Enlightenment was European in spirit and substance. And the
American and Russian societies were on the periphery
of European civilization as its two cultural outposts.
Nonetheless, both societies borrowed and imitated
Enlightenment ideas and values.

The American Enlightenment is, in essence, a
political enlightenment because natural rights were
conceived as the moral species of power. In addition,
the "ethical revolution" accompanying the Enlightenment, as Alfred Cobban[1] pointed out, included America
but not Russia. Seeing America and Russia as passive
recipients of European Enlightenment does not constitute a disclaimer against Henry Steele Commager's
thesis[2] that only in America did the Age of Reason
forge its political empire. Enlightenment in America
means, first and foremost, political enlightenment,
and, second, it coincides with laying the moral
foundation of the Republican form of Government.

In this sense, America is both the product of
and major contributor to the Enlightenment. But Russia
is neither the product nor the originator of the Enlightenment. Though Russia became a modern state in
the eighteenth century, Russian society had no eighteenth century. This is often construed as condescension
toward Russia, a throwback to Muscovite-Mongol despotism
on civilized Europe's Euro-Asian hinterland.

Yet Russia, indeed, escaped the eighteenth century
if the latter is interpreted in a specific political
sense. The Russian tsars and intellectuals grappled
with the spirit of Enlightenment and what it meant
for Russian civilization. In his major work, National
Consciousness in Eighteenth Century Russia, Hans Rogger[3]
sees the rise of national consciousness, or national
self-determination as the terminus ad quem of Russia's
eighteenth century. Undeniably, under the impact of
Enlightenment ideas Russia's educated strata begins
to strive for national identity. And by comparing
Russia's native values to those of Europe's, Russian
thinkers delineated the nature of autocracy and its
social-political ideals. But Russia's political-
intellectual speculations do not comprise, in any
remote sense, an "ethical revolution" we associated
with the Enlightenment.

From political perspective, Enlightenment laid the foundation of modern age in three respects. First, the philosophes have dissected political power and analyzed it in terms of its relation to individual rights. Second, the philosophes in general and Jefferson in particular were committed to the legitimacy of government. Third, and most important for our comparative approach, the Enlightenment thinkers investigated the relationship of political and constitutional thinking.

When one considers the long-range consequences of the American Enlightenment, one can see how deletirious was the absence of eighteenth century on Russian political development. Russian political theory addressed itself neither to the legitimacy of political power and its justifiable conduct, nor did it delineate between political and constitutional thinking. While Russian enlightenment can be characterized as a sustained apology for enlightened despotism, American Enlightenment is synonymous with constitutionalism. The contrast, then, of the Russian and American Enlightenment is the contrast of enlightened despotism and constitutional absolutism.

The antithetical values of the American and Russian political systems become even more revealing when we impose absolutism and constitutionalism on the means-to-end axis. In enlightened despotism, the means-to-ends are subordinate to the paramount values of survival and security of the state. In constitutional government, unless the individuals expressly consent to, civil rights cannot be subordinate to the state.

In the eighteenth century we witness the shift from the safety principle of the state to the welfare principle of the individual as the priority of good government. The welfare principle, or the pursuit of happiness, is embodied in the American Republic. But in Russia, there is no corresponding shift from the security of the state to the individual welfare.

Neither in the eighteenth century nor later is there any attempt in Russian political thought to define the ends of government in terms of the expanding welfare of the individual. Russian autocracy, as evident in Catherine's constitutional reforms, was only adept in wrapping itself in constitutional principles in order to be more presentable to Europe.

With the exception of Hobbes, Western political thought is not noted for its justification of absolute, indivisible political authority, without any counter-vailing powers. Just to stay with the Enlightenment, the political self-limitation of absolute power is explicit in Montesquieu's formula of self-tempered monarcy, and even in Voltaire's concept of "constitutional absolutism."

By contrast, the Russian approach to government, first under the Muscovite princes and then under the tsars and the All-Russian Emperors, can be conceptualized as samoderzhavie (autocracy). The autocrats and tsars proudly referred to themselves as samoderzhets, roughly the Russian equivalent of Hobbes's Leviathan. Interestingly, the Russian Empire proclaimed itself an "autocratic monarchy" until the rise of Lenin's "proletarian dictatorship" in 1917.

Despotic form of government is both separate, conceptually, and differs markedly from constitutional government. Commonplace wisdom holds that individual rights, in addition to a garantiste constitution protecting civil and political liberties, is the arch-stone of constitutional democracy. Undeniably, rights and liberties are the crucial, historical ingredients of a free society. But when the latter is compared with Russian society, we discover the structural conditions of free society. What prevented the evolution of free society in Russia is the complete absence of checks and balances on an otherwise over-whelming political power, centralized and personified in the tsar. Samoderzhavie is the very antinomy of free society. For society to be free, at no time can any single force, whether wielded by class, party, or bureaucracy, be overpowering (samoderzhets). Over-whelming and irresistable power, denoted by the Russian word vlast, is the death knell of free society.

The cognate issue of unlimited vs. limited forms of government is recognized in Western thought both as a rational and practical choice. In Russia, however, Enlightenment took the form of apology for enlightened despotism, rather than delineating constitutional first principles. Thus natural rights failed to have any measurable influence on Russian political thought. Nor is it a negligible factor for Russia's political destiny that Marx lacked the Enlightenment's confidence in reason as the morally acceptable final authority in resolving conflicts.

The Enlightenment, then, not only by-passed Russia, but by mid-nineteenth century the intelligentsia in Russia is absorbing Marxism, at war with the doctrine of natural laws. It cannot be overemphasized enough that the language of natural rights, in Europe as well in America, is the language of those who sought to curb political power.

In Russia, by contrast, natural rights became a strange, if not un-invited guest. We referred to Shcherbatov's Hobbesian reading of Locke's natural law thinking. Another Russian liberal thinker, S. E. Desnitsky (1740-1789), whose studies under Adam Smith exposed him to the "moral sentiment" approach to natural laws, confined natural rights to the Hobbesian right of self-preservation.[4]

To Hobbes, human nature and society are attenuated to survival (perseverae in esse quo) which, in turn, is equated with natural law. Whether human nature is detachable from moral ideals, as Hobbes would lead us believe, or it can be confined to the Hobbesian quest for survival, are issues that remain contested. The moral ideals man aspires to very from thinker to thinker. While Aristotle, for instance, associated human ends with the disinterested cultivation of intellect, Aquinas equates ends with the knowledge and love of God. Those who are sympathetic to Aristotle or Aquinas' teleology, will find little comfort in Hobbes's stark realism.

But even Hobbes and Hume, who lowered their sights of man, are not without a teleological element in their system of thought that counters the empirical emphasis on survival. Hume admitted that,[5]

"Human nature cannot by any means subsist without the association of individuals: and that association never could have place where no regard is paid to the laws of equity and justice."

In Russia, the moral necessity of the state to survive has consistently superceded any consideration for the welfare and rights of the individual. The rights and powers of the state, not the common good, became the constitutive element of Russia's social arrangements and the unique feature of its political thought. By contrast, natural law doctrines are the bedrock foundations of America's social and political arrangements. The question of how men should live in

132

political society, though metaphysical and moral in
scope, is not inconsistent with the Hobbesian right of
self-preservation. But self-preservation, universal as
it may be, cannot exhaust the total meaning of man as
a political animal. Indisputably, a society's social
arrangements to ensure survival also express its
political and moral aspirations.

Conversely, political systems also differ because
they respond differently to the right of self-preservation. Take Peter Chaadayev (1794-1856), whose in-
sights into Russian civilization and its destiny
compare with Tocqueville's famous study of American
civilization. Comparing Russian political values to
that of Europe, Chaadayev sadly observed,[6]

> "To behold us it would seem that the general
> law of mankind had been revoked in our case.
> Isolated in the world; we have given nothing
> to the world, we have taught nothing to the
> world; we have not added a single idea to the
> mass of human ideas; we have contributed
> nothing to the progress of the human spirit
> . . . . For people to notice us, we have had
> to stretch from the Bering Straits to the Oder."

As so many Russian thinkers after him, Chaadayev
reproached the Russians for allowing themselves to
be so exclusively guided by government. In his famous
First Letter, never intended for publication, he
ascribed Russia's political backwardness to its
deviation from the European heritage, Chaadayev
associated with the law and the legacy of Renaissance.
Chaadayev's comparative look produced the anguished
conclusion that Russia lacked the "moral essence,"
which enabled the West to inculcate the individual with
the values of "justice, law, and order."[7] Chaadayev's
philosophical incursion into Russia's past enraged
Nicholas I. The tsar declared the philosopher
insane and ordered that he be "treated." This is the
"humane" precedent for the Soviet regime's "psychiatric
wards" where dissidents are "treated" for mental illness,
known in the West as nonconformism. The mind recoils
at the spectre of committing Soviet dissidents to the
black roster of psychiatric inequity. According to
a handy Soviet theory, propounded by Andrei V.
Snezhnevsky, individuals who have repeated difficulties
with authorities suffer from "reformism"--a stubborn
penchant to reform Soviet society. Diagnosed as
disturbed, dissidents are treated with disabling drugs

and physically brutalized. The boundaries of acceptable political behavior have been left, throughout Russian history, to the discretion of its rulers. In Russia, questioning sacred and absolute political norms is considered a mental derangement. In the West, at least since Socrates, courage is the term for nonconforming behavior.

All told, Chaadayev's politically diagnosed "insanity" is not the first, nor the last instance that Russia's rulers, from tsars to commissars, converted critical analysis into a rank political heresy. What Nietzsche dismissed as the "wretched ephemeral babble" of ideas and politics, in Russia assumes the reality of few courageous individuals voicing independent opinion against a state.

The heartbeat of Russian civilization is set by the state, not individual conscience. The Socratic invitation to "Know Thyself" and the determined quest to lead an examined national existence are mostly unknown in Russia. With much truth, James Billington wrote,[8] "The Socratic method of Plato and the individualism of Socrates never took root in Russia." In place of individualism, with its belief that conscience is the repository of truth and judgment in private and public sphere of actions, Russian political tradition places the collectivity which allegedly enjoys special access to truth.

Not surprisingly, Russia's political ideal is a hyperthrophied state which, as embodiment of absolute knowledge and virtue, is to instill piety and obedience in society's errant members. The Russian playwright and astute observer of Europe, D.I. Fonvizin (1745-1794) sternly declaimed against individual liberties. "Freedom is an empty name," he declared, "and the right of the stronger remains a right which is above all laws."[9] Like so many Russian intellectuals, to Fonvizin the formal legal system was devoid of substance, and, he argued, individual rights in Russia lacked historical tradition and support. Not unlike Solzhenitsyn, Fonvizin put more faith into the so-called "law" of the heart, or human affection, than into cold impartial legalism. According to Fonvizin, the "laws of the heart" are uniquely Russian.

> "The best laws are meaningless if the first law, the first bond between men has left their hearts—good faith. We have little of it, but here (France) there is not even a trace."[10]

The concept of "feeling heart," as it appears in

134

Fonvizin's writings, was spawned, one need hardly add, by Rousseau's romanticism. It is noteworthy and germane that Hermann Melville, that yea-sayer of light out of his own darkness, had a special place for the "reason" of human heart in his vision of society. Yet Melville, whose embattled and tortured soul was schooled in what he called the "Dark Ages of Democracy," knew that man, at times reaching for the stars and at others playing pygmy parts, can never attain the unity of the self. Even at his best, as maker and inheritor of democracy in the New World, man is but a pure unit because, caught between heavens and hells, his heart and mind constantly duel for supremacy.

Compare this concept of man to Fonvizin's "natural man" who, staggering under the piled up despotic centuries, could not metamorphose himself into a New Adam, like Melville's "upright barbarian" (Billy Budd). Thus Melville, despite his transcendental gospel against the shoddy democracy of his time, paid respect to her. But even Russian writers who were influenced by European romanticism showed hostility not only to representative but to direct democracy, and above all, disdained eqalitarian ideas. Fonvizin, for one, saw the Russian political tradition as inimical to the concept of equality before the law. And Scherbatov, one of the more progressive figures of his time, extolled pre-Petrine civilization as morally superior to the reform-oriented new Russia. Finally, there was Alexander Sumarokov (1718-1777) who, like Fonvizin and his contemporaries, argued against extending rights to the peasants.

Russia produced its own share of aristocrats whose intellect and commitment to human ideals transcend the rigid social distinctions autocracy erected. The piled up despotic centuries crushed any potential Tocqueville in Russia. Russian political thought, therefore, is silent of the moral voice such as the aristocrat Tocqueville uttered[11].

> "A state of equality is perhaps less elevated, but it is more just: and its justice constitutes its greatness and its beauty. I would strive then, to raise myself to this point of the Divine contemplation, and thence to view and to judge the concerns of men."

For clarity, and for profound suggestion for all the implications of comparing the American and Russian political thought, Tocqueville's statement is matchless.

We started this discussion by briefly comparing
the political residue of Romantic movement in Russia
and Europe. To sum up, it was contended that European
romanticism contains an egalitarian, radical thrust.
By contrast, this is not the case in Russia. This
is particularly evident when one considers the exagger-
ated view of the Russian peasant, a point of contact
between the Slavophiles and Westerners despite their
disagreement. At least since the eighteenth century,
the God-bearing Russian peasant, muzhik, was conceived
as morally superior to the worthless "bourgeois
man" of the more civilized Europe. The Russian
peasant was cast into a paragon of virtues that were
either corrupted or corroded by "progressive" European
civilization.

To a European liberal like J. S. Mill, the bourgeois individual was a "progressive" being who, as
citizen, enjoyed equal legal and political rights with
others. But in Petrine Russia, equality meant
equal state service for all ranks of society. Whether
peasant or aristocrat, each was subject to Peter the
Great's service-state, and all took the subject's
oath. Peter not only made the state the decisive
organ of politics and society, but all members of
society were servants of the state. To Christian
thought, the Fall of man, his loss of innocence, means
forfeiture of Eden.

In Petrine Russia, the state is transfigured
by an autocratic fiat into a new Eden, which peasants
and aristocrats can enter only upon condition of
serving and obeying it. It is worth recalling that
St. Augustine viewed the state as a necessary evil,
the punishment of Fallen man, felix culpa. Thus, in
Paradise Lost, Milton speaks with magnificent irony of
the knowledge of good and evil as knowledge of
"God lost, and Evil got." The loss of innocence,
significantly, is the learning process of man in the
ways of good and evil. And acquaintance with the
necessity of evil - the all-to-human experience of
Christian man-includes the acquaintance and involve-
ment with the state. For Milton's protestant conscience,
man's domicile in the state is paradise lost. To the
Russian soul, self-conscious identification with a
Hobbesian state is paradise regained.

The political consequences of this can be measured,
paradoxical as it may sound, even in Russia's leading
anarchists, Michael Bakunin, Peter Kropotkin, and Leo

Tolstoy, all members of the aristocracy. As a service-class, Russian aristocracy was under relentless pressure to comply and conform. It is hardly surprising, therefore, that Russia's aristocrat-anarchists could not shake off the Russian past even in their utopian designs.

Bakunin's distrust of legal and parliamentary methods is not atypical among Russian anarchist thinkers. The following may serve as representative sample of Bakunin's thinking.[12]

"The time for parliamentary life, constituent and national assemblies is over. . . . I don't believe in constitutions and laws. Even the best constitution would not satisfy me. We need something else--life, a new world, without laws and thus free."

Bakunin left no doubt of his preference for a republic dominated by what he called a "strong dictatorial power with the exclusive task of raising and educating the popular masses."[13] Even in post-revolutionary Russia, he argued, political power must be "limited by no one and nothing."[14]

In Bakunin's political philosophy the reader finds a complete abridgment, if not negation, of the law and government. Equally revealing is in this respect Nikolay Chernyshevsky (1828-1889) whose epoch-making utopia, What is to be Done?, contains the main ingredients of the Leninist party dictatorship. In essence, Chernyshevsky, as Lenin after him, merely inverted Russian absolutism in delineating his own populist model of politics. Summing up his reflections on the Russian past, Chernyshevsky said[15], "Far better anarchy from below than from above."

Like the Russian populists, Slavophiles, and even Solzhenitsyn himself, Chernyshevsky had little use for European style legalism. At the same time, he also despaired over the Russian character, disarmed and deformed by autocracy. "Wretched nation," exclaimed Chernyshevsky, "wretched nation, nation of slaves from top to bottom. They are all only slaves."[16] Born of the Russian experience, similar Job-like despair was voiced by a historian who, studying the Russian masses, pronounced the verdict, "What horrors they allow, and yet they are dumb."[17]

The Russian masses, inert, indifferent, and deprived of civic education, could not develop a strong legal sense or judicial outlook. But neither were the Russian intelligentsia, the Platonic "soul" of the cave-dwelling Russian masses, or, for that matter, the Bolshevik leaders, noted for their respect of the concept of law and rights. Maxim Gorky's change of heart is instructive on this point. Once a friend of Lenin and sincere advocate of the birth of a New Man, the Soviet man who will read "Shelley in original," by 1918 Gorky realized that Lenin and Trotsky were the "maniacs of a beautiful idea." Gorky's dark prophesy merits full quote.[18]

> "Lenin, Trotsky, and their companions have already become poisoned with the filthy venom of power, and this is evidenced by their shameful attitude toward freedom of speech, the individual, and the sum total of those rights for the triumph of which democracy struggled. . . . Does not Lenin's government, as the Romanov government did, seize and drag off to prison all those who think differently?"

Gorky left us as revealing testimony on the crisis of the 1917 revolution as those of Madison's papers on 1776. Gorky could not find harsh enough words to reproach Lenin, his former friend, for building socialism with bullets, bayonets, and fist in the face. These methods, cried out Gorky, kept us in abject slavery through Russia's dark centuries. Gorky's god-that-failed disenchantment presages Russia's national tragedy for generations to come.

Lenin's recourse to torture by the right to avenge torture, Gorky protested, mocked the declared ideals of the revolution: conscience, justice, and respect for man. But Lenin's autocracy of political savagery embodied that countervailing force the Russian revolutionaries dreamed of in order to unhinge the ancien regime. In addition to this "arithmetic of madness," whereby the Soviets matched tsarism's efficient power, another element in the Russian political tradition was also absorbed into Communist ideology. Namely, the approach to politics from the presumed organic unity of the individual and society.

In Anglo-American political theory, on the other hand, we see an analytical-conceptual separation of

the individual and society. Even the "natural
sociability" of man, first propounded by Aristotle,
is not an exclusive concept, but a dialectical aspect
of individualism which, in Western thought, poses
the dilemma that Socrates posed in <u>Crito</u>. The legacy
which Socrates bequeathed to the common thought of
Europe is that individual conscience can and must
transcend the values of the political realm. Yet
it is the "natural sociability" of man that enables
the Socratic individual to challenge the normative
values of society.

The asocial individuality, associated with
Socrates, has no counterpart in Russian thought
which is consumed by the desire to eradicate the
antithesis between political society and the individual.
It is not accidental that Tolstoy, that penetrating
gazer into the Russian soul, rejected the concept of
individual liberty, and of civil rights guaranteed
by some impersonal system of justice   Another Russian
philosophical anarchist, Kropotkin, in his classic,
<u>Mutual Aid: A Factor of Evolution</u> (1902), had assembled
impressive data to prove that "society" is the "law
of nature." To Kropotkin, progress depends on the
spontaneous development of the instinctual bases of
social solidarity. Compare to it the views of Emerson
and Thoreau, the closest kins to Kropotkin's anti-
political philosophy.

Emerson's political idea was a "nation of friends,"
a "political brotherhood" based on inward unity of
spirit and power of love. The historical conflicts
that sundered men will end one day and "all men will
be lovers," and all mankind will bask in the "universal sunshine."[19] Much as he praised the "common soul,"
Emerson refused to dissolve or blot out individualism
in an abstract solidarity. To him each man, ideally
at least, was to be a "state," rather than each subsumed in the state.

Like Kropotkin and Solzhenitsyn, Thoreau had his
share of quarrel with politics. And yet Thoreau's
vision of man, a mere mass of "thawing clay" seeking
common values in friendship and fraternity, remained
irrovocably bound by the American intellectual-
political heritage. Above all, the concept of limited
government restrained Thoreau's enthusiasm for fulfill-
ing human aspiration in a gregarious collective. To
him modern government was but a device for developing

our individual values. In his own words,[20]

> "Now that the republic--the res publica--has been
> settled, it is time to look after the res private
> --the private state. . . ."

To give one more example of the divergent American-
Russian approach to the relationship of individual to
society, consider the argument of B. A. Kistyakovsky,
a leading Russian legal philosopher. Member of the
neo-Kantian school in Germany of 1900s, completing his
studies under George Simmel and Max Weber, Kistyakovsky
contended that the state exists not only as an essential
reality--incidentally, a notion that Hans Kelsen[21]
borrowed from Kistyakovsky--but also as a duty. Now
duty to the state, embodying universal laws, is a
Kantian postulate. Hence the Kantian duty to the
state is predicated on the general principle that the
state conforms to universal laws. The latter affirm
the pre-eminent good of man as a rational-moral being.
These universal laws were defined by Kant as lending
universal validity to the personal ends of rational
beings. In short, the Kantian concept of the state
supports the "kingdom of ends."[22]

By contrast, Kistyakovsky treats the law as the
totality of norms, safeguarded by the coercive
power of the state. He argued that representative
government would make Russia a "legal state" (pravovoe
gosudarstvo). The latter, Kistyakovsky added somewhat
prophetically, is not the result of political evolution, but the necessary precondition for the realization of the socialist state. In parenthesis we can add,
morality and legalism as precondition of socialism
is a conviction shared by those neo-Kantian intellectuals who, for one reason or other, committed themselves
to Marxism. The neo-Kantian Marxists, Lukacs in Hungary
and P. B. Struve in Russia, to name only two, have
argued that as a transpersonal value, socialism is to
be interpreted as subspecies of ethical values. In
short, neo-Kantian Marxists sought to connect the
concept of socialism, connoting a civilization based
on transpersonal values, with Kantian ethics. In
direct opposition to Soviet orthodoxy, neo-Kantian
Marxists insisted, and paid dearly for it, that socialism can neither transcend nor dispense with individualistic ethics. It should be kept in mind that the
Kantian concept of "community" is not an empirical
proposition. Significantly, it refers to certain
universal principles and values proper to man as a
moral being.

Even when adhering to Marxist views, Struve adopted
Kant's standpoint in Critique of Practical Reason when
arguing that ethical norms are the essence of human
society. The absolute universal norms Struve and Lukacs
injected into Marxism came from Kant. The neo-Kantian
Marxists, attacked by Lenin, argued for the need of
universally obligatory moral code within Marxism,
standing above the proletariat's historical interest and
strategic goals.

Neo-Kantianism is not our concern. Yet the issue
they raised, concerning the relation of individual
ethics and socialism, have deep roots in Russia's
past and, in Soviet setting, continue to haunt
Communism. Triumphant Communism, inheriting Russia's
antagonism to legalism, had little use for neo-Kantian
Marxists. Lukacs himself was silenced and his books
proscribed by Moscow. Nor should this surprise us.
For one can search in vain the voluminous corpus of
Russian political literature, from Radishchev (1749-
1802) to Lenin, to find a single work on legal theory,
constitutionalism, or the rights of man. In the West,
on the other hand, the concept of law and its moral
ideals have preoccupied virtually all major political
theorists from Aristotle to Montesquieu, and from Kant
to the Federalists. Yet no leading Russian thinker
attached any significance to legal philosophy.

Alexander Herzen, the giant of Russian thought,
considered the absence of legal rights in Russia as
something of a blessing. He referred to Western
legalism as "Barbaro-Roman justice."[23] And in his
turn Chernyshevsky pointedly observed that the
"constitutional minutiae" has little meaning for the
destitute Russian masses. The rule of law and
constitutional rights he dismissed as "political
deserts."[24] Intent on legitimizing the autocracy's
organic wholeness, Russian political theory failed
even to define the autocrat as legibus solutus.
Consequently, the autocrat's personal power was ascribed
not only primacy over the law and its procedure, but
the concept of political morality took a strange
turn in Russia.

Political morality, as understood in the West,
asserts that the government must treat those whom it
governs not only with concern and respect, but with
equal concern and respect. In Russia, as indicated,
the survival and safety of the state, rather than

141

political morality, attained a priority and dominant value. There are historical reasons for this In the West a powerful nobility, invoking its privileges and historical rights, managed to restrain and limit the scope and ambition of royal absolutism. By contrast, the servile and serving Russian nobility was not at liberty, which Machiavelli defined as absence of external impediments to political action, to counter the monarch's personal power and ambition. Unlike the English nobility, the Russian nobility was hardly interested in an independent judiciary that could have curtailed the nobility's vested privileges.

The Russian nobility played no role as an intermediary to expand the scope of royal justice.[25] As absolute masters in administrative and judicial spheres over their serfs, the Russian nobility had no interest in judicial supremacy. The result was a deep seated aversion to legal procedure that is deeply rooted in the very texture of Russian past and political history.

As John Dewey has shown,[26] democracy owes much to the constitutional struggles between the monarchy and aristocracy. Russian autocracy, on the other hand, was not challenged and tamed by an assertive aristocracy, jealous of its historical privileges and power. Undeniably, Russian autocracy had aspired to the scope and fame of European royal absolutism. Yet this Machiavellian ambition for power and prestige was not checked by the countervailing ambition of Russian aristocracy. The struggle between kings and nobility contributed to the creation and expansion of the judicial space in the West around the citizen. Even at its height, Western absolutism was not powerful enough to temper destructively with the concept of legalism and subordinate it to state interest. But in Russia, anti-legalism was written into the nature and outlook of autocracy, no less than that of aristocracy.

In the West, law has adjudicated the nasty and tawdry affairs of homo politicus. Real and grave abuses of the law there were. Yet Western legalism remained, on the whole, untainted. As Judith Shklar[27] pointed out, the Western intellectual heritage is deeply legalistic. We want to underscore that legalism, when compared with Russian political development, is an act of political choice.

At least since the seventeenth century, civic consciousness emerges in Europe as a frame of reference for political society. Civic consciousness we understand as the elementary perception that there is a public or social order which compels the government to show equal concern and respect toward all citizens. In Russia, the rights of nobility have not expanded to encompass the dignity and moral worth of all persons, nor were the peasants accorded the elementary perception as civic individuals.

Differently put, all subjects of Russia, from nobles to peasants, were equal in their civic duty to serve a Leviathan state. "All members of society," wrote Dimitrij Pisarev (1840-1868), "must, each in his own place, be of service to society."[28] The "dark folk" of Russian history were not only denied dignity and rights, but were to remain ignorant lest education would make them rebel against their fate. The distinguishing feature of the Russian autocracy was the absence of any constructive interplay between the absolutist state and its subjects The "father" of Russian Marxism, George Plekhanov (1856-1918), noted, in summing up the Russian political past, the "complete helplessness of the population vis-a-vis the state."[29] The Russian individual was "helpless" against the state because, to summarize, neither the constitutional limitations of political power nor the legitimacy of moral and civil rights against the state have developed in Russia or were conceptualized in its political theory.

Analyzing the American approach to politics, Socrates's name was invoked more than once. His influence on Western thought gains perspective against the Russian political past. The moral atmosphere and ethical discourse created and initiated by Socrates has changed Western values. Their absence in Russia was poignantly captured by G. S. Skovoroda (1722-1794), a "wandering" philosopher-monk, or what the Russians call strannik. These philosopher-minstlers enjoyed popular support in Petrine Russia for their Socratic mission of tending to the lonely, submissive, obedient Russian souls. "There are lost souls in every country," confessed Chaadayev, "but in ours (Russia) it is the general characteristic."[30]

Conscious of his role, Skovoroda composed
a prayer, asking God to bless Russia with a
Socrates.

"Our Father who are in Heaven, wilt Thou
send down Socrates to us soon. . . . Hallowed
be Thy name, in the thoughts and intentions
of Thy servant, who has intended with his
mind and desired with his will to be a
Socrates in Russia . . . . Thy Kingdom come,
and at that time the sown seed, according to
Thy word, will spring up like a lily."[31]

Russia was not blessed with Socrates.
Skovoroda's moving evocation of Socrates recognizes
that the feeble voice of justice and the law of
individual conscience, to counter unjust power, was
stilled in Russia. With Socrates, politics in
Europe begins to speak in terms of ethics and
individual conscience. The cultivation of justice
combined with wisdom is the way of redemption
for Socratic men seeking political power. The
Russian concept of politics approximates more the
Hobbesian model. The state is a field of force
for contending groups and factions, defined as
power units without moral or constitutional
restraints.

Nothing underscores this better than isolated
attempts in Russian history to introduce constitutional ideas and principles. The most renown
constitutional experiment is associated with
Catherine the Great, that Semiramis of the north
and avid correspondent of Voltaire, Diderot,
Grimm, and other philosophes who enjoyed her
bounties and gifts. The Empress, by her own admission, consulted the writing of Hobbes, Grotius,
Montesquieu, and Pufendorf to gather luminous

principles for the Russian constitution or Nakaz. Her philosophes-pensioners praised the great libertarian law-giver, the Solon of Russia. Yet her famous constitutional draft, Instructions for Composing a New Code of Laws, or Nakaz, demonstrates the incompatability of Russian political tradition and legalism.[32]

Even a cursory reading of the Nakaz shows that the Empress interpreted the writings of Hobbes, philosophes, and especially Montesquieu for providing the theoretical bracings to sovereign power and unconditional obedience to its incarnate-herself. Hobbes had sacrificed all rights but one, self-preservation, to the dominant interest of the sovereign. The latter's will is the will of all. The sovereign is under no obligation to his subjects, but is the source of all obligations. Hobbesian political theory contains an explicit rationale for the concentration of national power. Not surprisingly, Hobbes's prestige and influence in Russia parallels that of Locke in America.

In Russia, Hobbes became admired for his concept of a strong state, free from division, schism, and capable of fighting foreign invasions. Neither Peter nor Catherine, who gave modern Russia body and soul, have any use for Locke, recommending minimal state power and maximum individual rights. Russian autocracy needed a Hobbesian philosophy to legitimize state absolutism. In Hobbes's theory, man's duty to the state overrides the dictates of his conscience. Since the primary duty of the sovereign is to keep peace and maintain order, men's opinions and actions cannot be freely propagated if they subvert authority. It follows that the Hobbesian suppression of an opinion is justified when found "repugnant to peace." The diseases which bring about the dissolution of commonwealths, Hobbes never tired warning, are seditious opinions and pernicious doctrines. In essence, Hobbes gives ghostly power to the sovereign to challenge ideas and doctrines "repugnant to peace." And the suppression of an opinion or dissent, as demonstrated in the Soviet Union, must also be the suppression of error and private beliefs. To Hobbes there cannot be a moral-spiritual realm independent of the civil authority.

There is little doubt that the Hobbesian legacy of centralized and absolute state power has impacted Russian political thinking. In fairness to Hobbes, however, there is a democratic core to his political

theory. Though known for his brilliant yet dark
conceptual definition of the politics of egoistic
self-preservation, Hobbes conceded that the "people
rule in all governments."[33] In Russia, needless to
add, the democratic "core" of Hobbes's political theory
was ignored or glossed over. Hobbes is not the only
thinker subject to a "political" reading in Russia.
While in America Pufendorf's writings were used as
a primer of natural rights, Peter the Great ordered
the Russian translation of Pufendorf's On the Duties
of Man and Citizen, which stresses "duty" over "rights."

Somewhat similar fate overtook Montesquieu in
Russia. Undeniably, in Montesquieu's political theory
two strands are woven together, one moralistic and the
other positivistic. The relevance of this is that in
America Montesquieu is read for his moralistic and
natural law orientation. The Founding Fathers saw
in him a confirmation that natural-law principles are
the touchstone of political right. Above all, Montesquieu's sensitivity to the separation of powers played
prominent role in shaping American constitutional
thinking. The separation of powers was mentioned in
the Virginia Declaration of Rights of 1776 (Sec. 5),
and in the preamble to the Massachusetts Constitution
of 1789 (Sect. 30).

Montesquieu has linked the separation of powers
with the concept of constitutionalism. This became
embodied in Article 16 of the French Declaration of
the Rights and Citizen (1789). The article declares,

"Any society in which the enforcement of rights
is not guaranteed and the separation of powers
not definitely stated, does not possess a
constitution."

To the lasting credit of Montesquieu, he made the
separation of legislative and executive powers the
precondition for the realization of liberty. "There
is no liberty," he declared, "if the power of judging
be not separated from the legislative and executive
powers."[34]

Let's consider now the Russian perception of
Montesquieu. Catherine's avowed prayer book was The
Spirit of Laws. Of its author she said, "Were I Pope,
I would canonize him."[35] Montesquieu's book served as
a model of Catherine's constitutional draft, the Nakaz.

She herself admitted that the "spirit" of her proposed Nakaz was "stolen from president Montesquieu" (obobrala presidenta Montesquieu).[36] In her Nakaz, the Empress wrote: "A society of citizens requires a certain fixed order. There ought to be some to govern, and others to obey."[37] Article 9 of Nakaz states, "The ruler is absolute." One is hardpressed to find in Montesquieu's writings a justification for a fixed political order, let alone implicit endorsement of unlimited power. Montesquieu repeatedly stated that the best government is that which suits the particular people for whom it is established.[38] He categorically denied having favored one form of government over another.

The tsarina not so much "stole" ideas from Montesquieu as she subverted the spirit and meaning of his political ideas. Few examples will suffice to illustrate it. Montesquieu talks about aristocratic monarchy. Catherine translates it into "bureaucratic monarchy."[39] In delineating the concept of "bureaucratic monarchy" in the Nakaz, she follows the Russian "historical tradition."[40] Strikingly reminiscent of Hobbes, the Empress declared that individuals who disturb public peace (Art. 214), and refuse to submit to the laws, are to be excluded from the community. Dissidents, to use her immortal phrase, are "politically dead." The Soviet dissidents' fate, analyzed in the next chapter, lends tragic reality to the phrase.

But to return to Catherine. In a true Platonic fashion, she said the role of education is to "train citizens" (Art. 348). Few students of politics would find in Montesquieu support for what Catherine purports to be in The Spirit of Laws. More to the point, Montesquieu warns specifically against making the monarch or his council the "proper depository" of the fundamental law. Catherine, however, contends that only the "governmental power can be the depository of laws" (Art. 21,23). Compare this with Montesquieu's statement, "It is not enough to have intermediate powers in a monarchy; there must be also a depository of the laws."[41]

Montesquieu insisted that "express laws" distinguish limited from absolute power. Catherine, in her turn, ignored this crucial distinction. In fact, she was unhappy with Montesquieu's characterization of the Russian form of government as despotic. Despotism, declared Montesquieu, not only deforms human nature,

but it denotes a "government in which a single person
directs everything and by his own will and caprice."[42]
The Empress countered Montesquieu by arguing that
Russian autocracy is a special form of European monarchy.
But as we have tried to show, Russian enlightened
despotism recognized no "express laws" or "express
conventions" that limited the autocrat's personal rule.

Characteristically, the two principal ideas of
Montesquieu, the "division of power" and "ideas of
uniformity", were ignored by Catherine. Nor did she
find in The Spirit of Laws a strong endorsement of
liberal and humanitarian politics. Though she diligent-
ly copied Montesquieu's observations on geography and
climate as invariables of politics, the Russian ruler
ignored Montesquieu's conclusion, "Countries are not
cultivated in proportion to their fertility, but to
their liberty."[43] Montesquieu declared judicial powers
as an obstacle to absolute power. And trial by jury--
like his great successor Tocqueville--he considered the
essence of republicanism because it "places the real
direction of society in the hands of the governed, or
of a portion of the governed, and not in that of the
government."[44] Even in the 1880s some Russian thinkers
could still argue that,

"... the so-called omnipotence du jury is perhaps
understandable in Western Europe, where the
state is founded to some degree on the principles
of democracy, but this direction to jury's activity cannot be justified by anything in Russia."[45]

To summarize, natural law thinking had not penetrated Russia. Nor is it accidental that Rousseau
became something of an intellectual rage in post-
eighteenth century Russia. It was Rousseau who, in
his draft of Social Contract, removed lengthy discussion
of Diderot's conception of natural rights. As a
celebrated philosophe, Diderot was guest of Catherine
in 1774-1775. In one of his memoranda to the tsarina,
Diderot wrote,[46]

"It seems to me that in general your subjects err
on the side of one extreme or the other, either
in believing their nation too advanced or in
believing it too backward. ... I seem to have
observed quite generally a circumspection, a
distrust which seems to me to be the opposite of
that attractive and straightforward frankness
which characterize spirits that are lofty, free
and secure. ..."

In the Russian people's attitude toward authority
Diderot saw a nuance of "panic terror," the result of
prolonged despotism. He left Russia deeply disappointed
and even burned his personal notes on it. The reason
for it can be guessed from what Diderot wrote to
Mme. Necker in 1774:

> "I will confess to you very much under my
> breath that philosophes, who give the impression
> of best having known what despotism is, have seen
> it only through the neck of a bottle. What a
> difference there is between a tiger painted by
> Oudry and a tiger in the forest."[47]

5. Bentham and Russia

The Russian state was truly a veritable "tiger in
the forest." Diderot saw at first hand what the
"tiger" was like when not caged by natural law which,
together with "liberty" and "justice," Jeremy Bentham
dismissed as folly and self-conceit. Consistent with
his disdain for natural rights, Bentham was quite
impressed with Catherine's constitutional draft and
code of law. In fact, Bentham and Russia had an
elective affinity for each other. Making no secret
of his contempt for the American Revolution for
declaring "rights" the centerpiece of government,
Bentham was admired in Russia. Upon reading Jefferson's Declaration of Independence, Bentham declared
himself anti-American. He attacked the concept of
rights on grounds they confuse "is" and "ought"
which, according to Hume, were to be kept analytically
distinct and separate.

As a utilitarian, Bentham insisted on the need of
responsible power. Hence the emotional values that
attached to concepts like "rights" and "justice,"
he felt, were more of a curse than blessing for mankind,
seeking a happy and efficient political existence.
To Bentham, the moral history of man and his public
policy were two different propositions. He broke
sharply with liberal thought over the theory of law.
Defining law as public command whose primary consideration is to increase the efficiency of courts and
procedural principles, Bentham abandoned almost
entirely the checks and safeguards, emanating from
the natural law, deemed necessary to protect the individual's rights. From utilitarian perspective, natural
rights, relying on private judgment, were meaningless
superstitions. Bentham also attacked Locke and Jefferson's concept of rights by contending that subjection,
not freedom, is man's natural state.

Utilitarian philosophy had something of a rough
going both in England and America. Approached by
Bentham to propagate his utilitarian creed, which
involved purging the Anglo-American political vocabu-
lary of "rights," Benjamin Franklin remained distant
and unresponsive. Bentham, however, was confident
that autocratic Russia was ready for his utilitarian
gospel. Nor was he altogether mistaken in this.
After all, Russian autocrats possessed power and were
efficient. The efficiency of political power Bentham
defined in terms of the ruler-ruled's relationship.

When the sovereign speaks, Bentham said, the subjects
must obey rather than invoke rights. In the words of
Bentham,[1]

> "Machiavel supposes his statesman a villain and
> then teaches him how he may fulfill his purpose.
> I suppose my statesman a patriot and a philanthro-
> pist or, what comes to the same thing, a man
> of understanding."

In the Russian Empress, Bentham found a natural
"understanding" for his utilitarian philosophy.
But like so many others since who hoped to awaken
Russian despotism to its moral-legal responsibility,
Bentham misjudged the Russian talent for "legislation."
Catherine's constitutional design came to naught. In
Bentham's view not because the sovereign was not
willing, but because the national intelligence was
not "up to it."[2] Despite Bentham's high hopes in
"Saint Catherine," as he called the Russian ruler,
and her interest in utilitarian principles, nothing
came of the utilitarian conquest of Russia. When
Bentham finally visited Cahterine's Russia in 1785,
he realized that it was a society of violent contrast
between civilization and barbarity.[3]

Though the contrast of civilization and barbarity
has narrowed, it has not disappeared in Soviet Russia.
Russian despotism fell and Sovietism rose in its
place. Contrary to Solzhenitsyn, the Bolshevik
Revolution also marks the rebirth, if not triumph, of
Russian political values. When a nation is seized
with the pangs of labor, like America in 1776 and
Russia in 1917, the nations are, in the words of Milton,
"amazed at what she means."[4] Six decades after its
revolutionary birth, scholars and historians are
still grappling with the "meaning" of Soviet Russia.

Like all great questions that probe the political
universe in terms of human capacity to understand, the
question of what Soviet Communism "means" can only be
answered at the personal level of the inquirer. We
tried to demonstrate that, at least since the eighteenth century, Russian political theory had consecrated
the "rights" of the state and defined its subjects'
"duties." The state-oriented man (gosudarstvennyi
chelovek) is ontologically specific to Russian culture
as Aristotle's zoon politikon was to Athens. As early
as the fifteenth century, foreign literature on
Russia (skazanniia inostrantsev) discerned a distinct
pattern of illegalism in Russian autocracy. Giles

Fletcher was astounded by the power of Russian rulers and the nobility's habit to call themselves the monarch's "slaves" (kholopy). Nor has Soviet Communism brought about any qualitative changes in the rulers and ruled relationship. Georgi Malenkov spoke as a true Homo Sovieticus when he said, "We are all servants of the state."[5]

The "meaning" of Russia, then, does not reside in individual rights or the dignity of man. Put another way, the ideal "meaning" of Russia is neither natural rights nor freedom under law. It needs repeating that natural rights, as understood and developed in the American political system, acknowledge the gap between what "We, the People" have and what they aspire to is not an abyss, but a relation.

The interplay of rights and political power has yet to permeate Russian political culture. Hence the Soviet citizen is denied an independent ground, judicial and moral, upon which he can oppose the state. In the Soviet Union, neither religious nor moral values are acknowledged as carrying real or potential strictures against the government. The immunity of the person's internal domain, involving liberty and dissent, and the internality of morals whose confidentiality is upheld by Judeo-Christian thought, are absent from Russian political thought.

Nor is it atypical that Dostoevsky, in whose genius the Russian spirit resides as nowhere, repudiated the whole tradition of natural law. Dostoevsky's implacable hostility to rights is worth quoting,

> "Merciful heavens! But what do I care for the laws of nature and arithmetic, when, for the same reason, I dislike those laws and the fact that twice two makes four."[6]

Dostoevsky makes no concessions to natural rights. He counters the lofty assertion, l'homme de la nature et la verite, with the statement that man is but a mouse. To grasp the full implication of Dostoevsky's deflation of man, it is the enslaved and timorous Russian subject, the man-mouse, that enabled Lenin to subvert Communism into étatisme. Though Dostoevsky's faith in man recalls Rousseau's principle of man's radical goodness, his disclosures of the chaos and foul-smelling underground in man balance, if not outweigh, man's ethical aspirations. In the Grand

<u>Inquisitor</u>, containing Dostoevsky's most profound
revelations about man, he shows that freedom is a
burden too heavy to bear. The mystery of freedom,
argues Dostoevsky, is that man readily surrenders
it for bread. Man can live without freedom, but not
without bread. And those who supply the bread also
enforce social harmony, which means the suppression
of human freedom. Not surprisingly, Dostoevsky regarded Europe, with its freedom and what he called
the "comedy of bourgeois unity," as a "precious
cemetery." In Dostoevsky we can recognize, <u>de pro-
fundis</u>, the political destiny of Soviet-Russia.

Obedient subjects, ready to sacrifice abstract
freedom for a loaf of bread, not civic individuals,
is the conviction and expectation of Russian political
thought.

Unlike the American Revolution, the Russian Revolution was neither preceded nor did it coincide with
the development of Marxist legal philosophy. We
alluded to the legal aspects of the American Revolution. Lenin's primary concern, however, was the sei-
zure of state power. In his classical work, <u>State and
Revolution</u> (1917), and in his lectures delivered at
Sverdlov University (1919), Lenin strikes a Machiavellian tone in grappling with the problem of state and
the use of force. Associating the state with violence
and law with class oppression, Lenin calls upon the
proletariat to destroy and throw on the "scrap heap"
all this state rubbish.[7]

Lenin's nihilistic approach to the law is by no
means unique among Marxists. Lukacs, recognized as
the leading Marxist philosopher of this century, also
denied the autonomy of law. He defined law as the
legal mediation of the "dialectics of force." Like
legal positivists, Lukacs saw in law the ultimate
unifying force reconciling contradictory elements.
Associating law with a unifying force, Lukacs revealed
his debt to Hans Kelsen, father of legal positivism.
In fact, Gustav Radbruch,[8] noted exponent of legal
positivism, dedicated his book, <u>Grundzuge der Recht-
sphilosophie</u>, to Lukacs. In his work, Radbruch sees
the state both as the source of law and the ultimate
moral authority.

Though Lenin associated the state with the ultimate
force behind the law, he had nothing but contempt
for the whole legal profession, the "intellectual

cesspool."[9]   He stated bluntly that the dictatorship signifies "unlimited power which rests upon
force and not upon law."[10]   In the light of Marxism's
scathing attack on Western legalism as parasitic
upon society, Joseph Cropsey's statement that,[11]
"The war of Marxism against the ruling principles
of Western constitutionalism must never be mistaken
for a mere skirmish," is penetrating and matchless.

6. The Soviet Political Mind

It is a commonplace truth that there are substantive differences between imperial and Soviet Russia. Nonetheless, in terms of political values, we stressed the theme of continuity, rather than discordance between Russian and Soviet values. The continuity in Russia intrudes on visitors in small yet deeply symbolic gestures. The base of the Bronze Horseman, the equestrian statue of Peter the Great in Leningrad, is always covered with flowers left by common people. Peter built his city on human bones and blood, as the Russians are fond of saying. Yet in Leningrad, the Bronze Horseman's base is garlanded with fresh flowers. And stories are told of men, tortured during the Stalin purges, etching pro-Stalin slogans on the walls of their own cells with their own blood. As the poet Yevgeny Yevtushenko said, "To be Russian is to suffer."

Fresh flowers gracing the Bronze Horseman-- the great symbol of human sacrifice for Russia's greatness as a state--is a vivid reminder that Soviet-Russia remained a state-centered society. Russian political thought expresses it with its ingrained aversion to legal procedure and individual rights. Russian political culture, in its turn, insists on the unity of man and society.

The Slavophiles and the Westerners have differed on many doctrinal points, but were united in their dislike of Cartesian duality of mind and reality. To Russian thinkers, this duality was false and unfortunate. Be it the Cartesian cogito, Jefferson's self-evident truths, or the Kantian thing-in-itself, they all introduce an element of uncertainty into the human order that is difficult to calculate. As a result, the Russians stress more the psycho-ethical relatedness of the individual and collectivity than Western culture in any period.

Russia's two leading thinkers, Vladimir Solovyov and Alexander Herzen, endorsed emphatically the organic unity of individual and society. To Solovyov, "The relation between the individual members of society must be brotherly."[1] And Herzen's passionate search for an ideal solution to Russia's "cursed" despotism culminates in laying the foundation of Russian socialism. In this respect, Herzen invites comparison with

Mill, who, in the last part of his famed On Liberty, embraced collectivism. Yet the contrast of Mill and Herzen is subtle and revealing. Mill saw Socratic individualism as the instrument of collectivism. Herzen, on the other hand, combining Slavophil sentiment and socialist aspirations, saw the Russian muzhik as the harbinger of socialism. To Herzen, the West was reaching the dead end while the Slavic East held out the hope for the coming of the good society. Convinced that the middle class was degenerate, Herzen idealizes the Russian muzhik as a potential shortcut to socialism. Turgenev, who prophesied that socialist Russia will be just as "broad bottomed slut" as old Russia, warned Herzen against expecting salvation from the Russian masses who "loath all civic responsibility."[2]

Though Herzen gave his allegiance to civilization, justice, and the French Revolution, he saw in the immemorial obshchina, involving collective land tenure and communal self-government, the special dowry of the Cinderella among the nations, Russia. Herzen's Slavophilism is also evident in his negative attitude toward the West and "the Disunited States", where the Civil War was playing ducks and drakes with his United States bonds. Herzen's anti-liberalism owes much to German idealism. The structural ribbings of nineteenth century Russian intellectual life were constructed by ideas borrowed from Schiller, Fichte, and Hegel. Significantly, none were sympathetic to natural rights. Herzen's writings also show unmistakable traces of Max Stirner.[3] In his book, The Ego and his Own, Stirner unleashed one of the most savage attacks ever written on parliamentary democracy. Herzen's credo, "The truly free man creates his own morality,"[4] was inspired by no other than Stirner.

Next to Stirner, Schiller also influenced Herzen's political views. Though humanistic-liberal in tone, Schiller's works contain a call for a reconciliation with political authority. In his famous plays, Don Carlos, The Robbers, or Maid of Orleans the declaration for the rights and dignity of man are balanced by pleas for enlightened despotism. In common with German idealism, Schiller's political liberalism is more susceptible to the "pure" form of liberty than to the democratic ideals of liberty.

Not surprisingly, Herzen's brilliant and sparkling epigrams on man's transpolitical values, residing in the obshchina, were incompatible with individual rights. Reading Herzen's works one can detect a shift of emphasis in values. As a general rule of thumb, the further East one travels the more abstract and metaphysical ideas become. In England, Burke insisted on the historical rights of Englishmen; Rousseau advocated the universal rights of man. Across the Rhine, Schiller and Marx sought freedom in the "pure" realm of ideas or in men's "species being." The "whole man" and his essence, not liberty under the law, are the concern of Schiller and Marx. As Bertold Brecht observed, "With us, even materialism is abstract."[5]

By the 1820s German idealism had overwhelmed the Russian intelligentsia. The notorious "German empire of the air," where men walk on their heads, produced even more grotesque results in Russia. Though intent on belonging intellectually to the genus Europaeum, Russia, in reality, travels a non-European road to politics. One example will suffice. In Tocqueville's Democracy in America, Herzen ignored the penetrating analysis of democratic values. He was more taken by Tocqueville's reference to the future of Russia. As Herzen put it,[6]

"The work of Tocqueville filled me with sorrow and sadness. . . two countries bear in themselves the future: America and Russia. But where in America is the principle of future development? A cold, calculating country. But the future of Russia is unbounded--oh, I believe in her progressiveness."

Herzen not only endorsed socialist Russia but saw it as the long-overdue realization of the Enlightenment ideals. This theme re-appears in Boris Pasternak. "Thus Greece gave way to Rome," he wrote, "and the Russian Enlightenment has become the Russian Revolution."[7] It is not without paradox that some of Herzen's ideas, ostensibly liberal and humanistic, foreshadow Soviet thinking. By arraigning bourgeois Europe before the Russian "spirit", Herzen inadvertently anticipates Lenin's bitter strictures of bourgeois civilization. Ironically, Marx dismissed Herzen's notion that "young Russia" will be the rejuvenator of "dying" Europe as

both preposterous and outright silly. Marx's dislike
of Herzen[8] was so intense that he categorically
refused invitations to socialist gatherings, attended
by Herzen. Marx wrote to Engels,[9]

> "I at no time and no place want to be associated
> with Herzen since I do not adhere to the opinion
> that 'old Europe' can be renovated by Russian
> blood."

Marx had neither patience nor use for Herzen's
infatuation with the Russian muzhik, the Russian
narodnichestvo, let alone the redeeming virtues of
the un-educated Russian masses. By contrast, Herzen
persisted with the notion that,[10]

> "Europe is sinking because it cannot rid itself
> of its cargo--that infinity of treasures accumu-
> lated in distant and perilous expeditions. In
> our case, all this is artificial ballast;
> out with it and overboard, and then full sail
> into open sea!"

Against bourgeois individualism, Herzen juxtaposed
the Russian conception of collectivism, or sobornost, that
differs substantially from collectivism as understood
in Western political theory. To Herzen sobornost
denoted an emotional rallying point for the Russian
intelligentsia, rather than an alternative social form.
The intelligentsia's approach to reality was neurotic-
emotional, rather than cognitive and practical. Herzen
himself drew up a devastating indictment of the
Russian intelligentsia,[11]

> "We are great doctrinairies and raisonneurs.
> To this German capacity we add our national
> . . . element, ruthless, fanatically dry:
> we are only too willing to cut off heads.
> . . . With fearless step we march to the very
> limit, and go beyond it."

Herzen's own apocalyptic expectation is a classical
instance of Russian intellect marching to the
"very limit" of reason and reality.

This is not to deny the extraordinary role
dissident intellectuals play in Russia's political
destiny. Though always small in number and invariably
isolated from the silent, sullen masses, Russia's
intellectual revoltés constitute a bright chapter in

Russian history. Dissidents are knots of brave
individuals arrayed against the vast rope of a
despotic state. The harder they pull against the
state the tighter the governmental rope becomes.
Conversely, the larger and more conspicuous the knot
of dissidents, the tighter the state loops its rope
around society.

Pasternak said with a first-hand knowledge that
the Russian Revolution was made by the sons and heirs
of the intelligentsia who created the Russian Enlightenment. This is true of the cultural and aesthetic
elite that supported at least the initial phase of
1917. But the political design of 1917, as Lenin
came to recognize it before his death, amounted to
no more than a metamorphosis of autocratic despotism
into a bureaucratic despotism. Already in 1904
Rosa Luxemburg forewarned of the bureaucratic
despotism that awaits Lenin's Russia, and saw
autocracy transfigured in Lenin's political vision.
As Luxemburg expressed it,[12]

> "It is amusing to note the strange somersaults
> that the respectable human 'ego' has had to
> perform in recent Russian history. Knocked
> to the ground, almost reduced to dust, by
> Russian absolutism, the 'ego' takes revenge by
> turning to revolutionary activity. In the shape
> of a committee of conspirators, in the name
> of a nonexistent Will of the People, it seats
> itself on a kind of throne and proclaims it
> is all-powerful."

The revitalized "ego" of autocracy is the
Communist Party-Machiavelli's Prince with an apparatus.
No sooner did Lenin seize power than the Russian
past, like the ghost of Hamlet's murdered father,
begins to haunt and close in on new Russia. In
his classical work, The Spirit of Russia, Masaryk
has pointed out that "red Tsarism" is historically
and sociologically a more natural successor to
tsarist absolutism in an illiterate, backward society
than the democratic republic that was set up, however
briefly, in March 1917. After nearly seven decades
of revolutionary transformation of society, Russian
political thought would still rather have subjects
void of freedom and rights than a state void for its
totalitarian purpose and pre-eminent right. There
is a haunting resonance to Nietzsche's observation
that Russia is the "only power with endurance."[13]

160

In many respects, Russia is the most revolutionary among modern societies. "The Russians are extremely revolutionary," said Masaryk, "but not very democratic."[14] The Pantheons of revolution are populated with Russians. Try to get away from Russian ideas and names in the history of the revolutionary movements of the last century and you will understand that it cannot be done, for to do so is to deform the over-all picture. But try to find one Russian revolutionary who has Paine's qualities, namely, the goal of revolution is democracy, not tyranny. Revolutionary messianism, extremism, and intracranial Russian past have conferred a stubborn halo on Soviet Russia.

Russia's tragic irony, the continuity of state absolutism despite revolutionary discontinuity (1917), is personified in the dissident movement. Soviet dissidents are just as removed from Communist reality as the intelligentsia was from tsarist reality. In large measure, this is due to the peculiar relationship that developed between the Russian state and the intelligentsia. Very briefly, beginning with the Europeanization of Russia, an isolated civilization up to the eighteenth century, the intelligentsia postulated the ideals of freedom, equality, justice, and human dignity. Though the Russian state was judged deprived of human and philosophical ideals, it was the sacred symbol of national unity for lifting the Mongol and Tartar yoke.

The intelligentsia's commitment to ideals, however, was so strong that it refused reconciliation with reality that profaned its ideals. In collision with reality, the Russian intelligentsia created its own ideal world, noted more for its philosophical idealism than common-sense. In due course, the word intelligentsia connoted an opposition to the state. The more oppressive the autocracy, the more pronounced the conflict between the educated mind and reality. As reality and truth part, the intelligentsia creates its crystal palaces of ideals.

But much as they opposed the state, the intelligentsia, especially under the magic spell of Hegel, could not disassociate autocracy from personal rule. Hegelianism, in essence, provided rational interpretation of the inchoate Russian reality. From European standpoint, Russian absolutism was a throwback to barbarism. But the Hegelian dictum that what is real

is rational and what is rational is real, was eagerly
seized by the intelligentsia who were passionately
concerned with "reality." Thus, the despised
"reality," state absolutism, was now to be understood
rationally. As a result, the tsar, seen as Hegel's
world-historical individual, embodied rationality.
Consequently, submission to autocratic rule was not
submission, but liberation. Hegel served the Russian
reality by tranforming the symbol of arbitrary
power, the tsar, into the personification of higher
reason.[15]

The intelligentsia, caught between a despotic
state and the imperative to define Russian "reality,"
has been shaped by the very forces it opposed.
Hatred for the existing reality on the one hand,
and Hegelian necessity to rationalize state absolutism
on the other, lends a tragic dimension to the intelligentsia. For one thing, hatred of state absolutism
has weakened the intelligentsia's sense of justice
and quest for good society. Heroic sacrifice,
asceticism, martyrdom, not prosaic struggle to widen
the social base of their ideals became the ideal
type of behavior among the intelligentsia. The
historical-cultural abyss, frequently referred to
in Russian literature, that separates the intelligentsia from society is a political tragedy of major
proportion.

We can find no better illustration of this
than Dostoevsky's image in The Possessed. He
describes a dream of one of his characters, Maria
Lebyatkin. In the dream, the setting sun cuts across
a lake and splits an island in half. Suddenly there
is darkness; and she has a baby whose gender is
unknown, and even its existence uncertain. The
only thing Maria believes is the death of her baby.
The father-sun does not inseminate mother-earth,
but splits it in half. The result is darkness without
light, night without day: incompletion. The sun is
not reconciled with the earth. Hence its offsprings
are the symbol of rebellion and death, not resurrection
and life. The offsprings of earth, and herein lies
Dostoevsky's relevant message, strive for self-
destructive justice The tragedy of Russian intelligentsia is that it evolved with the state, the symbol
of national unity and force. Just as the Russian
state resorts to despotism to attain social harmony,
the intelligentsia seizes absolute values to build
its crystal palaces. Consequently, neither the

state nor its adversary, the intelligentsia, developed
any interest in converting the power of force into
a power of law.

No one can remain impartial to the moral courage
of Russia's dissidents as, out of the vast spaces
of despotism, they continue to ring the bells of
conscience and humanity. Dissidents confirm our
democratic faith that even in Russia there are men
in tune and step with the constellation of moral
principles. We in the free world see the Russian
dissidents' wish, will, and woes as expressions
of the Socratic noumenal character, crowned with ivy,
ready to drink hemlock for truth and tending to the
soul. But Solzhenitsyn's idee fixe as those of other
lesser known dissidents should caution us against
projecting the dissidents as a democratic alternative to
Soviet rule.

Solzhenitsyn's art is woven of such moral strands
that to inquire into the political tradition that
spawned his genius may appear forced. A Russian
Prometheus hurling cosmic defiance at the Kremlin
is awe inspiring. Nonetheless, his own expectation
of the Soviet rulers is not without serious problems.
While still in Russia, Solzhenitsyn believed that
his own moral appeal to the rulers' conscience can
and will bring about changes in Russia. Reflecting
on his own frame of mind as he paced his prison cell,
Solzhenitsyn wrote,[16]

> "I was mentally in conversation with the
> Politburo. Something told me that given two
> or three hours, I could budge them, shake
> their certainty. There would have been no
> getting through to the fanatics in Lenin's
> Politburo, or the sheep in Stalin's. But these
> people I (foolishly?) thought could be reached.
> Why, even Khrushchev had shown some signs of
> understanding."

What a sobering confession on the poverty of common-
sense politics

Admiration for the dissidents' courage ought not
to blind us to their reductionist view that society
is hapless victim of an oppressive Soviet regime.
There is more affinity between Soviet power and the
Russian mind than Solzhenitsyn, among others, lead
us to believe. For one thing, the most fundamental

and inalienable power of the Russian state is its
tutelary power. This teaching power of the state
ensures the continuity of Russian political tradition.
Though oppressive and tyrannical, the Russian state
is not without strong national foundation. Let's
not forget those fresh flowers on the base of the
Bronze Horseman. And it is to this Russian state
that Soviet dissidents appeal in pressing for change
and reforms.

Soviet dissidents, with the possible exception
of Sakharov, fail to realize that respect of human
rights presupposes the legal value of the individual
that is non-existent in Russian political thought.
Hence the pathos of distance between the Russian
"spirit" and Western "legalism" upon which Russian
moralists, from Tolstoy to Solzhenitsyn, insists
upon. From the viewpoint of Western political theory,
which predicates political society on the civic-
legal relationship between individual and the government, Soviet society is lawless.

Nor can one overlook the intelligentsia's share
of responsibility for the lawlessness of Russian
society. Rosa Luxemburg understood well that Russian
despotism will condition the vision of those seeking
a "new" Russia. The intelligentsia itself viewed
the concept of government by law as something wholly
un-Russian and antithetical to its "spirit."
Tolstoy himself rejected the concept of individual
liberty, of civil rights guaranteed by an impersonal
system of justice. And Tolstoy is by no means atypical
in preferring the Russian "spirit" to the Western
notions of law and reason.

In a profound essay, "The Russian People and
Socialism" (1855), Herzen answers the criticism of
Jules Michelet (1798-1874) that Russia lacks all
vestiges of freedom, individualism, and legalism.

> "We see clearly that the distinction between
> your laws and our ukazy lies principally in
> the formula with which they begin. Ukazy
> began with the crushing truth: 'The Tsar com-
> mands'; your laws are headed with the insulting
> lie of the threefold republican motto and the
> ironical invocation of the name of the French
> people. The code of Nicholas is directed exclu-
> sively against men and in favor of authority.
> The Code of Napoleon does not seem to us to

have any other quality. We are dragging about
too many chains that violence has fastened
on us to increase the weight of them with
others of our choice. In this respect we stand
precisely on a level with our peasants. We
submit to brute force. We are slaves because
we have no means of freeing ourselves; from the
enemy camp, none the less, we accept nothing."[17]

Herzen forewarned that "Russia will never be
Protestant. Russia will never be juste-milieu."[18]
He stigmatized Russia for sacrificing innocent people,
without qualm or scruple, on the altars of abstractions
like "progress," or "social equality." Herzen's
undaunted eyes discovered two icy climates in Russia:
Siberia and the freezing of free thought. As for the
much acclaimed "popular sovereignty," he said in Russia
the "people" smell of burned bodies, torture, and
blood. Russian history demonstrated that the
"triumph of order"[19] is the universal lot of man.

Herzen was critical of republicanism and monarchy.
He saw the principle of salus populi as much a crime
as lese majesté. As for socialism, though he endorsed
its ideals as we saw, he was less than sanguine
about its curative power in Russia

"Socialism will develop in all its phases until
it reaches its own extremes and absurdities. Then,
there will again burst forth from the titanic
breast of the revolutionary minority a cry
of denial. Once more a mortal battle will be
joined in which socialism will occupy the place
of today's conservatism, and will be defeated
by the coming revolution as yet invisible
to us. . . ."[20]

Socialism occupying the place of conservatism
in Russia! Herzen's prophecy became the grim reality
in Soviet Russia. The fate of Soviet dissidents is
well known. Comparing the tsarist treatment of its
dissidents with the Western one, Herzen wrote,[21]

"However low government sank, Spinoza was not
sentenced to transportation, nor Lessing to be
flogged or conscripted."

The continuity in Russian political tradition is
also evident in the state's elemental pattern of

ruthlessness toward dissidents. It is not without
relevance to note here that President Truman, in a
newly discovered handwritten journal he kept, made
this entry (26 July 1945): "The Communist Party in
Moscow is no different in its methods than were the
Czar and the Russian nobleman (so-called: they were
anything but noble)."[22]

Not without reason, Solzhenitsyn quoted St.
Augustine to the Soviet rulers, "What is the state
without justice. A band of robbers."[23] In his tragically
brilliant satire, The Yawning Heights, Alexander
Zinoviev sketches unforgettable vignettes of the
"lawless" Soviet civilization. Zinoviev has been
compared to Swift and Rabelais. When these two
geniuses dissolved in satire the pretenses of Irish
and French politics, their works became a national
treasure. But Zinoviev, whose book is one of the
most important studies of Soviet society in the last
half a century, was expelled from the Communist Party.
And when allowed to leave the Soviet Union to teach
in Munich, Brezhnev signed a decree revoking his
Soviet citizenship for "behavior damaging to Soviet
prestige."

Zinoviev's devastating satire on Soviet society
verifies Aristotle's dicta that the same action can
be represented as tragic or comic. Behind the hilarious
puns, searing ironies, and dazzling oxymora of
famous Soviet figures, e.g., the Boss (Stalin),
Hog (Khrushchev) and Truth-teller (Solzhenitsyn),
Zinoviev captures the terse tragedy of Soviet society.
In Russia concepts like "justice" and "government
by law" are meaningless, linguistic platitudes,
and remain as such as long as the Party and state
interests override all considerations of morality
and legality. As Zinoviev reminds us, a society
which officially boasts that the state's interest
transcends individual rights is a lawless civilization

Marxism-Leninism, indeed, boasts that its
"rights" are superior to bourgeois rights. The
superiority of Soviet "rights" was demonstrated
when the state-owned Soviet television refused to
televise the traditional July 4 (1977) speech by
U.S. Ambassador Malcolm Toon. Each year since 1974,
the American Ambassador has presented an Independence
Day speech to Soviet television audience. Toon's
prepared text, however, contained this passage:

"The United States of America itself was founded
on the principle that each human being is
endowed with fundamental and inalienable rights
which cannot be arbitrarily infringed or
removed by governmental authorities. But we
recognize, more than those who watch us afar,
that we are not perfect. We recognize as well
that a man cannot live up to his ideals,
however, if he ignores them. Americans will
continue to state publicly their belief in human
rights and their hope that violations of these
rights wherever they may occur will end."[24]

As if fate would have it, three months later,
October 1977, Brezhnev addressed the opening session
of the Supreme Soviet, the nation's rubber-stamp,
legislative body. Chastizing the detractors of
the Soviet Union's human rights policies, he staunchly
defended the individual rights clauses in the new draft
constitution. Soviet rights, argued Brezhnev, are
different from the capitalist rights to "unemployment,
racial discrimination, lawlessness and overpriced
medical care." Scorning Western legal experts'
opinion that the proposed "rights" in the Soviet
constitution were offset by "obligations" and
"duties," Brezhnev declared,[25]

"It seems that from the standpoint of our class
adversaries Soviet citizens should evidently
be granted only the 'right' to fight against
the Soviet state, the socialist system, so as
to gladden the hearts of the imperialists.
We must disappoint such critics of our constitution. Their wish will never be satisfied by
the Soviet people."

Brezhnev's constitutional theory merits two
observations, one borrowed from Max Weber and the
other from Voltaire. Weber underscored the pre-
eminence of the politically guaranteed legal order
and legal norms in the West.[26] Legal norms, as evident
from Brezhnev's statement, have no recognized standing
in Russian political culture. Brezhnev's view that
citizenship precludes rights against the Soviet
state recalls Voltaire's futile attempt to impress
upon his Russian admirers the dignity of man.
Voltaire's axiom, "Remember your dignity as a man,"[27]
testifies to the normative value of individual reason
and conscience in the political order.

To Russia's rulers individual conscience is
analogous to what Hobbes called the "worms within
the entrails of the body commonwealth."[28] The
primacy of the state in Russia was acknowledged by
Vissarion Belinsky (1811-1848), the father of the
Russian radical intelligentsia. In Russia, he wrote,
"the government has always marched ahead of the people,
had always been the people's guiding star toward its
high destiny."[29] Insisting on the individual's
organic unity with the state as his higher "destiny,"
Russian political theory summons the individual to
the morality of duty, rather than informing him of his
rights. The Anglo-American approach to politics is
rights-standard oriented, the Russian approach to
politics is duties-standard oriented.

The rights-standard allow the individual to
do certain things and expressly forbid others,
including the government and its elected representatives,
to hinder it. By contrast, the duties-standard
forbid the individual to abstain from performing
functions that are designed to benefit the state.
In the Soviet Union the duties-standard is normative
and, in essence, subsume and cancel out the rights-
standard.

The deputy director of the Government and Law
at the USSR Academy of Sciences, A. Tikhomirov
provided a classical statement on this. Analysing
the new Soviet Constitution, Tikhomirov said it
"reflects the expansion of the Soviet state's sphere
of activity."[30] By sanctioning the state's expanding
activity, the Soviet Constitution contains, in
Tikhomirov's words, a "distinctive class of normative
demands."[31]

The 1977 Soviet Constitution demonstrates
that the duties-standard (Articles 1-9) lay down ground-
rules the citizen must comply with to be entitled
to certain rights. The morality of duty conditions
the Soviet citizen's "natural rights." The late
Russian dissident historian, Andre Amalrik, reminded
his Western readers that the vast majority of Soviet
people not only associate freedom with "disorder,"
but human rights arouse "bewilderment" in popular
thinking.[32]

Needless to say, the Soviet Constitution contains
its own impressive Bill of Rights. Cynics would observe

that they are included because nobody takes rights
seriously in the Soviet Union and thus there is no
harm in "liberalizing" the Constitution. It would
be more accurate to argue that the Soviet Bill of
Rights are confined to the functioning of power and
the relationship between citizens.

To illustrate the distinction between Western
and Russian approach to "rights," consider the following. Marxism assigns a higher priority to social
purpose than to individual rights. Social purpose
is invariably defined in collective, not individual
terms. One social purpose or social ideal is
Communism's avowed determination to improve the
lot of workers and raise the standard of living.
Theoretically, the Soviet people have the right to
decide what their social purpose is. In reality,
the "vanguard" Party defines and implements the
social purpose. In so many words, the social
purpose in the Soviet Union coincides and is identical
with the oligarchic interests of an elite-based
Party.

Lenin's Party takes inordinate pride in the
ascribed "unity" of the Soviet people. But as
Nadezhda Mandelstam observed, whose works provide
a Dantesque guide to Soviet society, the people
can only be united by something that has meaning for
them, not by "a goal that somebody sets for them."[33]

Consider another social purpose in Soviet
society: the moral and social obligation to work.
As early as May 1917, Lenin defined his slogan,
"He that does not work neither shall he eat," as
the "primary rule of Communism."[34] Consequently,
the "Declaration of the Rights of the Toiling and
Exploited People" (1918), issued by the Soviet
state, asserted the general obligation to work.

This was repeated in the first Soviet Constitution
(1936) and retained in the Brezhnev Constitution (1977).
In the latter, article 40 states, "Citizens of the
USSR have the right to work." The "right" to work,
on first impression, appears to enlarge the concept
of human rights. In practice, it involves a "direction" of labor. Most significant from our perspective,
virtually every article in the 1977 Constitution refers
to the need and concern of the Soviet "state."
The right to work, not surprisingly, precludes
the "right" to strike. By Soviet logic, the workers
cannot strike against their own interest as owners of

169

national assets. The intra-bloc implications of
this logic were dramatically demonstrated by the
Polish trade union movement, Solidarity.

In the summer of 1980, the Polish workers, led
by Lech Walesa, organized a free trade union,
Solidarity, numbering some 10 million members.
Solidarity had no ties with the party and for some
17 months it searched for change without violence
to reform a bankrupt Communist regime. Then in
December, 1981, Moscow struck and extinguished
Solidarity and Poland's hope for freedom. The Polish
army, headed by General Jaruzelski, declared martial
law in Poland and arrested all the leaders of
Solidarity. The silence of bayonets fell on Poland
as it was sealed off from the outside world. As
many as 50,000 Poles were interned and some 36 million
people were held virtually incommunicado by its own
army. The Moscow instigated Pantzerkommunismus
imposed on Poland gave dramatic demonstration to the
world of the limits of trade union movement within
Communism.

Polish workers were forced to return to work
at gunpoint, and factories were patroled by armored
cars. The right to work, then, includes work at
gunpoint and the threat of prison, even death.
The most serious implication of the right to work,
however, is in the area of human rights. In a full
employment economy, guaranteed by the Soviet Constitution (Art. 14), social rights against the state,
guaranteeing jobs, housing, education, and culture
to its citizens, is a logical fallacy. As should be
obvious by now, social goals come before individual
rights. The preamble to the Soviet Constitution
declares, the "law of life is the concern of all for
the good of each and concern of each for the good
of all."

The imperative to make the "law of life" the
concern of all means that the postponement of
human rights becomes the moral duty of Soviet
citizens. The Communist Party itself determines not
only what the "law of life" is, but when and how it
becomes the concern of all. In addition, Soviet
Marxism insists on a trade-off between basic
liberties and economic goods. Liberal philosophy,
on the other hand, is reticent to justify a trade-off
between rights and bread. Once we grant the general
validity of Tolstoy's utilitarian assertion that a

pair of boots is preferable to Shakespeare's sonnets, the road opens to the kind of political madness which can inspire a Gulag Archipelago.

Summing up, it is useful to juxtapose the American and Soviet constitutional thinking. The American Constitution lacks provisions for the suspension of law, or a government by decree even in emergency. Nor does it make individual rights contingent on the performance of explicit duties. In America only the privilege of the writ, habeas corpus, can be suspended (Art. I, Sect 9) and only by Congress. It was suspended during the Civil War, and individual rights were curtailed during the relocation of Japanese-Americans in World War II. Despite these lapses in American legalism, the independence of legal principles and norms is intact and enforced.

But in Russia even those responsible for millions of innocent victims, whose unmarked mass-graves cover the vast Gulag Archipelago, cannot be brought to justice. Very simply, Stalin's henchmen cannot be judged because an independent legal principle, by which the guilty can be judged, is non-existent in Soviet Communism. What an awesome abyss opens for society when the law is cònsigned by the Revolutionary Fathers of that society to a transitory "superstructure."

In Soviet society law is the ratio scripta of arbitrary power, better known as the Communist Party. The Brezhnev Constitution, legitimizing six decades fo Soviet rule, can be summed up as a Soviet styled Rechtasstaat. In short, it is a handy legal framework for the Party to control and guide society without, in any sense, limiting the scope of political power. The Brezhnev Constitution is then a sort of "magic wall," which, with its impressive democratic facade and appealing rights, conceals the personal rule and lawlessness in Russia.

In the Soviet Constitution and the political system, the center of gravity is the state. It can strip at will dissidents of their citizenship when their acts or words damage the spurious "Soviet prestige." The famed cellist, Mstislav Rostropovich was deprived of his citizenship by a Supreme Soviet decree. Even the French Communist Party, by and large sympathetic to Moscow, felt "saddened and stupified" by the decree.

171

The conflict of power and intellect is as old as Plato's Republic. Political power prefers and demands disciplined minds and ideas. Artistic genius, industrious and remote, estranged or modest, is a winged animal that soars on the thermal winds of freedom and seldom alights on stern political power. Much as he flouted mores, the state, and the gods, Goethe was neither exiled nor stripped of his citizenship. But Soviet artists, who contribute to the Kantian end of man--culture--can be denied the right to live and die in their native land. Deprived of his citizenship, Rostropovich wrote the epitaph on lawless Soviet Communism.

> "Can we be found guilty on account of our artistic activity abroad? For this--by the stroke of a dictator's pen--can we be deprived of our homeland without even the legal right to justify ourselves? We know that here abroad a dog thrown out on the street will be protected by a Society for the Prevention of Cruelty to Animals, which is often able to call its former owner to account. It is possible that in our world there is no society capable of defending those who are cursed and cast out?"[35]

PART THREE

1. Introduction

1. Everett, America (Philadelphia, H.C. Carey & Lea, 1827), p. 300.

2. Kennan, "Nuclear War," The New York Review 28 (21 January 1982):8.

3. For a contrasting view on U.S.-Soviet relations, see Commentary 70, no. 4 (October 1980), pp. 21-22.

4. Kant, Eternal Peace, Reiss ed., p. 438.

2. Russian State Tradition

1. Tocqueville, Democracy in America, 1:521-22

2. Mason, Free Government, p. 81.

3. Time, 12 November 1979, p. 97.

4. Hegel, The Philosophy of History, trs. J. Sibree (New York: Dover Publications, 1956), p. 85.

5. S. V. Utechin, Russian Political Thought (New York: Praeger, 1963), p. 53.

6. Pope, Essay on Man, Epistle III.

7. G. R. Derzhavin, Uzbranniia sochineniia [Selected works] ed. A. A. Kasparin (St. Petersburg: Rodina, 1843), p. 91.

8. Dante, Convivio, IV, IX, X: "Cavalcatore de la umana voluntade" refers to the Emperor as the source of law.

9. Augustine, The City of God, ed. Vernon J. Bourke (New York: doubleday, 1958), pp. 88-89.

10. Jacques Truchet, Politique de Bossuet (Paris: Armond Colin, 1966), p. 150.

11. Robert Filmer, Patriarcha, ed. Peter Laslett (Oxford: B. Blackwell, 1949), p. 62, 104.

173

12. T. S. Eliot, Murder in the Cathedral, in Complete
    Poems and Plays (New York: Harcourt, Brace &
    World, 1971), p. 212.

13. Ibid., p. 208.

14. Dostoevsky to Maikov, 20 March-2 April 1868,
    in A. G. Dostoevsky, Dostoevsky: Letters and
    Reminiscences, trs. S. S. Koteliansky et. al.,
    (New York: Knopf, 1923), pp. 63-64.

15. T. S. Eliot, Murder in the Cathedral, p. 212.

16. Quentin Skinner, The Foundation of Modern Politi-
    cal Thought, 2 vols. (Cambridge: Cambridge Uni-
    versity Press, 1978), 2:128.

17. Leonard Schapiro, Rationalism and Nationalism
    in Russian Nineteenth Century Political Thought
    (New Haven: Yale University Press, 1967), p.8.

18. N. I. Popov, V. N. Tatishchev i ego vremenia
    [Tatishchev and his time] (Moscow, 1861), p. 118.

19. Tatishchev, Istoriia rossiskaia [Russian history]
    7 vols. (Moscow: Izdatel'stvo Akademii Nauk
    SSSR, 1962-68), 1:541-45.

20. Madame de Stael, Ten Years of Exile, trs. Doris
    Beik (New YOrk: Saturday Review Press, 1972),
    p. 203.

3. Alexander and Jefferson

1. Jefferson, The Works of Thomas Jefferson, ed.
   P. L. Ford (New York: Putnam's Sons, 1905),
   9:404-05; to Joseph Priestley, 29 Nov. 1802.

2. Alexander to Jefferson, 3 November 1804, in
   Novaia i noveishaia istorii [New and contemporary
   history] (Moscow, 1959, no. 2), pp. 154-55.

3. Jefferson, Writings, 19:227.

4. See, M. Szeftel, "La monarchie absolue dans
   l'etat moscovie et l'empire russe," Recueils de
   la Societe Jean Bodin 22(1969): 727-41; also
   M. Szeftel, "The Form of Government of the
   Russian Empire Prior to the Constitutional Reform

4. cont.
   of 1905-16," in J. S. Curtiss, ed., Essays in
   Russian and Soviet History in Honor of G. T.
   Robinson (Leiden, 1963), p. 105.

5. Marc Raeff, Origins of the Russian Intelligentsia
   (New York: Harcourt, Brace & Jovanovich 1966),
   ch. 3.

6. Schapiro, Rationalism, p. 13.

7. M. M. Speransky, Proekti i Zapiski [Projects and
   notes], ed. A. I. Kopanev et. al., (Moscow:
   Akademia Nauk SSSR, 1961), p. 147.

8. Schapiro, Rationalism, p. 17.

9. Ibid., p. 20.

10. Ibid., p. 23.

11. Shakespeare, Macbeth, Act I, Scene 4, II, 12-13.

12. Karamzin, Karamzin's Memoir on Ancient and Modern
    Russia, trs. & ed. Richard Pipes (New York:
    Atheneum, 1969), p. 139.

13. Ibid., p. 183.

14. Ibid., p. 185.

15. Ibid., p. 198.

16. Homer, Iliad, ii. 204-05.

4. Enlightenment in Russia

1. Alfred Cobban, In Search of Humanity (London:
   Jonathan Cape, 1960), p. 7, pp. 241-45.

2. See Henry Steele Commager, The Empire of Reason
   (New York: Doubleday, 1978).

3. Hans Rogger, National Consciousness in Eighteenth
   Century Russia (Cambridge: Harvard University
   Press, 1960), see also, J.G. Garrard, The
   Eighteenth Century in Russia (Oxford: Clarendon
   Press, 1973), pp. 53ff.

4. Interestingly, the "first" theoretical jurist
    of Russia, Desnitsky, rejected natural law as
    abstract; cf. Andrzej Walicki, A History of
    Russian Thought (Stanford University Press,
    1979), p. 12.

5. Hume, Treatise of Human Nature, III,ii.

6. Peter Chaadayev, The Major Works of Peter
    Chaadayev, trs. R. McNally (Notre Dame:
    University of Notre Dame, 1969), pp. 37-38.

7. Schapiro, Rationalism, p. 38.

8. James H. Billington, The Icon and the Axe,
    (New York: Vintage Books, 1970), p. 62.

9. D. I. Fonvizin, Pervoe polnoe sobranie sochinenii
    D. I. Fonvizina [First complete works of Fonvizin]
    (St. Petersburg-Moscow, 1888), p. 895; for an
    informative study of Fonvizin, see Moser Charles,
    Denis Fonvizin (Boston: Twayne Publication, 1979).

10. Fonvizin, Op. Cit., p. 896.

11. Tocqueville, Democracy in America, 2:410.

12. M. A. Bakunin, Sobranie sochinenii i pisem
    1828-1876 [Complete works and letters 1828-
    1876]ed. Yu. M. Steklova, 4 vols. (Moscow, 1934-
    35), 3:317-18.

13. Ibid., 4:153.

14. Ibid.

15. Chernyshevsky, Polnoe sobranie scohinenii
    [Complete works]ed. V. Ia. Kirpotina et al.,
    16 vols. (Moscow: Goslitizdat, 1939-51), 1:357.

16. Chernyshevsky, Prolog, ed. A.P. Skaftymov et.
    al., (Moscow, 1936), pp. 237-38.

17. Lev A. Tikhomirov, Russia, political and social,
    trs. Edward Eveling, 2 vols. (Westport, Conn.:
    Hyperion Press, 1969), 2:17.

18. Melvin Lasky, Utopia and Revolution (Chicago:
    University of Chicago Press, 1976), p. 115.

19. Emerson, The Journals of Ralph Waldo Emerson,
     ed. E. W. Emerson & W. S. Forbes (Boston:
     Houghton Mifflin, 1909-14), 3:235, 5:380;
     6:336, 7:115-16.

20. W. C. McWilliams, The Idea of Fraternity in
     America (Berkeley, Los Angeles: University of
     California Press, 1973), p. 295.

21. For the distinction between the "legal" and
     "sociological" aspects of the state, Kelsen is
     indebted to Kistyakovskii. cf. Hans Kelsen,
     Der soziologische und der juristische Staats-
     begriff, 2nd ed. (Tubingen, 1928), pp. 106-13.

22. Kant, The Essential Kant, ed. Arnulf Zweig
     (New York: Mentor Book, 1970), p. 334.

23. Alexander Herzen, My Past and Thoughts, trs.
     Constance Garnett, 4 vols. (New York: Knopf,
     1968), 4:1673.

24. Chernyshevsky, Polnoe sobranie sochineniia,
     1906 ed., 4:158.

25. I. V. Gassen, ed., Istoriia russkoi advokatury
     [History of Russian solicitor] (St. Petersburg,
     1914-15), 1:26.

26. Dewey, The Public and Its Problems, pp. 82-86.

27. Judith Shklar, Legalism (Cambridge: Harvard
     University Press, 1964), pp. 1-28.

28. Dimitrij Pisarev, Sochineniia, 4 vols. (Moscow:
     Gosudarstvennoe Izd. Hudozhestvennoi Literaturii,
     1955), 3:289.

29. George Plekhanov, Sochineniia, ed. D. Riazonov,
     24 vols. (Moscow: Gosudarstvennoe izdatel'stvo,
     1923-27), 21:37-40. Plekhanov defined the
     nobility as "state-slaves" and referred to the
     Russian concept of "equality without rights"
     (ravenstvo bezpravia), 21:39.

30. Chaadayev, Philosophical Letters, in V V. Zen-
     kovsky, A History of Russian Philosophy, 3 vols.
     (New York: Columbia University Press, 1953),
     1:114.

31. Gregory S. Skovoroda, Sochineniia v stikah i proze Skovorody [Poetic and prosaic works of Skovoroda] (St Petersburg, 1861), pp. 288-89.

32. G. A. Gukovski, Ocherki po istorii russkoi literatury i obshchestvennoi mysli XVIII veka [Sketches on Russian literacy and social thought in the 18th century] (Leningrad: Hudozhestvennaia, 1938), pp. 17-19; see also the same author's work, Russkaia literatura 18 veka [Russian literature in the 18th century] (Moscow: Narkomprosa RSFSR, 1939), partic. pp. 246-48 where Gukovski's quotes Catherine's boast to Voltaire that in Russia there is "freedom of thought."

33. Hobbes, Hobbes's English Works, ed. William Molesworth (London: Longman, Brown, 1845), 2:100, 160.

34. Montesquieu, The Spirit of Laws, ed. D. W. Carrithers (Berkeley, Los Angeles: University of California Press, 1977), pp. 202.

35. N. M. Druzhinin, ed., Absolutizma v Rossii XVII-XVIII vv [Absolutism in 17-18th century Russia] (Moscow, 1964), p. 391.

36. F. V. Taranovski, "Politicheskaia doktrina Nakaza" [Political theory of Nakaz], Sbornik statei po istorii prava posviashchennyi M.F. Vladimirskomu-Budanovu (Kiev, 1904), p. 47, pp. 44-86.

37. M. F. Reddaway, ed., Documents of Catherine the Great (New York: Russell & Russell, 1971), p. 256.

38. Montesquieu, Spirit of Laws, p. 104.

39. Taranovski, Op. Cit., p. 79.

40. Ibid., p. 84.

41. Montesquieu, Spirit of Laws, p. 114.

42. Ibid., p. 113.

43. Montesquieu, Mes Pensees, in Oeuvres Completes, ed. Roger Caillois, 2 vols. (Paris: Plaeiade, 1949), 1:XVIII, 3.

178

44.   Mark Hulliung, Montesquieu and the Old Regime
      (Berkeley, Los Angeles: University of Califor-
      nia Press, 1976), p. 219.

45.   Quoted by Theodor Taranovski, "The Aborted
      Counter-Reform: Murav'ev Commission and the
      Judicial Statues of 1864," Unpublished MS, p.51.

46.   Diderot, Memoirs pour Catherine II, ed. Paul
      Verniere (Paris: Garnier Freres, 1966),
      pp. 66-67.

47.   Diderot, Correspondence, eds. Georges Roth &
      Jean Varloot, 16 vols. (Paris: Editions de
      Minuit, 1955-70), 14:72-73.

                5. Bentham and Russia

1.   M.P.Mack, Jeremy Bentham (New York: Columbia
      University Press, 1973), p. 362.

2.   Bentham, The Works of Jeremy Bentham, ed. John
      Browning, 11 vols. (Edinburgh: William Tait,
      1843), 1:364.

3.   Bentham, The Correspondence of Jeremy Bentham,
      ed. Timothy L.S. Sprigge et. al., 3 vols.
      (London: Athlone Press, 1968-71), 3:596-610.

4.   Milton, Works of John Milton, 18 vols. (New
      York: Columbia University Press, 1931), 4:344.

5.   G. M. Malenkov, O zadachakh partiinykh organiza-
      tsii v oblasti promyshlennosti i transporta
      [The task of Party organization in industry
      and transportation] (Moscow, 1941), p. 39.

6.   Dostoevsky, Notes from Underground, trs. Con-
      stance Garnett (New York: Dell, 1974), p. 48.

7.   Lenin, State and Revolution (New York: Inter-
      national Publishers, 1977), p. 68.

8.   Gustav Radbruch, Grundzuge der Rechts philosophie
      (Leipzig: Quelle & Meyer, 1914), see Preface.

9.   Sovetskoe Gosudarstvo i Pravo, no. 7 (1940):120.

10. *Ibid.*, no. I (1930):9.

11. Joseph Cropsey, <u>Political Philosophy and the Issues of Politics</u> (Chicago: University of Chicago Press, 1977), p. 95.

6. Soviet Political Mind

1. Solovyov, <u>A Solovyov Anthology</u>, trs. Natalie Duddington (New York: Greenwood, 1974), p. 163.

2. Avrahm Yarmolinsky, <u>Turgenev</u> (New York: Collier, 1959), p. 216.

3. Max Stirner, <u>The Ego and His Own</u> (New York: Harper & Row, 1971).

4. Herzen, <u>Sobranie Sochinenii v tridsati tomakh</u> [Collected works in thirty volumes] (Moscow: Akademii Nauk SSSR, 1954-65), 6:131.

5. Bertold Brecht, <u>Schriften zum Theater</u> (Frankfurt am Main: Suhrkamp, 1964), 7: #75.

6. Herzen, <u>Sobranie sochinenii</u>, 21:386.

7. Boris Pasternak, <u>Doctor Zhivago</u> (New York: Pantheon, 1958), p. 518.

8. For a brilliant comparison of Herzen and Marx, see John Berger, <u>Selected Essays and Articles</u> (Penguin Books, 1972).

9. Marx-Engels, <u>Werke</u> (Berlin: Dietz Verlag, 1953), 28:434-35. See also, Henry Eaton, "Marx and the Russians," <u>Journal of the History of Ideas</u> 41, no. 1 (Jan-March 1980):89-112.

10. Herzen, <u>Sobranie sochinenii</u>, 5:13-14.

11. *Ibid.*, 12:56.

12. Rosa Luxemburg, <u>The Russian Revolution and Leninism or Marxism</u> (Ann Arbor: University of Michigan Press, 1961), p. 107.

13. Nietzsche, <u>The Portable Nietzsche</u>, ed. Walter Kaufmann (New York: Viking Press, 1954), p. 543.

14. T. G. Masaryk, The Spirit of Russia, 2 vols. (London: George Allen & Unwin, 1961), 2:527.

15. See V. Belinsky, "The Russian Nation and the Russian Tsar," in Russian Philosophy, ed. J. Edie, et al. (Chicago: Quadrangle Books, 1969), pp. 296-99.

16. Solzhenitsyn, The Oak and the Calf, trs. Harry Willets (New York: Harper & Row, 1980, p. 438.

17. Herzen, My Past and Thoughts, trs. Constance Garnett, 4 vols. (New York: Knopf, 1968), 4:1673-74.

18. Ibid., p. 1674.

19. Herzen, Sobranie sochinenii, 6:140.

20. Ibid., p. 110.

21. Ibid., p. 15.

22. New York Times, 5 July 1980, A14.

23. Solzhenitsyn, ed., From Under the Rubble (Boston: Little, Brown, 1974), p. 105.

24. New York Times, 5 July 1977, A17.

25. New York Times, 19 October 1977, A5

26. Weber, Economy and Society, 2:904.

27. Voltaire, Oeuvre completes, ed. M. Beuchot (Paris: Lefevre, 1934-40), 2:127.

28. Hobbes, Works, 3:624.

29. V. Belinsky, Polnoe sobranie sochinenii [Complete collected works], 13 vols. (Moscow: Akademii Nauk SSSR, 1953-59), 1:247.

30. Iu. A. Tikhomirov, "Gosudarstvo v razvitom sotsialicheskom obshchestve" [The state in the development of socialist society] Voprosy filosofii, no. 10 (1979), :7.

31. Ibid.

32. Andrei Amalrik, _Will the Soviet Union Survive until 1984_ (New York: Harper & Row, 1970), p.34

33. Nadezhda Mandelstam, _Hope Abandoned_ (New York: Atheneum, 1974) p. 496.

34. Lenin, _Works_, 21:263.

35. _New York Times_, 17 March 1978, A4

Part IV

The Soviet government asked for trouble, of
course, when it signed the Helsinki declaration
of human rights.

-George Kennan

Belief in the primacy of human rights over other
claims is the first principle that separates
pluralist from centralized societies.

-Isaiah Berlin

The Soviets gave 1/1000th of what natural
law should provide.

-Solzhenitsyn

SOVIET-AMERICAN CONFRONTATION

1. The Helsinki Conference

Some thirty years after the second world war,
ushering in a divided Europe whose destiny was
arbitrated by two non-European superpowers, ambassa-
dors of thirty-four nations met on November 22, 1972,
at Helsinki to prepare a Conference on Security and
Cooperation in Europe (CSCE). After three years of
protracted and complex negotiations to settle issues
left unresolved at the end of World War II, including
the normalization of East-West relations, the Helsinki
Final Act was signed on August 1, 1975, by every
European country--except Albania--as well as the
United States and Canada.

The Helsinki Accord covers four broad areas in
which expanded East-West cooperation and the furthering
of peace and international security are to be sought
and implemented. The four areas are: 1) political
and military security questions, including confidence-
building measures and the status of frontiers; 2) economic, trade, technology and environmental protection;
3) cultural and information exchange--what in the
West became known as "the free flow of people and
ideas" and; 4) permanent European security arrangements.
The Helsinki Conference has produced a 40,000 words
document known as the Final Act or Accord. It became
the most quoted, and most misread document in diplomatic history. In the East it was hailed as the triumph of Soviet diplomacy. Soviet enthusiasm was

understandable. Ever since 1945 the USSR has relent-
lessly pursued the formal diplomatic sanction by the
West of the postwar status quo in Eastern Europe.
That sanction was ultimately incorporated in the Final
Act by various agreed upon principles. For instance,
"Refraining from the Threat or Use of Force"
(Principle II), "Inviolability of Frontiers" (Prin-
ciple III), the "Territorial Integrity of States"
(Principle IV), and "Nonintervention in Internal
Affairs" (Principle VI).

Indisputably, the CSCE and the concurrent negotiations on Mutual Force Reductions (MFR) and the
Strategic Arms Limitations (SALT II) promised to
augur a new era in European diplomacy and open a
new chapter in Soviet-American relationship. We
cannot review here the postwar international relations
whose dominant reality was and remains the nuclear
capability of the two non-European superpowers--
the USA and USSR. The chilling reality of our generation is Pax atomica as pax timoris. In plain
English, the balance of terror imposed armed truce
is modern civilization's version of peace. Kant's
generation believed peace can be made "perpetual."
But the Soviet-American rivalry has stripped peace
of its "perpetual" follies and made international
reality naked, as at its birth.

2. Morality and Foreign Policy

In the Enlightenment, physiocrat Jacques Turgot proclaimed the irreversible, upward progress of mankind. A century later, Mill asserted that nationalism makes man indifferent to the "rights and interests of any portion of the human species, save that which is called by the same name and speaks the same language as themselves."[1] It is not without irony that the rights of man and nationalism were products of the Enlightenment. And as Isaiah Berlin[2] argued recently, nationalism, once the bridge between the individual and community, paved the way for the abyss of 1914 and 1939.

In the coming decades of our century nationalism will be more upsurgent as the Soviet and American political systems continue to confront and challenge each other as standard bearers of opposing ethical ideals. The United States will continue to be the principal champion of the moral imagination in our century. The moral imagination aspires to the apprehending of right order in the individual and right order in the polity. It was the gift and heritage of the American Founding Fathers.

The origin and causes of the Cold War cannot detain us here. But this much needs to be said   America's moral idealism and the entry of the Soviet Union on the world stage during 1945 became the principal determinants of the Cold War. Russia's traditional imperialism, the unquenchable revolutionary aspiration of Bolshevism, the deviously suspicious brutality of Stalin--all are elements of which the cold war guilt of the Soviet Union is composed. In comparison, America in the early 1950s appears to be well meaning but bumbling, anxious to close the bloody chapter of war quickly and decisively, without defining with any precision its postwar objectives in a world reshaped by Soviet military thrust. Though virtuous and idealistic, the U.S. is ineffective when faced with the ruthless ambition of an expansive Soviet power.

Russia's imperial grasp and its ideological vestment known as Soviet Communism on the one hand, and the democratic aspirations of the United States on the other have locked the two superpowers into a power and value confrontation   The geopolitical and strategic interests of the two adversaries shouldn't be minimized. Nonetheless, the two superpowers, as great powers throughout history, have considered the maintenance of their power position in terms of the primacy of their respective political values

One cannot separate the Soviet-American relationship apart from their value rivalry. A classical instance was provided by the Helsinki Accord. Moscow and its East European allies chose to give more weight to Principle III and IV, dealing with the inviolability of frontiers and the territorial integrity. Recognition of the Soviet conquered lands as <u>status-quo</u> of postwar Europe has been the underlying aim of the Soviet Union in proposing and actually signing the CSCE. By contrast, the West and United States in particular placed stronger emphasis on Principle VII, concerning human rights and fundamental freedoms. The inclusion of Principle VII has been considered by many in East and West as the most important, if not basic, achievement of the Helsinki Accord.

Many Soviet and East European dissidents actually wept when they read the Helsinki Accord because they interpreted it as Western capitulation to Soviet territorial gains and dominance since 1945. In short, many dissidents viewed the Helsinki Accord as betrayal of the cause of freedom in Communist countries. Solzhenitsyn pronounced the Helsinki agreements as the "funeral of Eastern Europe."[3] Undeniably, the Helsinki clause on "inviolability of frontiers" was conceived by Moscow as a substitute for a World War II peace treaty covering Central Europe, with formal international endorsement of map changes imposed by the Red Army.

On the other hand, there is little doubt that the U.S. Administration supported the Helsinki agreement as manifestation of the broader detente policy of which Henry Kissinger was the principal architect. The Helsinki Accord was a dramatic culmination of the era of negotiations on which European international politics embarked in the early 1970s. The postwar world saw the emergence of the United States, a non-European power, and its rivalry with the Soviet Union, half-European power with a strong "Asiatic component."[4]

The perpetual and restless desire of power after power, "that ceaseth only in death,"[5] and the intangible yet real realm of ideas have contributed to the Soviet-American labyrinth from which there is no magic exit. The superpower conflict of postwar years was also the conflict of two different political cultures. Soviet ideology insists on a state-enforced absolute order, whereas the American civic culture considers justice the regulative principle of democracy. In addition, there is the accompanying power impulse of the two nations, irrespective whether the competition for destructive power is designated in terms of "parity" or "superiority."

The nuclear arms race is the strangest military competition the world has ever seen. A nuclear exchange would mean a leap into an abyss. Some fifteen years ago the U.S. Department of Defense estimated that if one hundred nuclear warheads landed on the Soviet Union, 37 million people, or 17 percent of the population would die and 59 percent of the industrial capacity would be destroyed. As the Reagan Administration takes office, the American stockpile is almost 16 times more "overkill" than some fifteen years ago. Yet we continue to talk about not only the United States "falling" behind the Soviet military momentum, but the idea is gaining currency that either superpower could emerge victorious from a nuclear war. Vice President George Bush expressed belief that there was such a thing as a "winner in a nuclear exchange."[6] And some American strategists, including the Hudson Institute's Colin Gray and Keith Payne, have argued that "the U.S. must possess the ability to wage nuclear war rationally."[7] No wonder that Henry Kissinger once exclaimed, "What in the name of God, is strategic superiority?"

All the statistics of death and the tangled issue of nuclear arms race can be reduced to a psycho-political question: Would a rational leader, either in the Kremlin or White House, begin a war if he believed that at least 50 million people would die? If the answer is no, there is no justification for Soviet-American arguments to improve or add to their nuclear arsenal. If the answer is yes or even maybe, there is no escape from the escalating arms race. We incline to the view that incompatible political values, more than the immutable reality of power, create the Soviet-American labyrinth.

187

Postwar America provides convincing evidence that
a democratic civilization cannot escape the Sisyphean
task of translating its domestic ideals into a workable
concept of international relations or foreign policy
objectives. Influenced by its conspicuous beginning,
the American political mind designed a correlation
between pacifism and democracy. The tension between
self-interest and democratic ideals, though not unique
to America, becomes an American problem in the postwar
years. The German-born Hans Morgenthau could write
a classic textbook on American foreign relations as a
story of idealistic self-deception.[8]

In his attempt to define modern man, Walter
Lippman stumbled on the challenge facing America.
He wrote,[9]

> "The modern man is an emigrant who lives in a
> revolutionary society and inherits a protestant
> tradition. He must be guided by his conscience.
> But when he searches his conscience, he finds
> no fixed point outside of it by which he can
> take his bearings."

Few would dispute that postwar America entered
the international world with distinct hopes, pre-
scribed by the domestic society's protestant conscience. The American reluctance and half-hearted
attempt to translate its postwar military-political
power into a "right" is an important factor in understanding the Soviet-American relations. Moral idealism
has colored postwar America's perception of the Soviet
power. Nothing captures America's idealism better
than William Gladstone's brilliant image. Comparing
England and America, he said the mother-country was
praxis and her prodigy a poiesis.[10] Unlike England,
which has grown and developed, America was a choice
and inspiration of an epoch.

The heritage that weighed on postwar America was
the preeminance of domestic values over foreign policy.
Differently put, at home the rule of reason and legality,
abroad tyrannies and the unchecked sway of force. The
American moral cosmos received its first major
earthquake as its wartime ally--Russia--became its
principal adversary. Despite the cracks and fissures,
the Republic managed to survive the Hobbesian-
Machiavellian postwar world which, lacking a coherent
moral foundation, pursued the morality of states.
The morality of states recognizes foreign policy,

rather than domestic social justice, as the primary obligation of the state, seeking autonomy.

One historian, John Lukacs, has argued that 1945 heralds the beginning of the Post-Modern Age, demanding new outlooks, new modes of statecraft, and new priorities. In the Post Modern Age, America assumes the posture of a gladiator, its nuclear weapons pointing, and its eyes fixed on the Soviet Union. In post war decades the Hobbesian model of international relations attained reality. As Hobbes put it, whatever international principles exist, they apply in foro interno but not in foro externo.

Compare America's Post Modern Age with 1905 when James Bryce, America's most astute observer, could still talk about the Republic's "indifference" to and detachment from foreign policy as an "unspeakable blessing." Throughout its formative years, America rarely concerned itself with clouds boiling over her "external horizon." In America, observed Bryce, one mentions foreign policy as a traveler mentions "snakes in Iceland,"11 only to note their absence and count it as blessing.

In Bryce's updated metaphor, with the Soviet-American rivalry, the snakes appeared in Iceland. A complex international reality forced itself on America for which it was unprepared by tradition or national psyche. The vexing problem of "ends and means," so brilliantly resolved in the American Constitutional system, presented itself in a basically Hobbesian international setting. Consequently, postwar America had to preserve democracy and freedom against Soviet challenge and seek moral validity for democratic ideals beyond the peculiar historical conditions of its transatlantic birth.

The postwar "American problem" is foreshadowed in Tocqueville's premise that democracy is inferior to non-democracies in the conduct of foreign policy. Democracy is better adopted for the peaceful conduct of society than for the prolonged "endurance of the storms which beset the political existence of nations."12 The democratic people, said Tocqueville, are reluctant to concentrate effort and combine resources upon a "single point."13 With his customary prescience, Tocqueville foreshadows the difficulties America will face in confronting Soviet despotism. He wrote,14

189

"In order, therefore, to appreciate the sacrifices which democratic nations may impose upon themselves, we must wait until the American people is obliged to put half its entire income at the disposal of the Government, . . . or until it sends forth a twentieth part of its population to the field of battle. . . ."

Few students of the Soviet-American relations would dispute the appropriateness of Tocqueville's prophecy. The superpower conflict is more than relentless tension between American ideals and national interest. Schooled in security and legalism, the American mind was unprepared for the Hobbesian postwar years where the state's pursuit of national interest invalidates the moral constrain binding on domestic politics.

The atom bomb and military technology not only challenged the "safe" transatlantic civilization, but they dethroned America's special geographical providence. In addition, the rapidly expanding technology has enhanced the destructive potential of states which are indifferent, if not outright hostile, to the "self-evident" truths associated with the American civilization. The thrusts and probings of Soviet power have revealed what could be termed the Lockean-premise of American politics. Locke postulated that nations are friends in peace and enemies in war. By contrast, the Soviets had interpreted detente as relaxation of tension between states, without relaxing the ideological confrontation between democracy and Communism.

Another aspect of the Lockean premise of American politics is the sanctity of consent and rights in a democratic polity even when it wages a war. To be sure, Locke admitted that the conducts of war and foreign policy do not admit "plurality of governors."[15] Unlike Soviet foreign policy, American foreign policy appears to suffer because of its pluralistic and constitutional setting. A democratic polity is less prone to re-align its domestic priorities to accord with the foreign policy goals. When Locke looks at foreign affairs, he sees great uncertainty which demands strong executive leadership without, and herein lies America's democratic dilemma, undermining the consensual basis of political power. Locke recognizes that a society's conduct of foreign affairs depends on the actions, designs, and interest

190

of other societies.[16]

Consequently, American foreign policy is burdened with more restraints than the Soviet one. Simply put, Soviet society and international relations are more congruent than American society and international relations. Seizing and maintaining power by force and fraud, Communism has existential understanding of the cynical opportunism that is the touchstone of international relations. By contrast, American democracy, engaged in promoting domestic social justice and tranquility, finds the international disorder and ambition[17] unsettling. Put another way, unlike the Soviets, America cannot emancipate itself completely from moral principles in order to become the lion and the fox in international relations.

To Locke the role of foreign policy is to defend and express the political order from which it derives its force and direction. Clearly then, American democracy has a legitimate concern for external security and effective military force. As Locke put it, the remedy against violence and force facing a nation lies in "arms, riches, and multitudes of citizens."[18] If external security is the first concern of democracy, the criteria for the security of the United States ought not to be its moral idealism, but must be determined by comparing America's power and arms with that of the Soviet Union. Equality between two nations, forewarned Locke, invariably invites aggression.

By agreeing to a symmetry or "parity" of nuclear capability, the United States has weakened its position vis-a-vis the Soviet Union. A despotic power attains advantage over a democratic polity, as Locke noted, when their powers are equal. The differentia, of course, resides in the national psyche of a despotic system like the Soviet Union. Thus Moscow insists that "parity" with the United States is the sole guarantee of a peaceful world-order. For reasons that cannot detain us here, the United States lost its nuclear monopoly and the Soviet Union enjoys better than parity with its adversary. The "equivalence" argument failed to produce a more rational and predictable Soviet power. On the contrary, the Soviet Union displays less "good will" and moral restrain today than when it was weaker in arms. To put it bluntly, the achievement of "nuclear parity" has not produced any of the consequences originally anticipated and expected.

Very few people would be prepared to assert categorically that the recent Soviet thrusts--from Africa to Afghanistan--are entirely explicable as the actions of a great power taking advantage, however cautiously, of the military weaknesses of its adversary--the United States. On the contrary, the Soviet threat is congruent with the Lockean axiom that equality of power invites aggression.

Signing the SALT II treaty in Vienna, and bestowing the peace of kiss on President Carter, Leonid Brezhnev said the treaty guarantees the "most sacred right of man--the right to live." But no amount of technical agreements and parchment declarations of good intent can remove the psychological variants of war and peace. Like every mortal being, the superpowers want to "survive." They disagree on how to survive largely because the Soviet and American political systems embody opposing ideals and principles about man and his political destiny. The Soviet-American rivalry, despite all the SALT treaties and its future variants, will continue because its cause lies in the very hearts of men.

Undeniably, the Soviet people desire peace and prosperity. Before drawing a too optimistic conclusion from this, it ought to be remembered that the Soviet state, with a national product of about 60 percent of the United States, enjoys a military clout comparable, if not superior, to its rival. Addressing the Berlin Conference of the Communist Parties of Europe (Summer 1976), Brezhnev dismissed as myth the "Soviet threat." He declared:[19]

"The Soviet Union is the only great power which does not increase its military spending every year, and which is working for a generally agreed reduction of military budgets "

Such olive-branch statements cannot hide that "proletarian internationalism," rather than an innocent linguistic formula, connotes intervention, aggression, and Russian expansionism. Sakharov reminds the West that,[20]

"Everything is as it was under the system of power and economy created by Stalin. The leaders carry on the arms race, concealing it behind talk of their love of peace. They interfere in troubled areas around the world, from Ethiopia to Afghanistan, in order to increase prestige, to strengthen the nation's power and ensure that the guns don't get rusty. They round up dissidents, returning the country to quiet 'predissident' period. . . ."

Sakharov's stark analysis raises the question not only about the nature of Soviet power, but, more fundamentally, how to contain or respond to it. We have seen that "proletarian internationalism" means imperialism and Soviet adventurism. Soviet history, in essence, is a record of the struggle between Russia and communism. Russia won. Marxism-Leninism is Marxism modified by the Russocentric Lenin, and adjusted to Russia after the 1917 revolution. The history of tsarist Russia as that of Soviet Russia is a history of expansionism in all directions except north, the artic circle. Soviet history and policies, especially in the last decade or so, can hardly inspire any hope for the emergence of socialism with "human face" under Soviet tutelage. Both the theory and practice of Marxism has been subverted into an ingenious rationalization and preservation of an unchecked, corrupt power. The geriatrics in the Kremlin and in communist Politburos around the world are symptomatic of a corrupt power. Yet sychophant intellectuals still write learned dithyrambs about "humanistic" communism.

Whatever the Marxist potential for "good" society may be, the reality is that communism is impervious to any ideals other than state and party idoltry. The massive buildup of conventional and nuclear forces of the Soviet Union testify to the communist idols. Some could argue that the Soviet arms buildup is rooted in Russian history, national psychology, and the dynamics of Kremlin's politics, rather than symptomatic of an aggressive, sinister intent. In short, Soviet intentions, whether in Kabul or in Warsaw, are not as sinister as actual, or potential Soviet military interventions suggest. The inordinate influence of military in Soviet power should, therefore, be scaled down by taking into account the traditional Russian obsession with security, stemming from its ingrained inferiority complex. The logic of this argument then forces one to conclude that no matter what the United States does with its military power, Moscow will continue its strategic buildup because its momentum is dictated by Russian history and Soviet politics.

Once more the American tradition influences our perception of Soviet power. Referring to the Lockean-premise of American politics, we stated that security and peace are firmly fixed in American and popular thinking. The "poesis" of their political creation has conditioned Americans to understand peace in non-strategic terms. The New World's privileged remoteness from Hobbesian European powers has contributed to the popular image that America's unique values, rather than the United States's strategic non-involvement with external adversaries, is the source of American concept of peace and progress. The notion of deliverence from Old World politics dates back to the Founding. An early version, commemorated in the phrase <u>novus ordo seclorum</u>--"a new order of the ages"--on the reverse side of $1 bills, cast the U.S. as a moral exemplar to the world. This is the source of America's attempts to reform the world through worldwide application of its domestic values and ideals. Each war to end wars and the formula for lasting peace, whether Woodrow Wilson's League or the United Nations, was a splendid page torn from American history which celebrates man's readiness to compromise and sacrifice for the happiness of all.

Many Americans continue to believe that only if the Soviet Union could "liberalize" internally the world would be cleansed of conflict and, above all, Russians and Americans could start to build a paradise. This dream dies hard. It took the <u>Realpolitiker</u> Henry Kissinger to remind us,

> ". . . The one thing that the Communist systems do better than any other one thing is the accumulation of arms, and there is an almost inevitable tendency to do those things which a nation does well--to continue doing them." [21]

As long as Russia continues to specialize in what it does best--deploy arms for its ideals--America has little choice but to follow the Lockean script of matching arms and power with the USSR. In practice this means that America must approach the concept of peace in strategic terms, not through moral idealism. This is easier said than converted into policy. Historically, two views have vied for primacy in American foreign policy. The first, as expressed by Henry Kissinger and the so-called political realists, emphasizes the morality of power. The second, the power of morality, is congruent with American idealism.

That American idealism is rooted in its Protestant
faith hardly needs documentation. Even in the contingent world of politics, the American credo holds,
alternatives are available because ethical principles
are the humanism of means, not of ends. As John F.
Kennedy expressed it, the rights of man come not
from the generosity of state but from the "hand of
God." In a created universe, man carries the imprint
of his creator, the measure of all things. One may
dismiss the ideal of human character, prophesied in
high religion, as nothing but a noble myth, unsuitable
to modern civilization. But if religion is nothing
but moonshine and cobwebs, or, at best, an eccentricity
of the soul, how is one to account for the prevasive
influence of religious outlook on modernity. There
is much that recommends itself to modern man in the
political consequences of Biblical concept of man as
an ever precarious synthesis of beast and angel.
This makes the morally ambiguous man suspect in the
conduct of power and politics because political man,
ever prone to shift his interest from angel to beast,
creates a morally ambiguous world.

It is for this reason that in American political
thought, due to its Protestant heritage, the individual
is under the obligation to reconcile his political
nature with his moral destiny. Nor is it accidental
that in America the state is faced by an insurmountable
barrier in relation to the individual, in other words,
the state may not infringe upon the protective sphere,
drawn around the individual by natural rights and
religion. By contrast, in Hobbes's system of thought,
the protective sphere is missing as a matter of
principle, since he recognizes no stages precedent
to the establishment of the state, in which the unorgan-
ized individuals unite for fear that otherwise they
will destroy each other.

It is against the exclusive representation of
society by the state, inherent in Hobbes's system, that
the significance of James Bryce's remark, concerning
the influence of Protestantism on the American Constitution, becomes apparent. The Constitution, he
wrote, "is the work of men who believed in original
sin, and were resolved to leave for transgressors no
door which they could possibly shut."[22] With Puritanism enters legalism whose aim is not only to secure
good government, but to prevent any form of power
from threatening the dignity and rights of person.
The leading exponent of political realism, George
Kennan has frequently reproached Americans for equating

principles with reality. Yet the same Kennan said that the American people can respond more effectively to Soviet challenge not through arms, but by the example they set and "what we are."[23]

That there is internal inconsistency between Kennan the "realist" and Kennan the American is not difficult to see. What Americans are and aspire to is precisely what compels them to inject "legalistic-moralistic" values into foreign policy Kennan objects to. Reflecting on the troubled Soviet-American relations, he wrote,[24]

> "There is not greater American error than the belief that liberal institutions and the rule of law relieve a nation of the moral dilemma involved in the exercise of power."

The tough-minded conclusion of political realists is best captured in Spinoza's blunt statement, "Liberality of spirit, or courage, is a private virtue; but the virtue of a state is security."[25] Nor can one ignore Kennan's compelling logic on the inherent difficulty of all powers to shape events in other societies to their own liking. Kennan may rail against the American penchant for launching moral crusades to secure the Holy Sepulchre that invariably ended in failure, yet polls repeatedly show deep seated respect for a "moral dimension" of foreign policy. To America moral principles are applicable to international relations because national experience teaches that nations form a community, bound to moral values.

Political realists, insisting on the invariable morality of power, ignore that even our century was shaped by two idealistic events. One was the Bolshevik Revolution, and the other the entry of United States into the Great War of 1914. As A. J. P. Taylor concluded, these two events have determined the shape of the world "in which we still live."[26]

Indisputably, a complex international system produces its own discontinuity between moral stance and the reality of power. Yet in evaluating moralism, we must not overlook that the American foreign policy objectives are the objectives of American democracy. Democracy is cherished because it is the tested instrument to secure individually designed social ends. From the Hobbesian perspective of international politics, this can be viewed as democracy's

liability. Those who wish to argue that the insertion
of human rights into Soviet-American relations, both
by the Carter and Reagan Administrations, reflects the
American moral-religious bias, they should ponder
Bryce's foresight.[27]

"The future of democracy is therefore a part
of two larger branches of enquiry, the future
of religion and the prospects of human progress."

The American political tradition is an intricate
weaving of idealism and pragmatism. The United States
has always insisted that it was not merely concerned
with preserving the global balance of power and with
protecting its interests around the world, but rather
that it stands for certain values and for a certain
concept of human rights. As a historical rule,
democracies generalize from their domestic values to
international relations. Nor is it accidental that
democratic statesmen speak in terms of values when
discussing foreign policy. Winston Churchill, a
consumate lion and fox when Anglo-American interests
required, had great respect for principles in foreign
affairs. Deep convictions and principles, he said,
enable policy makers to maintain a steady course among
shifting interests and power gyrations. More than
once Churchill spoke in the House of Commons on the
need of "moral outlook on world affairs."[28]

Spinoza's axiom that "security" is the state's
chief virtue needs qualification. The spiritual oxygen
that kept alive America's basic liberties and values
ought not to be traded off for the promise of "world
peace" on Soviet terms. Security of the state, yes.
But it cannot come at the expense of democratic values.
America and Russia are adversaries because, among others,
they disagree over the necessity and degree of trade
off between state "security" and democratic values.

The political destiny of Atlantic democracies
must not be resolved in Moscow or arbitrated by
Soviet arms. In a physical sense, the USSR can destroy
Western democracies. Hence the United States, despite
all its idealism, can hardly expect to stop Soviet
aggression by appealing to heaven, which served America
so well in a more innocent past. The survival of
democracy is the basis of Western civilization we have
known, cherished, and sacrificed for. Facing Soviet
power, we ought to remember Plato and Aristotle's
prediction that governments yielding absolute power

have a short life-expectancy. The reign of Stalin and Mao testify that deep, inside communism is buried despotism, using terror, torture and the usual human skulduggery.

Winston Churchill got it somewhat backwards when he described the Soviet Union as a "riddle wrapped in a mystery inside an enigma." On the contrary, there is no mystery to communism. Inside communism is despotism and the mystery wrapper is to conceal that there really is not much higher meaning to Soviet communism. The sooner we remove the veils from our dazed eyes concerning the "mystery" of communism, the sooner democracy will manage rationally its relation with the Soviets. As demonstrated by the twelfth year cycles of Soviet invasion of its satellites--Budapest of 1956, Prague of 1968--Communism is not only crisis-ridden, but it is not as solid as the shell of secrecy makes it seem. Communism is a primitive system because at its very core it writhes with fear and ambition.

American foreign policy options should take into account that, though the Soviet regime continues to change, the geopolitical position of Soviet imperium is weak and bleak. Moscow may command formidable military force to contain pluralistic pressures in its far-flung yet restive empire. Arms and tanks may suppress and silence freedom. They cannot extinguish the people's aspirations for dignity and bread. Gun barrels can shore up a tottering, corrupt power. But it is the ballot box that, in the long run, captures human allegiance. The Soviet-lead invasion of Budapest and Prague, and the Soviet inspired Pantzerkommunismus in Poland symbolize an arriviste empire's mortal weakness, not its strength. The United States should take note of Francis Bacon's insight. Upon the "breaking and shivering of a great state and empire," he wrote, "you may be sure to have wars."29

One way the West can weaken Soviet despotism is to induce realization in its subject people, at all levels of personal and social life, that freedom and bread are inseparable issues in a good political order. When the suppressed, misled masses realize that free people do not form bread-lines, the deathknell of Communism will sound. We must not underestimate the entrenched Communist elite's fear of spontaneous, mass-based changes. No other than Khrushchev admitted

198

the Hobbesian fear that grips Communist leaders.

> "We were scared, really scared. We were afraid
> the thaw might unleash a flood, which we
> wouldn't be able to control and which could
> drown us. How could it drown us? It could have
> overflowed the banks of the Soviet riverbed
> and formed a tidal wave which would have washed
> away all the barriers and retaining walls of
> our society."[30]

Khrushchev's confession proves that Communism
is denied the moral base of political choice, namely,
reconcile self-preservation of the state with obedience to moral principles. Lord Bolingbroke once
compared England to amphibious animals. Like the latter,
England must come occasionally to shore. "But the water
is," he said, "more properly our element, and in it,
like them, as we find our greatest security, so
we exert our greatest force."[31] Communism's natural
element is force and fear. As Bolingbroke noted,
even amphibious animals must come occasionally to shore.
Indeed, the Soviet regime occasionally signs human
right declarations and embraces humanistic principles.
But let there be no illusion, Communism's natural
element is force and fear.

No sooner did Moscow sign the Helsinki Accord
than the consequences of human rights instilled fear
in the Kremlin. Human rights assert immediate and
non-postponable satisfaction of basic human need--free-
dom. Rights are not identifiable, despite dialectical
interpretation, with social goals associated with
laying the technological foundation of Communism.
As successor of natural rights, human rights constitute
a veto over state-sponsored social goals.

There was a revealing exchange between Sidney
Hook and a Soviet Marxist, Vitali Korionov, on the
concept of "rights" and "goals."[32] Hook expressed
puzzlement over the fact that Khrushchev, while
denouncing Stalin's horrible crimes and political
purges, failed to indict the system that produced such a
tyrant. Korionov responded by defending and justifying
Stalinism on grounds that the necessity of the state
demanded it. As Korionov put it,[33]

> "First of all, you must not forget that the Soviet
> Union was encircled on all sides by countries
> that wanted to destroy it. The United States

also invaded. We owe the defeat of imperialistic powers to Stalin."

As evident from Korionov's argument, Stalinism contains its own justification for the massive violation of human rights. To Hook, on the other hand, individual rights are not suspendable by the invoked necessity of the state to survive. To be sure, Montesquieu postulated that every socio-political system has a law of survival which sanctions certain actions and prohibits others. But Montesquieu would hardly support the Soviet practice of subordinating individual rights to state survival. The Stalinist regime's goal was to make the state invincible, against its internal and external enemies. According to Solzhenitsyn's estimate, the "enemies" of Stalin's regime may have numbered from 15-20 millions, whose dead souls inhabit the Gulag Archipelago.

Should we master "cognitive respect" for the argument that Stalinism, though its maw swallowed tens of millions of people, saved the Soviet state. To accept the logic that Stalin "saved" Communism is to subscribe to an "internal" definition of human rights, i.e., rights as understood by Stalin and his successors. From Western perspective, the necessity of the state, real or contrived, cannot override the moral base of political choice. To argue that Stalin had no "choice" other than disposing millions of people in order to strengthen the state, from within and without, is to acknowledge state survival as an absolute value. When this happens, society is left naked to unchecked tyranny.

Stalin's brutal methods have become the exception rather than the rule in Communist lands since his death. Yet his most significant legacy, the Stalinist state, remains the basis of power in every Communist country. To criticize Stalin's "excesses," as Khrushchev did in his secret speech, is one thing. But to question the ends or goals for which these "excesses" were committed is to challenge, even in the 1980s, the legitimacy of today's Communist regimes. Stalinism, minus the Gulag Archipelago and the bloody purges, is recognizable political feature of every Communist state today.

In 1979, the Communist world marked the centennial of Stalin's birth. As Stalin's second century began, Moscow intensified its assault on dissent by arresting Andrei Sakharov (January 1979) and exiled him to Gorky, a city closed to foreigners. Sakharov's banishment to Gorky, his gilded cage where his apartment is next door to a police station, unfolds once more the endless Russian drama of conflict between government and genius. By placing Sakharov, winner of the 1975 Nobel Peace Prize for his rights activities, under police surveillance, Moscow served notice to the United States on the limits of human rights as the arbiter of Soviet-American relations. The treatment of Sakharov, who won some of the Soviet Union's highest awards, including the unusual distinction of three-time award of Hero of Socialist Labor, for his work on the hydrogen bomb in the 1950s, underscores the fate of the Helsinki Accord as it begins to haunt the Kremlin. As the un-anticipated consequences of Helsinki Accord's human right provisions begin to dominate Soviet-American relations, the Kremlin turns irritant and repressive toward Soviet dissidents. Commenting on the Helsinki Accord, Brezhnev said,[34]

"These provisions are imbued with respect for man, with concern for ensuring that he might live in peace and look to the future with confidence."

The Soviets hardly anticipated that its dissidents will seize the Helsinki Accord as beacon of hope. As human rights received international attention, Moscow began to interpret Principle VII as an abridgment of Principle VI, obliging the signatory powers to "refrain from any intervention, direct or indirect, individual or collective, in the internal or external affairs of the participating states." To contain human right activities, Moscow argued that the major conclusions reached at Helsinki was that "no one should try to dictate to other people" the manner in which they ought to manage their internal affairs. However, the Helsinki text defined human rights not as a privilege extended by government, but as something inherent in the human condition. Human rights, states the Helsinki text, derive from "the inherent dignity of the human person and is essential for his free and full development." Moreover, the signatories agreed that human rights carry a transcendental significance. Respect for human rights is declared to be "an essential factor for peace, and is a key element in the nations' mutual relations." Just how Moscow interpreted and implemented the Helsinki Accord deserves separate treatment.

A life, fit for the Dignity of Man

-Richard Hooker (1594)

I want private conscience, not public loyalty

-George Konrad (1978)

3. Dissent: The Soul of Men Under Socialism

Democracy had entered America, literally,
in a ship with religious dissenters. As a nation
of dissenters, and descendents of pilgrims to truth,
to Americans the Russian voices of dissent are constant reminder that even shackled souls aspire to the
dignity of man, and retain the courage to be. Courage
means, pace Spinoza, the desire whereby every person
strives to preserve his own being in accordance of
conscience and the dictates of reason.

In Russian history, the poets and writers
played a conspicuous role in defending human dignity
against despotic power. Solzhenitsyn, the great
dissenting voice of our troubled century and for years
the conscience of Russia and scourge of Communism,
in analyzing Soviet power, wrote:[1]

"The Communist regime has not been overthrown in
sixty years, not because there has not been
any struggle against it from inside, not because
people docilely surrendered to it, but because
it is inhumanly strong, in a way as yet unimaginable to the West."

Solzhenitsyn's description of the Soviet Leviathan
recalls Ovid's lines,[2]

Just look
How big I am! Jove up there in the sky
. . . he can't be bigger

It is against the state, an earthly Jove, that
Russian literature is burdened with its special humanistic mission. More than any world literature,
Russian literature is full of search and longings for
truth and justice. Russia's great writers are never
disinterested observers of the human condition,
racked by poverty, ignorance, and injustice. Russian
literature, on the whole, comprises a series of social
documents that record the depthless agony of a nation

deprived of freedom.

Russian creative talent, throughout history,
assumes an oppositional role against an unjust state.
Deprived of constructive political role by despotism,
Russian genius transmutes its anger, loneliness, and
suffering through art and literature. By contrast,
talent in America gravitates, from colonial period on,
toward law and government. American literature mostly
celebrates the miraculous feat, in R.P. Warren's words,
that[3]

> "Two hundred years ago a handful of men on the
> Atlantic seaboard with a wild continent at
> their back, risked their necks and their sacred
> honor to found a new kind of nation, and thus
> unleashed an unprecedented energy that succeeded
> to a power and prosperity beyond their most
> fantastic dreams."

Compare to it the oppositional role of Russian
literature. In America the self is proclaimed not
only in the Declaration and the Constitution, but is
embedded in the very structure of government,
which depends upon the single vote of a man who speaks
his conscience. In Russia, literature champions the
concept of self against the state. This little world
of art, arrayed against the vast state, creates the
righteous empire of conscience and self by which the
state is judged. To powers that be, literature, this
little world apart, is but a toy. Yet this toy,
whether crafted by Tolstoy or Solzhenitsyn, teaches
man to know himself and lead an examined life. Facing
tyranny and bearing witness to suffering, great works
of Russian literature speak of pity for the pitiable.
In Russia it is art, not constitutionalism, that
speaks of freedom and reclaims man's lost dignity.

Not surprisingly, autocratic Russia has been
producing an endless stream of dissidents. In a world
of lies and enforced orthodoxy, the refusal to lie is
a hard currency. In a closed society, loyalty to
humanity and affirmation of moral principles in themselves constitute dissent. It is in such atmosphere
that Russia continues to breed its sacrificial
elite, recruited from literature, science, and academia.
Lenin, for instance, treated dissent as opposition to
"correct" political activity. Soviet dictionary thus
defines a "dissenter" (inakomysliaschi) as one who
thinks differently. In official connotation, the

term "dissenter" is pejorative. It implies an
ideologically unbalanced or counter-revolutionary
individual.

Indicative of the Soviet treatment of dissent is
the growing use of "political psychiatry." The
1977 World Congress of Psychiatry has condemned
the Soviet diagnosis of dissidents as mentally ill.[4]
Political psychiatry is a hienous chapter in an
otherwise inquisitorial Communism. Essentially it is
a secret police tool to intimidate, suppress, or terror-
ize into recantation through drug treatment the open
critics of the regime. This too has roots in the
Soviet past. Lenin attributed mental illness to
his foreign minister, Chicherin, because of the views
he held. "We will be fools," Lenin declared,
"unless we immediately and forcibly send him to a
sanitarium."[5]

Forcible psychiatric interment of the regime's
opponents, without reference to statutes or laws,
condemns innocent people to drug-induced deaths:
the sickness-unto-death of Soviet Communism. The
activities of the infamous Soviet political psychiatry,
Serbsky Institute[6], is well documented and need not
detain us here.

The typical Soviet dissident is mysliaschi, or
intellectual, who disagrees with Soviet orthodoxy.
The regime brands their spoken and written words as
"anti-Soviet." Basically, dissidents try to remove
spheres of human condition from official jurisdiction
and state control. They insist, with Justice Louis
Brandeis, that "the right to be let alone" is the
"most comprehensible of rights and the right most
valued by civilized men."[7] In his famed philosophical
novel, The Rebel, Camus compared the intellectual
protester to a metaphysical or artistic rebel.
The typical intellectual rebel, said Camus, is the
"slave who had taken orders all his life," then
suddenly decides that he cannot "obey some new command,"
or there is a "limit beyond which you shall not go."[8]

In Sakharov's refusal to collaborate with the
Soviet regime in developing newer and deadlier
weapons of destruction, we can recognize that moment
when the "slave" discovers his "freedom" and thus
dissent is born. Dissent in Soviet society has an
existential stance: the inner need of the individual

205

to speak or act in the name of ideals, even when no
concrete means exists to realize them. You speak because you cannot remain silent. It must be stressed
that the inner compulsion of the dissenter is a moral
one, an obligation to speak out against real or
perceived injustice, rather than to subvert Communism
by alternatives. This makes Soviet dissenters opti-
mists without much rational hope. They are cast into
the role of Sisyphus, who, trying to roll a boulder
to the mountain top, labors in vain yet keeps hoping.
Dissidents shoulder a giant boulder, the Soviet
state, and try to roll it off society.

    Civil courage appeals to free people everywhere
because it expresses the moral responsibility of the
free individual. In despotic Russia, then, the dissenter is thrust into the role of l'homme engage.
But individual engagement, relying on conscience's
instructed judgment, spells dissent in Communism.
Since by definition the Soviet citizen is an approximation of the normative Homo Sovieticus, a dissenter
must be pathologically skewed, a political reprobate.
In the Orwellian world of Communism, courage thus
becomes madness and political dissent a disease.

    By Soviet logic, discussion presupposes the dis-
cussant's adherence to the principal tenets of
orthodoxy. Hence an act of dissent indicates that
the individual extracts himself, via conscience or
independent judgment, from the collective pursuit
of Communism. Soviet citizens, in so many words, are
denied the right to travel in the "wrong" direction
or take the unbeaten path to Communism. Because
Communism proliferates ultimate values and essences
beyond what is humanly necessary, Soviet society is
victim of its own Occam Razor. It states that entities
and essences must not be multiplied beyond what is
humanly possible. One example will illustrate the
Soviet variant of Occam Razor. A totalitarian system's
ambition is to control all aspects of life, political,
social, and cultural. Thus, it is estimated that at
least a fifth of the adult Soviet population is
engaged in some part or other of the system of power.
Since such multitude can only have negligible share
of power, it naturally compensates itself by inventing
tasks and roles in order to enhance its position in
the apparatus. The result is the power of misery
or what we called the Soviet Occam Razor.

It must not be overlooked that Communism, as a
political form, denotes ideocracy. The latter means
the supreme rule of a governmental ideology. In
Communist societies no ideas can compete with Marxism-
Leninism. Consequently, neither the concept of truth
nor, for that matter, reality can be interpreted
from a private point of view and then air it in public.
The imposition of official truth, known as propaganda,
also means that in Communism truths express a complex
of prohibition, directed optimism, real and potential
threats. If imposed truths prevailed, no child could,
in Communist society, shout the fairy tale version
"but the King is naked." Ideally, everybody must
participate in the grandiose ideological sham that
the emperor is clothed, even though we know that
political power is often naked.

Consequently, the communist regime does not have
an enemy that is more frightening than conscience.
Communism continues to produce the pilgrims of conscience, who, like the child in Anderson's fairy
tale, shout in public, but the Commissar is naked.
By speaking truth according to conscience and reporting
reality as reason understands it, dissidents discredit
the Leninist dogma that the individual can only
attain salvation as the ward of the party. Left to
his own conscience and judgment, the individual may
continue to stand at streetcorners and shout, "but
the King is naked." Consequently, Lenin's party cannot
be subject to the incalculable temper and mood of the
masses. Enlightenment and knowledge, meaning
communism, must be brought to the masses from outside.

Not surprisingly, the Soviet transcript for
communism calls for the masses's forced march under
paternalistic gerontocracy. The lock-step-march took
Soviet society through industrialization, collectivi-
zation, and state socialism. None of these enforced
stages on the road-to-Communism had provision for the
development of human values, civil rights, and procedural guarantees appropriate even for Homo Sovieticus.
This regime in the hurry could dispense with basic
civil rights. But the orthodox rites of sacrificial
times sound hallower, if not sepulchral, to a growing
number of people. The regime, nonetheless, is mellu-
fluous in praising the Soviet people.

"Everything that has been achieved today is the
fruit of your truly golden hands, dear comrades,
of your inquiring minds and creative efforts."[9]

207

The golden hands! They are guided by a vanguard
Party whose "guardian" spirit intensifies, rather than
slackens, as society draws closer to Communism.

"The further along the road to Communism our
country advances, the stronger will grow the
guiding role of the Party in the life of our
society."[10]

As long as one abides the Party's "guiding" spirit
and manifests no overt opposition to the regime, the
Soviet individual is secure in his "citizenship."
Soviet citizen is an organic part of the ideal,
symbolic universe known as the "Soviet state."
Hence dissidents, by challenging the truth of authority
by the authority of truth, give incontrovertible
evidence of having broken and escaped the organic
links to the state.

Though signatory to the Helsinki Accord, the
Soviet regime was willing to stand condemned by world
opinion just to rid itself of hard-core dissenters.
Seeking order without anarchy, the Soviet rulers
must deny national affiliation to Joseph Brodsky,
Andrei Sinyavsky, Mstislav Rostropovich, Alexander
Ginzburg, Valentin Morozov, Edward Kuznetsov, and scores
of lesser known dissidents. When Moscow released
from prison in early 1979 five dissidents, in exchange
for Soviet spies, they were stripped of their citizenship before leaving Moscow for New York. One dissident,
Ginzburg, spending much of his adult life in prison,
quoted Thoreau: "There comes a time when an honest
human being should spend some time in prison."[11]
Speaking on behalf of the five freed dissidents,
Kuznetsov said, "Yesterday, we were still deprived
of all rights. Today, we are in a country which for
more than two hundred years has been the symbol of
freedom."[12]

The American Constitution can neither prescribe
orthodoxy in politics or culture, nor strip, without
due process of the law, individuals of their citizenship. Commenting on the American concept of citizenship, Chief Justice Earl Warren wrote,[13]

"Our government was born of its citizens, it
maintains itself in a continuing relationship
with them, and in my judgment, it is without power
to sever the relationship that gives rise to
its existence. I cannot believe that a government

208

conceived in the spirit of ours was established
with power to take from the people their most
basic right."

By democratic standards, Soviet citizenship is
the simple idea of a primitive political system.
Treating Sakharov as a common criminal confirms just
how primitive the Soviet regime is. That Soviet
dissidents have a special claim on America's commitment to humanitarian principles is not surprising. At
the same time, to make the Soviet pilgrims of conscience
the litmus test of the U.S.-Soviet relations is not
without problems. Soon after his inauguration,
President Carter sent a letter to Sakharov, the leading
voice of "democratic" Russia. The President promised
to "continue our firm commitment to promote respect
for human rights."[14] This was hardly an ordinary letter.
The hard-bitten Realpolitiker, Hans Morgenthau observed
that nothing like this had happened since Gladstone
rose up against Disraeli to protest atrocities in
Bulgaria. No other American president had intervened
so directly in the internal affairs of other countries
in defense of their people's rights. In Morgenthau's
view, the Carter-Sakharov correspondence was not only
"terribly naive," but a "nonsense" that "won't do
anybody any good."[15]

Predictably, Sakharov released Carter's letter to
the Western press, adding he welcomed it as an
"expression of support" for the human rights movement
in Communist countries. Significantly, Sakharov
added,[16]

"If he (Carter) has taken such a step, it will
not, I think, be an isolated one. After such
steps, others always follow. I do not believe
that President Carter intends to step away
from his principled position on human rights.
If he were to do this, it would be a catastrophe
on a world scale."

The Carter-Sakharov exchange drew an angry,
apprehensive response from Moscow. The government
news agency, Tass, charged that Carter "assumed the
role of mentor to the USSR and other socialist countries"[17] by using concoctions about Soviet suppression
of rights. What fueled Soviet suspicion was that
Carter's letter coincided with the circulation of
Charter '77, drawn up by Czech intellectuals and
circulated in East Europe for signatures. Signed by

some 617 intellectuals, the Charter declared,[18]

> "Charter '77 is a free, informal, and open
> community in which various convictions, religious
> and professional, co-exist. Its members are
> linked by the desire to work individually and
> collectively for human and civil rights in
> Czechoslovakia and the world. . . . Thus Charter
> '77 is based on the solidarity and friendship
> of all people who share a common concern for
> certain ideals."

Significantly, Sakharov linked Soviet and East
European drive for human rights by acknowledging the
letter on behalf of East European dissidents. To
make matters worse from Soviet perspective,
Vice President Mondale followed up Carter's letter
saying the Carter Administration will not soft-
pedal human rights, even though it is difficult to
achieve internal changes in "closed societies."
Moscow's reaction was swift and angry. Anatoly
Dobrynin personally protested to the State Department
about Carter's letter to Sakharov, and conveyed
Moscow's stern message that human rights fall within
the "competence of states."

The Carter-Sakharov exchange highlights the
dramatic conflict of American idealism and political
realism. The heroic stance of Soviet dissidents to
claim the liberty of free-born men deserves high praise.
Yet between the human rights and Soviet power fall
two deep shadows. The nuclear bomb had frozen the
human spirit on the ice of peace between two superpowers.
Humanistic principles recede in numb prodigality before
the ever present potential of nuclear holocaust,
and the all-too-human instinct to survive. Realists
question the relevance of human rights in an age when
the survival of civilization overrides individualistic
moral ideals. On the other side, one hears the
arguments that Soviet human rights groups should be
taken seriously because they prove that man's fate is
not that of a fed, sheltered, and regimented slave.

The issue is not so much the validity of human
rights, but the question whether it can or should become the touchstone of American foreign policy. This
introduces the second shadow we referred to. It
had darkened the U.S.-Soviet relations when Carter
received the exiled Soviet dissident, Vladimir Bukovsky,
in the White House. Carter not only told the often-

jailed Russian that "our commitment to human rights is permanent and I don't intend to be timid about it,"[19] but affirmed his Administration's policy on human rights,

> "I want (human rights) to be productive and not counterproductive, and also to assure that our nation and countries other than the Soviet Union are constantly aware we want to puruse the freedom of individuals and their right to express themselves."[20]

Carter informed Bukovsky that their meeting will help him prepare for the Belgrade conference (June 1977) that was to review adherence to the provisions of the 1975 Helsinki Agreements. Moscow was stung by the White House reception of Bukovsky. Tass tersely reported that President Carter received Bukovsky, a "criminal law offender" who was expelled from the Soviet Union and is also known as an active opponent of the development of Soviet-American relations. The Carter-Sakharov exchange, and later the White House reception of Bukovsky prompted the Soviets to retaliate in kind. Moscow decided to raise the question of American "dissidents." The Literary Gazette declared that, five weeks prior to the Carter-Bukovsky meeting, James Baldwin wrote to Carter protesting the treatment of the so-called Wilmington Ten and Charlotte Three. Reporting on the Black prisoners in detail, the Soviet journal gleefully remarked that Baldwin had not received a reply, though Carter replied promptly to Sakharov's letter. The provocative campaign of defending human rights, argued Moscow, interferes in Soviet "internal affairs."

Responding to Carter's human rights crusade, the Soviets took the position that when letters were exchanged between Moscow and Washington in 1933, to establish diplomatic relations, each side promised to "refrain from interference" of this kind. Moscow denounced Carter's human rights stand as hypocritical because the United States refused to sign the ten years old U.N. Declaration on Civil and Political Rights, ratified by Communist nations. Kremlin's cup brimmed over when Bukovsky, addressing the biennial convention of AFL-CIO (December 1977), questioned the wisdom of the U.S. aiding Soviet economy.

"Every time that the Soviet Union's inefficient economy experiences need--in equipment, in support--Western countries readily come to its aid. It is completely evident that Western capital investments in the USSR, which are calculated to exploit cheap labor, are directly harmful to the interests of Western workers."[21]

In his turn, Senator Moynihan (D-N.Y.) questioned American economic cooperation with the Soviets without exacting commitments in return. While Russia is free to invest in U.S. capital market and use "North Dakota as its reserve granary," charged Moynihan, Moscow is also spreading its "tyranny and crushing its dissidents." Moynihan conceded that[22]

"We cannot make them do this, but we can make them understand that if they do it, if they go on with this pattern for repression and jail and blame every person who stands up for elemental human rights . . . then they goddamn well can feed themselves next Winter."

To add insult to injury, Sakharov's letter to George Meany was read to the convention delegates. Comparing the Soviet regime to a brontosaurus, Sakharov called upon the AFL-CIO to continue its active support of the struggle for "free choice of country and residence" and defend everywhere individual freedom from the "arbitrariness of the state."[23]

That the Carter Administration's human rights crusade proved counter-productive to an improved Soviet-American relations, entering the crucial and delicate phase of SALT talks, was brought home when the Soviet police arrested Anatoly Shcharansky. The arrest, on the eve of Secretary of State Cyrus Vance's visit to Moscow (March 1977) was a calculated and defiant challenge to the White House whether it will speak out and risk aborting the strategic arms talks and other detente discussions. Following Shcharansky's arrest, President Carter personally interceded with Soviet officials on the Russian dissident's behalf who was later accused of being a spy for CIA agents. The case took a dramatic turn when Carter declared,[24]

"I have inquired deeply within the State Department and within the CIA as to whether or not Mr. Shcharansky had ever had any known relationship, in a subversive way or otherwise, within the CIA. The answer is no."

Carter's stand put Moscow in a position where to pursue its case against Shcharansky would mean publically challenging the word of the President of the United States. Given the already heated U.S.-Soviet atmosphere that appeared to jeopardize progress in SALT negotiations, the White House decided to tone down its human rights campaign. While the Soviet press openly called Shcharansky a "traitor to his motherland," the President of the United States declared him innocent.

The official Soviet reaction to Carter's defense of Shcharansky was best summed up by Yuri Kornilov,[25]

"It would be interesting to see how the American authorities and the American judiciary would react if anybody outside, or inside, the country undisguisedly tried pressuring them in regard to a criminal case, and especially pressuring at the official level. We imagine that such attempts at pressuring would be rejected outright. But why is something which is inadmissible for American justice, considered by certain individuals in Washington quite acceptable when it concerns Soviet justice?"

The Soviet regime was not without a logic of its own. When it put Shcharansky on trial despite Carter's special intercession, members of the American Congress, led by Senator Frank Church (D-Idaho) spoke out in defense of the jailed Russian dissident. Brought over from Israel, Mrs. Shcharansky testified for her husband at a public hearing sponsored by the Ad Hoc Committee on Justice for Shcharansky, hosted by Senator Church. The Soviets had a legitimate point in objecting to American interference in "Soviet justice." But the American position was equally valid in voicing skepticism on the "impartial" trial of Shcharansky. Soviet political trials recall Theodor Mommsen's statement, "Impartiality in political trials is about on the level with Immaculate Conception: one may wish for it, but one cannot produce it."[26]

Shcharansky's trial and the Carter Administration's attempt to intercede in Soviet justice demonstrate the inherent difficulties of injecting human rights into inter-state relations. The incident serves notice on the wisdom of making U.S.-Soviet relations captive to the moral courage of dissidents, whether

that of Shcharansky or Sakharov. Carter would have
saved himself considerable trouble and embarrassment
had he remembered, declaring Shcharansky "innocent,"
Justice Learned Hand's opinion,[27]

> "If a community decides that some conduct is
> prejudicial to itself, and so decides by numbers
> sufficient to impose its will upon dissenters,
> I know of no principle which can stay its hand."

Morgenthau reached similar conclusion in declaring,
"Every society must decide for itself who shall have
what freedom."[28] He cited Lincoln in support, who,
in a famous image, compared the freedom of the sheep
with the freedom of the wolf. Since the two do not
agree upon a definition of "liberty," Lincoln concluded
that "precisely the same differences prevail today
among us human creatures even in the North, and all
professing to love liberty."[29]

By extending the Lincoln paradigm to the Soviets,
there is not much common ground between the Soviet
rulers and the ruled. Power to Russia's rulers
sginifies an opportunity for political dominance,
whereas freedom for the ruled, e.g. Sakharov, means
the absence of such domination. As Morgenthau understood Lincoln, justice and freedom depend on the
particular political order in which the individual
lives. Consequently, America's democratic principles
cannot become the evaluative standards of Soviet
Communism. Morgenthau's postulate of two different
conceptions of "freedom" tacitly acknowledges the
value-conflict of the American and Soviet political
systems.

Faithful to its historical heritage, the Soviet
regime is fast and loose with the Holmesian doctrine
of "clear and present" danger. As indicated, state
security is the absolute among Soviet values.
Nowhere in Russian political thought can one find the
disclaimer that the state, to be right, must be
reasonable. By contrast, the republican state,
expressing the will of the majority, "to be rightful,"
in Jefferson's words, "it must be reasonable."[30]
And to be reasonable is to be absolute about nothing
except about being reasonable. The Soviet regime's
case against Shcharansky was hardly "reasonable"
even by Soviet legal standards.

Be it as it may, the Carter Administration has

learned from the Shcharansky case. In his speech
on "Human Rights and Foreign Policy" (30 April 1977),
Cyrus Vance said, "our human rights policy must be
understood in order to be effective." In an essay
published in the Baltimore Sun (19 September 1977),
President Carter came around to the view that human
rights should not stand in the way of peace. "Human
rights," he wrote, "cannot be the only goal of our
foreign policy, not in the world in which peace is
literally a matter of survival."

Though giving a qualified support for Carter's
human rights initiative, Henry Kissinger warned
against trying to become the world's policeman.
In a lecture delivered at New York University
(19 September 1977), Kissinger declared,

> "If we universalize our human rights policy,
> applying it indiscriminately and literally to
> all countries, we run the risk of becoming the
> world's policeman--an objective the American
> people will not support."

Kissinger's views, drawing attention to the interplay
of power and rights, are not without merit. President
Carter himself began to tone down the initial flury
of human rights pronouncements. The differences
between principles and policies began to dawn on the
Carter Administration.

Though conceding that one cannot expect quick
results in the "struggle" for human rights which,
by Carter's own admission, has been going on "for
many centuries," he noted with pride his administration's efforts to weave a regard for rights into the
fabric of America's foreign policy. As for the role
of morality in foreign policy, Carter remained
optimistic that human rights will continue as the
cutting edge of foreign policy.

> "Changes will not come quickly, but they will
> surely come. History moves slowly and fitfully;
> but as long as we are true to ourselves, history,
> where human rights are concerned, is on our
> side."[31]

This still left unresolved the vexing issue of
how to reconcile American moral idealism, mandating
sympathy and support for Russian dissidents, and
the reality of Soviet power. In short, what policy

should praiseworthy American democracy adopt towards
blameworthy Soviet Communism? Kissinger has concluded
that the 1979-1980 crackdown on dissidents was aimed
at demonstrating to the United States the futility
of its human rights campaign. As a policy option,
Kissinger called for drawing a distinction between
authoritarian and totalitarian governments.

In its turn, the Reagan Administration took the
position that President Carter's human rights policy
failed to distinguish between the absolute evil of
Communism and the more limited and remediable lapses
of authoritarian regimes. Many of the latter, of
course, are claimed to be anti-Communist and thus
"friendly" to the United States. This raises the
rather interesting question, seriously propounded by
Leo Strauss[32] some years back, whether there is such
a thing as a "friendly" tyrant.

Whatever the case might be, the distinction
drawn between totalitarian and authoritarian regimes
implies that the latter are less inimical to human
rights. Whether the Soviet regime will eventually
evolve into a more relaxed authoritarian system is a
hope to some and illusion to others. The Soviet
regime today is less oppressive than during Stalin's
reign.[33] No one will deny that creative geniuses
can now dissent and live. But let's not conjure
crystal palaces of humanism in a land where the dictatorship of a vanguard Party is still absolute.

The transition to freedom is not an easy one. In
some countries, however, it is easier than in others.
Russian history counsels against any excessive hopes
that Communism will evolve toward a more "democratic"
polity. Spain has accomplished the transformation of
personal dictatorship into a pluralistic democracy
in less than five years in the post-Franco era.
What post-Franco Spain accomplished is beyond Marxism
and the structural capacity of Communism. Dictatorship and Sovietism are welded so tight that any sharing
of power on a wider base than the Leninist elite party
is inconceivable.

Poland today poses the gravest threat to the
Soviet Union since it forcibly formed the East bloc
after World War II. Events in Poland have already
stripped the clothes right off the Soviet empire.
Lech Walesa and his independent trade union, Solidarity,
discredited the doctrinal core of Marxism. The

Polish challenge came from below, from the workers, the only class of which Communism, by paradox and irony, is mortally afraid. Polish workers have undermined the legitimacy on which Communism rests by refuting the Party's claim to be the sole, authentic representative of the working class. The pluralistic forces in Poland, coalescing around three power centers, the party, the Church, and Solidarity, had to be crushed lest the Polish-disease infects the Eastern-bloc.

In Poland, Moscow has served notice, in masterminding the tragic denouement of Solidarity and the restoration of communism by terror, censorship, and mass arrest, that, though the pathological excrescences of the regime can be reformed, there cannot be any pluralistic overhaul of communism. Unlike in Hungary of 1956 and Czechoslovakia of 1968, Poland's bid for "renewal" and restoration of human rights was suppressed by proxy. A nation terrorized and silenced by its own army, rather than direct Soviet invasion, may constitute compelling evidence to some that Moscow has been touched by what the classical scholar, Gilbert Murray, called _Aidos_.[34] Reflecting on the legacy of Western civilization, Murray expressed conviction that even in the midst of lawlessness there will ultimately spring up some actions that make the unreformed tyrant uncomfortable. No one can tell where the exact point of honor will arise. Take Achilles. He sacked whole cities, slew Eetion, but "spoiled him not of his armour." In Murray's term, he had _Aidos_ for that. Stalin sent Ossip Mandelstam to his unknown grave. Khrushchev sent Russian tanks into Budapest and Prague, but Brezhvev used General Jaruzelski to extinguish the flame of freedom in Poland. Brezhnev then, it appears, was touched by _Aidos_.

All very true. But sparing Solzhenitsyn and Sakharov's lives, and suppressing Polish "renewal" by proxy hardly constitute conclusive evidence that Communism had foresworn its historical impulse to play Leviathan-the clerisy of power-to elements "hostile" to socialism. Soviet leaders, even when touched by _Aidos_, are consumate followers of Hobbes's axiom that rulers are obliged by law to lay the "burdens of commonwealth equally on their subjects."[35] And Brezhnev, like Stalin, cherishes nothing more than "obedient subjects" whose silence, not dissent, is the sweetest music to the Kremlin.

Though Solzhenitsyn denies it,[36] despotism reaches deep into the Russian past. As an ardent patriot, his defense of "old Russia" is understandable but untenable. Hannah Arendt[37] has offered a better insight into Soviet communism when she suggested that the pervasive sense of loneliness and rootlessness in modern society compels many people to long for strong rulers who suppress freedom. Rallies are still held to honor Franco, Hitler continues to spellbind some Germans, and Stalin's ghost has not been laid to rest in Russia. Stalin is not a dying god in Russia. Given the choice between democratic "anarchy" and despotic order, many Russians will choose the latter. In Russia of the 1980s despotism is as alluring to those in search of perfect order than during Stalinism of the 1930s.

The Soviet suppression of human rights induced pessimism even among Eurocommunists concerning the eventual democratization of Soviet Communism. Santiago Carrillo, the Spanish CP leader, declared that "the political system of the Soviet Union lacks democracy."[38] At the Madrid Eurocommunist summitry (1977) Carrillo was spawning new heresies by defending human rights and deploring Soviet violation of the Helsinki provisions. In his book, Eurocommunism and the State,[39] Carrillo compared the "deformed and degenerate" Soviet system to an imperial state.

The West European CPs human rights record is incomparably better than that of the Soviets. Eurocommunists profess to believe in an Europe, based, in Carrillo's own words, on "parliament, political, and philosophical pluralism."[40] Anxious to share political power in European democracies, Eurocommunism's independent stand appeals to dissenting voices in the Eastern bloc. Yet Eurocommunism's defense of human rights will not quicken the seeds of dissent that perenially sprout beneath the Soviet snow.

The spectre of Eurocommunism is bound to haunt Moscow in the coming years. The courage of Eurocommunists to speak on behalf of Soviet dissidents at least affirms, in Bernard Shaw's phrase, that the human "souls are still alive." Solzhenitsyn's suggestion that the enslaved people's liberation depends on democracies' moral-political support for dissidents casts the dissenter into a creature of hope. From Soviet perspective, suppressing dissent is punishing madness, or, in Hobbesian image, crushing the "worms" of body politics. From American perspective, dissidents

are the beacon of democratic and constitutional hope
for communism. Not surprisingly, Soviet dissidents
rely on others, especially the United States, to
reform or overthrow communism. This is the primary
reason why U.S.-Soviet relations are so frequently
on collision course.

As Norman Podhoretz put it,[41]

"In resisting the advance of Soviet Power we
are fighting for democracy and against totalitarianism."

The great ideological divide, separating the Soviet
Union and the United States, has historical and
structural causes which, in many respects, antedate
the cold war.

From the eighteenth century to the present, the
contact of America and Russia is the story of friendship and mistrust, rivalry and truce, but never
common visions. America's democratic seer, Walt
Whitman, captured vividly the relationship of the
Euro-Asian colossus and the Transatlantic Republic.

"You Russians and we Americans! Our countries
so distant, so unlike at first glance--such
a difference in social and political conditions,
and our respective methods of moral and practical development and the last hundred years:--
and yet in certain features, and vastest ones,
so resembling each other."[42]

Whitman noted the "deathless aspiration" in the
inmost center of each great nation; so vehement, so
mysterious, and so abysmic. Many Russians shared
Whitman's sentiment. Herzen believed that Russia
and America, expansive and seeking frontiers on the
opposite shores of the ocean, were the lands of the
future.

"We are two huge countries of the world peopled
by nations destined to reach great power, we
are the 'Mediterranean of the future.'"[43]

The "Mediterranean of the future" confront each other
across geopolitical and strategic lines as rivals,
each determined to maintain or re-establish an overall
position of superiority. Camus once described our
century as the "century of fear." This applies with
chilling relevance to the U.S.-Soviet relations,

entering the phase of containment and confrontation.

Looking back, America can hardly rejoice at the awesome spectable as backward Russia hurdled itself into the twentieth century, and in four decades attained superpower status. Even without Communism, Russia was fated to play dominant role in world politics. As Russia's greatest modern poet, Alexander Blok, expressed it, Russia was a "big ship destined for big sailing." Russia became communist and America's implacable adversary was born.

America's response to the Russian Revolution bears striking resemblence to Burke's response to and perception of the French Revolution when he wrote,[44]

"As I understood the matter, we were at war not with its conduct but with its existence; convinced that its existence and its hostility were the same."

One of the leading students of the U.S.-American relations, Adam Ulam, had argued that the conjunction of Russia's power and its universal creed embodied in Marxism-Leninism have, in effect, contributed to the emergence of Soviet imperium. According to Ulam, Soviet power has managed to destroy the rules of international politics as they prevailed during the supremacy of the West. In Ulam's words,[45]

"The problem here is not primarily U.S.-Soviet relations but rather how the Soviet Union has affected the general character of international relations and politics.

There is no denying that Soviet superpower status, upon which the Kremlin insists and will only compromise at our peril, has not only darkened the international horizon, but it exacted a terrifying human cost, which Sakharov equated with the "lumpenization" of Soviet society. It refers to the systematic disregard of basic human decencies that accompanied Russia's breakneck modernization under party-state monopoly.

In the 1960s, under the Johnson Administration and given formal expression by the Nixon Administration, the United States accepted the Soviet Union as an equal in strategic military power. What has

never been adequately explained under the detente
formula is what will effectively restrain the Soviets,
once granted equal status, from using their new
status for improving their military and strategic
position. We have been witnessing the visible decline
of American power and informed of the "disturbing
fear" that "we are no longer capable of shaping our
future."[46] The Reagan Administration's determination
to "reconsider" U.S. security is based on a new
assessment of the reality and intent of Communism.
Under detente, it was assumed that once the Soviets
reached nuclear parity with the United States, it
would become a status-quo superpower. The invasion
of Afghanistan and the crushing of Polish freedom
demonstrated otherwise. Though the unity of Communism
is shattered and the doctrine itself discredit, both
home and abroad, Communism demonstrates its vitality
and dynamism by an enhanced military posture throughout the world.

It is under Communism that Russia has steadily
advanced in power and influence. At the same time,
we must not overlook that Russia is also prisoner of
its own imperial design. Soviet imperialism demands
a large military establishment, which, in turn needs
a strong economic support. Hence Russia must divert
its industrial resources to other than consumer needs.
Russia is not a nation with an army, but an army with
a nation. And an army, like a serpent, travels on
its belly.

An additional source of Soviet weakness is the
pressure dissident intellectuals exert on Communism.
In the process of seeking basic liberties, dissidents
enlist the moral- political support of America. An
historical perspective, once more, helps to put into
proper focus the relationship between Russian dissidents and American democracy. As a general observation, the nineteenth century Russian radicals--Herzen,
Nicholas Ogarev, Michael Bakunin, Chernyshevsky,
Peter Lavrov, and Nicholas Chaikovski, found their
primary source of inspiration in Tocqueville's
Democracy in America. By contrast, Soviet dissidents--
Solzhenitsyn and others --are hardly impressed by
democratic values and ideals.

Our concern is with the implication of Soviet
dissidents' endeavor to gain the intercession of the
United States, rather than analyzing the strategy of
opposition with Soviet society. Dissidents attempt to

activate America on two grounds. First, they look to the United States as the superpower rival of the Soviet Union. Second, dissidents invoke Western ideals to bring pressure on the Soviet system. As a result, human rights will continue to play integral part in U.S.-Soviet relations. Given the existential and structural base of Soviet dissent, the Kremlin can no more suppress dissent than Neptune can command the sea to calm and recede. Political repression remains endemic to the Soviet system.

Postwar experience with the "closed" Soviet society, blocking domestic and foreign information channels necessary for democratic society, reveals a total lack of popular pressure to control politics. A closed society precludes any identification with the concept of human rights. Put it differently, in the Soviet Union the suppression of human rights is congruent with the traditional Russian mistrust of individual, including his liberties and rights.

America's most respected diplomat and public servant, whose knowledge of Russia was utilized by all presidents since Roosevelt, Averall Harriman wrote:[47]

> "A basic difference between the Soviet Union and us is our fundamental idea that government is here to be the servant of the people and not the reverse. That is a very fundamental difference and we certainly are not going to weaken our principles of representative government and civil liberties. It is going to take a long time to get Soviet convergence on that."

Liberal-humanitarian values have never enjoyed grass-root support in Russia. Sakharov and other dissidents like to talk about exerting "democratic control" over Communism. But whatever democratic interludes there were in autocratic Russia, they were eclipsed by an intense and rancorous struggle between different autocratic elements. Though courageous disclaimers of tyrannical power, Soviet dissidents betray strong autocratic-elitist tendencies. It compelled Kennan to observe,[48]

> "Our experience with Soviet defectors had shown us that however such people might hate their Soviet masters, their ideas about democracy were primitive and curious in the extreme, consisting often only of the expectation that

222

they would be permitted and encouraged by us to
line their recent political adversaries up
against the wall with a ruthlessness no smaller
than that to which they professed to be reacting,
after which they would continue to rule, with
our help, by their own brand of dictatorship."

Examples of Soviet dissidents' autocratic or
theocratic outlook could be multiplied at will.
Take Solzhenitsyn's Letter to the Soviet Leaders.
His prescription for an "authoritarian system"
in Russia is based on a scornful discussion of
democracy's "reckless debauchery" in the West. His
examples are: American presidential elections, the
acquittal of a scholar-pacifist who "stole and published" documents of the Department of Defense, and the
activity of labor unions which will tear off the
"best piece for themselves" in any difficult moment.
Like Plato, Solzhenitsyn sees democracy as hopeless
because it sanctions rampant individualism, diversity,
and is unstructured. Solzhenitsyn contends in his
Letter that an authoritarian system is humane and just.
He states,[49]

". . . Russia lived for a thousand years with
an authoritarian system. And toward the start
of 20th century, it still had greatly preserved
the physical and spiritual well being of the
people. . . . That authoritarian system. . . had
a strong moral foundation, not an ideology of
general coercion, but one of justice, ancient
justice: it was a seven centuries old Orthodoxy. . . ."

One may rightly wonder by what logic is an
authoritarian system "just." Solzhenitsyn himself
was aware of this when he wrote that he preferred
authoritarian rule as long as its leaders accepted
"their responsiblity before God and their own
conscience."[50] Be as it may, Solzhenitsyn, as most
dissidents who are product of the Soviet system, cannot
envision a "regime of law" in place of the "regime of
force." To add further paradox to Solzhenitsyn,
despite his brilliant Jeremiad against Communism and
the evils of Europe for cradling Marx, he also denounced American legalism.

Solzhenitsyn's attack on law as an evaluative
scale deserves full quote,[51]

"I have spent all my life under a Communist regime and I will tell you that a society without any objective legal scale is a terrible one indeed. But a society with no other scale but the legal one is also less than worthy of man. A society based on the letter of the law and never reaching any higher fails to take advantage of the full range of human possibilities. The letter of the law is too cold and formal to have a beneficial influence on society. Whenever the tissue of life is woven of legalistic relationships, this creates an atmosphere of spiritual mediocrity that paralyzes man's noblest impulses. And it will be simply impossible to bear up to the trials of this threatening century with nothing but the supports of a legalistic structure."

Had Solzhenitsyn read Madison he would have learned that, given man's inherent potential for evil, political and legal institutions are the safest guarantee to reconcile liberty and order in democracy. That American representative democracy has been a success owes something to the beneficial system of law, presiding over the political destiny of the Republic. Government by law means that political authority over the individual is formed by rules and habit of consent, not by the sudden jerk of authority. To call the American obedience to such legal humaneness "vulgar" reveals more about Russian political culture than Solzhenitsyn may have intended.

One of Russia's leading legal philosophers, Bogdan Kistyakovsky (1868-1920), has sketched a revealing historical perspective on the Russian intelligentsia's "dulled legal consciousness." Even the stormiest period in English history, the Glorious Revolution, produced Hobbes, Filmer, Locke, and the "legal ideas" of the Levellers. As for 18th century France, there was Montesquieu's The Spirit of Laws, and Rousseau's Social Contract. All these works, argued Kistyakovsky, contained "purely legal" ideas. Looking at Russia, without its own L'esprit des lois, or Le contrat social, Kistyakovsky observed,[52]

"It might be said that the Russian people set out on the historical path much too late; that there is no need for us to work out independently the ideas of freedom and the rights of the individual, of the legal process and the

224

constitutional state; that all these ideas have long since been advanced, developed in detail, and realized; and that therefore all that remains for us to do is borrow them."

But legal ideas, Kistyakovsky added, acquire their own unique nuances and their own shading to be effective by the borrowing country, which, like Russia, has no place for law in its political thought. Herzen himself complained of the "legal insecurity" hanging over Russians from time immemorial. Complete inequality before the law, he said, has killed any respect the Russian people may have had for legality. In Herzen's words,[53]

"The Russian evades or violates the law wherever he can do so with impunity; the government does exactly the same.

Natural law, as we have argued, is the invisible authority behind the visible state. But the Russian state, throughout the long centuries, has never depended on the invisible natural law-the apotheosis of law. Just how consequential was the removal of the "first principles" of good government can be surmised from the statement of Russia's leading populist. In the 1870s, N.K. Mikhailovsky bluntly announced that,[54]

"Freedom is a great and seductive thing, but we do not want freedom if it only increases our centuries-old obligation to the people, as happened in Europe."

And Plekhanov, the father of Russian Marxism, has concluded that the proletariat can limit the "political rights" of the upper classes just as they once limited the "proletariat's political rights." Plekhanov proposed that the democratic rule of salus populi suprema lex be replaced by the rule of salus revolutiae suprema lex. Plekhanov's prescription for the supremacy of force and revolutionary justice, rather than the supremacy of the law, opened the road for Lenin and his revolution.

By the 1920s the disastrous results of the Soviet "socialist" state divesting itself of all legal status became apparent. Unlike Lenin, who divorced socialism and legalism, Kistyakovsky emphasized the need for

225

"judicial socialism."[55] He saw human rights and socialism as compatible.

> "For us (in the Russian Empire) it should be clear that this question of human rights can only be properly solved when social forces are organized more equally. The complete organization of social forces leading to real individual freedom can only be realized in the government of the future or under a different social order."[56]

Russia has undergone the social transformation envisioned by Kistyakovsky. But Communism has yet to find a place for the cluster of liberties we call political and civil rights. Kistyakovsky knew his Russia only too well. "We Russians," he wrote, "are well acquainted with police repression. We always have been subdued by the statement that the leader will worry about it."[57]

The idea of a long-sword state casts an unbroken shadow on Russian history. By contrast, the idea of liberty and human dignity as individual rights became the normative values in the West, dating back to the Renaissance or the Reformation.[58] America's creed of political faith, the gift of its sages and thinkers, designates freedom and rights as the surest bulwark against tyranny. The American Republic had found its strength and unity in an idea. With the government restored to first principles, which Jefferson declared a new chapter in the history of man, the American experiment is launched and put to test. The greatest test, the unsettled question that now confronts America is its irrepressible historical conflict with the Soviet Union.

History and geopolitics has taught the Russians to invest the state with absolute rights, unburdened by constitutional or moral limitations. As a result, the U.S.-Soviet relations, transcending that of the conflict of arms and power, will continue to be afflicted by opposing moral and political ideals.

> The preponderant influence that Russia has won
> through surprise . . . frightened the people
> of the West, who accepted it fatalistically,
> and only resisted by fits and starts.
>
> - Karl Marx

4. Conclusion

Like a dark crystal, Russia continues to dazzle
and deceive the West. The peerless gazer into the
dark crystal of capitalism, Marx noted that other
empires in their infancy have caused similar fascin-
ation to arise, but Russia has become a "colossus"
without having dissipated them.

We stated that the United States and the Soviet
Union are not compossible. The doctrine of compossibility holds that there are nations whose political
ideals or desires can be gratified together and others
only through conflict. If one adopts Bertrand Russell's
maxim that the art of politics consists, to a large
degree, in finding as "numerous a group of compossible
people as you can,"[1] then, the Soviet-American conflict
is insoluble except by politics or war.

George Kennan, on the other hand, takes the
view that the direction in which Soviet society
evolves is determined and influenced, to a measurable
degree, by the American vision and "treatment of it."[2]
Kennan, therefore, sees America's role toward the
Soviet regime as pedagogical, if not maieutic. Not
unlike Socrates, the United States is called upon
to midwife evolutionary changes in Russia.

The acrimonious Soviet-American dispute over
human rights suggests the futility of educating Russia
by re-awakening its political soul to the blessings
of freedom and rights. If knowledge was the sort of
thing that flows by mere contact from a fuller into
an emptier vessel, the United States should have
already removed impediments to human rights in Russia.
For as President Carter put it in his Farewell Address,

> "America did not invent human rights. In a very
> real sense it is the other way around. Human
> rights invented America."

It is this human rights invented America, which happens
to be a nuclear superpower, that stands between the

Soviet Union and its imperial complex and political messianism. The U.S.-Soviet relations is the unfolding drama of our time whose unbound consequence only hope and faith can comprehend. Two great nations are caught in the casting net of destiny: the American resolve and confidence to endure as a democracy, and the Russian determination to advance the cause of Communism are pitted against the power to crush each other.

The United States and the Soviet Union are revolution-designed societies. The birth of these revolutionary societies was hardly an immediate political issue of international politics But in the postwar years they became such an issue, and, as we tried to argue, the Soviet-American conflict is the predominant issue determining the future of international political relations. The Soviet Union has now attained a superpower status and influence. Consequently, an intrinsically totalitarian philosophy has passed from the realm of theory into that of the practical political relations of the national states.

This has already injected perilous and sweeping changes in international politics. As for the future, one can only scan it with the eyes of gods. Americans are blessed with a disposition to trust the divine potter who works on the historical shapes and destinies of human nations. But divine intentions should not blind us to actually-happening history, demanding decision and responsibility. The actual-happening history of our generation is the Soviet-American conflict whose embodiment in values and principles forms the core of this book.

PART FOUR

2. Morality and Foreign Policy

1. J.S. Mill, Dissertations and Discussions:
    Political, Philosophical and Historical
    (Boston: W.V. Spencer, 1868 , 3:382.

2. Isaiah Berlin, Against the Current, ed. Henry
    Hardy (New York: Viking Press, 1980), pp. 333-55.

3. Solzhenitsyn, Detente (New Brunswick: Trans-
    action Books, 1976), p. 31.

4. Max Beloff, Foreign Policy and the Democratic
    Process (Baltimore: The Johns Hopkins Press,
    1955), p. 91.

5. Hobbes, Leviathan, Collier ed., p. 80.

6. Times, 12 January 1981, p. 22

7. Ibid.

8. Hans Morgenthau, In Defense of the National
    Interest (New York: Knopf, 1951).

9. Walter Lippmann, A Preface to Morals (New York:
    Macmillan, 1929), p. 59.

10. W. E. Gladstone, "Kin Beyond Sea," North American
    Review CCLXIV (Sept.-Oct. 1878), p. 185.

11. James Bryce, The American Commwealth, 2 vols.
    (New York: Macmillan, 1905), 2:522.

12. Tocqueville, Democracy, 1:265.

13. Ibid., p. 266.

14. Ibid., p. 264.

15. Locke, Second Treatise, #108.

16. Ibid., #147.

17. Ibid., #16,#17.

18. Locke, A Letter Concerning Toleration, in Works,
    5:42-43

19. Brezhnev, <u>Za mir, bezopostnost, sotrudnichestvo i socialnoi progress v Evrope</u> [For peace, security, cooperation, and social progress in Europe] , (Moscow, 1976), p. 5.

20. <u>The Economist</u>, 14 June 1980, p. 53.

21. <u>Encounter</u> 60 (November 1978): 17.

22. Bryce, <u>American Commonwealth</u>, 1:306.

23. George Kennan, <u>Russia, The Atom, and the West</u> (New York: Harper & Row, 1958), p. 98.

24. Kennan, <u>Russia and the West</u> (New York: Mentor Books, 1961), p. 372.

25. Spinoza, <u>The Political Works</u>, ed. & trs. A. G. Wernham (Oxford: Clarendon Press, 1958), p. 265.

26. A. J. P. Taylor, <u>The Trouble Makers: Dissent over Foreign Policy 1792-1939</u> (London: Hamish Hamilton, 1957), p. 146.

27. James Bryce, <u>Modern Democracies</u> (New York: Macmillan, 1921), p. 606.

28. <u>Parliamentary Affairs</u> (16 August 1945), Hansard vol. 413:95.

29. Bacon, <u>Works of Francis Bacon</u>, ed. James Spedding, 7 vols. (London: Longmans & Co., 1858), 6:515.

30. R. J. Barnet, <u>The Giants: Russia and America</u> (New York: Simons & Schuster, 1977), p. 54.

31. Bolingbroke, <u>The Works of Lord Bolingbroke</u>, 4 vols. (Philadelphia: Carey & Hort, 1841), 2:417-18.

32. Sidney Hook, <u>Revolution, Reform and Social Justice</u> (New York: New York University Press, 1975), p. 210.

33. <u>Ibid.</u>, pp. 211-12.

34. Brezhnev, <u>Following Lenin's Course</u> (Moscow: Progress Publishers, 1975), p. 583.

3. Dissent

1. Solzhenitsyn, *The Gulag Archipelago*, trs. Harry Willetts, 3 vols. (New York: Harper & Roe, 1978), 3:ix.

2. Ovid, *Metamorphoses*, 13, lines 839-42.

3. Robert Penn Warren, *Democracy and Poetry* (Cambridge: Harvard University Press, 1975), p. 30.

4. Walter Reich, "Diagnosing Soviet Dissidents," *Harper's* (August 1978), pp. 31-37.

5. L. Schapiro & P. Reddaway, eds., *Lenin* (New York: Praeger, 1967), pp. 18-19.

6. Victor Nekipilov, *Institute of Fools: Notes from Serbsky* (New York: Farrar, Strauss & Giraux, 1979).

7. Olmstead v. United States, 277 U.S. 438 (1928).

8. Camus, *The Rebel* (New York: Knopf, 1956), p. 106.

9. "The CPSU Central Committee's Appeal to the Soviet People," *Pravda*, 4 January 1974, p.1.

10. V. I. Evolokimov, *Vorastaiushchaia rol' partii v stroitel'stve kommunizma* [The growing role of the party in the construction of communism] (Moscow: Gospolitizdat, 1960), p. 27.

11. *Los Angeles Times*, 29 April 1979, A5.

12. *Ibid.*

13. Perez v. Brownell, 356 U.S. 44, 64-65 (1957).

14. *New York Times*, 17 February 1977, A1.

15. J. M. Perry, "God's Grace and a Little Guile," *National Observer*, 26 March 1977.

16. *Newsweek*, 20 June 1977, p. 53.

17. *Ibid.*

231

18. H. P. Riese, ed. *Since the Prague Spring* (New York: Vintage Books, 1979), pp. 13-14.

19. *Los Angeles Times*, 28 February 1977, A2

20. *New York Times*, 4 March 1977, A 4

21. *Los Angeles Times*, 13 December 1977, B1

22. *Ibid.*, p. 7.

23. *Ibid.*, p.2.

24. *Los Angeles Times*, 27 November 1977, part VI, p. 2; for a more extensive analysis of Scharansky's case, see *Times*, 24 July 1978.

25. *Newsweek*, 20 June 1977, p. 53.

26. Theodore Mommsen, *Romisches Strafrecht* (Graz: Akademische Druck-U. Verlagsantalt, 1955), Bk. 4., p. 782.

27. Justice Learned Hand, *The Spirit of Liberty*, ed. Irving Dilliard (New York: Knopf, 1963), p. 72.

28. Morgenthau, *The Restroation of American Politics* (Chicago: University of Chicago Press, 1962) p. 72.

29. *Ibid.*, p. 71.

30. Jefferson, *Writings*, 3:318.

31. *New York Times*, 23 May 1977, A12.

32. Leo Strauss, *On Tyranny* (New York: Free Press of Glencoe, 1963), pp. 95-109.

33. George Kennan, "The Time Has Come to Exorcise the Ghost of Stalin," *Los Angeles Times*, 18 December 1977, Op. Ed. page.

34. Gilbert Murray, *The Rise of the Greek Epic* (Oxford University Press, 1907), p. 80.

35. Hobbes, *De Cive*, ed. S. P. Lamprecht (New York: Appleton-Century Crofts, 1949), p. 148.

36. See a revealing exchange, "Solzhenitsyn and his Critics," Foreign Affairs 59, no. 1 (Fall 1980): 187-210. For a critical overview of Soviet dissidents, see V. Belotserkovsky, "Soviet Dissenters," Partisan Review 42, no. 1 (1975): 35-59.

37. Hannah Arendt, The Origins of Totalitarianism (New York: Meridian Books 1958), pp. 445-47.

38. Santiago Carrillo, Eurocommunism and the State (Westport, Conn.: Lawrence Hill, 1978), p. 90, 159, 168.

39. Ibid., p. 155.

40. Ibid., p. 105.

41. Norman Podhoretz, The Present Danger (New York: Simon & Schuster, 1980), p. 100.

42. Walt Whitman, Complete Writings of Walt Whitman, ed. Oscar Lovell (New York: G. P. Putnam's Sons, 1902), 2:259-60.

43. Max M. Laserson, The American Impact on Russia-Diplomatic and Ideological, 1784-1917 (New York: Macmillan, 1950), p. 218.

44. Burke, Works, 8:214-215.

45. Adam Ulam, Ideologies and Illusions (Cambridge: Harvard University Press, 1976), p. 307.

46. See Cyrus Vance's speech delivered at Harvard University, 5 June 1980, New York Times, 6 June 1980, A12.

47. Averall Harriman, America and Russia in a Changing World (New York: Doubleday, 1971), p. 167.

48. George Kennan, Memoirs, 1950-1953, 2 vols. (New York: Little, Brown, 1972), 2: 96-97.

49. Solzhenitsyn, Letter to the Soviet Leaders, p.52.

50. Solzhenitsyn, Iz-Pod Glyb: Sbornik Statei (Paris: YMCA Press, 1974), p. 26.

51. Solzhenitsyn, A World Split Apart (New York: Harper & Row, 1978), pp. 17-19.

52. Kistyakovsky, "In the Defence of Law," in Landmarks ed., Boris Shragin (New York: Karz Howard, 1977), p. 115.

53. Herzen, Collected Works, 7:121.

54. Mikhailovsky, Sochineniya (Works), 4:949.

55. Kistyakovsky, "Gosudarstvo pravovoe i sotsialis-ticheskoe," Voprosy filosofii i psikhologii, no. 85 (Nov-Dec. 1906): 495-96.

56. Ibid., p. 606.

57. Ibid., p. 490.

58. Isaiah Berlin, Four Essays on Liberty (London: Oxford University Press, 1969), p. 129.

4. Conclusion

1. Bertrand Russell, The Autobiography of Bertrand Russell, 1944-1969 (New York: Simon and Schuster, 1969), p. 30.

2. George F. Kennan, "A Risky U.S. Equation," New York Times, 18 February 1981, A23.

INDEX

blazhenny, 9, 10

Bloch, E., 98

Blok, A., 220

Bolingbroke, Lord, 199

Bolshevik Revolution, 151, 196,
see Russian Revolution

Bossuet, J., 117

Boutillier, C., 31

Boyd, Julian P., 43

Brecht, B., 158

Brezhnev, Leonid, 58, 167,
169, 171, 192, 217

Bryce, J., 89, 195, 197

Bukovsky, V., 78, 210-11

Burke, E., 158

Calvin, John, 16

Camus, A., 205, 219

Canon law, 22, 23

capitalism, 13, 78, 227

Carlyle, Thomas, 14

Carter, Jimmy, 192,209,210-11,
215

Carter Administration, 51, 197,
210, 215
Farewell Address, 227

Carrillo, S., 218

Catherine II, Empress (the Great)
114, 126, and Bentham, 151,

and Constitutional reforms,
130, 144, 150, and Nakaz,
145, and Montesquieu, 146-
48

Chaadayev, P., 133-34, 143

Chernyshevsky, N., 137, 141,
221

Chicherin, Georgi V., 205

Cicero, 19

civic consciousness, 31, 143,
28

civic humanism, 116

civic life, 39

civil rights, 226, 17, 78,
164, see human rights

conscience, 7-8, 15, 20,
25, and individual, 12,
16, 66, 68, 168

Cobban, A., 129

Cold War, 185

Coleman, F., 38-39

Commager, H. S., 129

Communism, 13, 73, 88, 152,
190, 198-99, 205-06,
214, 220-21, moral end of,
90, 191, Soviet communism,
152, 171-72, 185, 198,
205, 206

Communist, 15, 54, 125, 138
207

Communist Party of the Soviet
Union, 166, 169, 170, 171,
208, see Lenin

241